CW00501748

PLUTONIUM

HOW TO LOSE FRIENDS
AND INFURIATE YOUR BOSS

Jonar C. Nader is a digital-age philosopher and educator who has worked and consulted for some of the world's largest organisations, including Compaq and IBM. ★ He was the co-founder of the Information Technology Society and the New Leaders Foundation. ★ He is the author of several international bestsellers including, *How to Lose Friends and Infuriate People* and *How to Lose Friends and Infuriate Thinkers*. He is also the author of *Prentice Hall's Illustrated Dictionary of Computing*, and the technology writer for *Butterworth's Legal Dictionary*, and the *Concise Legal Dictionary*. ★ Jonar is a highly sought-after lecturer, corporate presenter, and consultant in the areas of technology, leadership, management, thinking skills, teamwork, marketing, advertising, and politics. Jonar can be contacted via:

www.LoseFriends.com
Jonar2@LoseFriends.com

PLUTONIUM

TAKE CONTROL OF
your career

JONAR C. NADER

PLUTONIUM

How to Lose Friends and Infuriate Your Boss

Published in Australia by

 **PLUTONIUM**

PO Box 15, Pyrmont NSW 2009
Plutonium@LoseFriends.com

1 2 3 4 5 6 7 8 9 • 06 05 04 03 02

National Library of Australia
Cataloguing-in-Publication Data

Nader, Jonar C.

How to Lose Friends and Infuriate Your Boss

Includes index
ISBN 0 9577165 5 9

1. Supervision of employees. 2. Career development.
3. Supervisors.
I. Title

658.302

For information on how to contact the author or the publisher, please visit www.LoseFriends.com

I am indebted to each one of my ex-bosses.

THE *vulgar* BOSSES
FORCED ME TO LEARN ABOUT RESPECT.

THE *selfish* BOSSES
HELPED ME TO UNDERSTAND COMPASSION.

THE *generous* BOSSES
ALLOWED ME TO SPREAD MY WINGS.

THE *patient* BOSSES
KEPT ME ON THE STRAIGHT AND NARROW.

THIS BOOK IS DEDICATED TO
THE *ghastly* BOSSES
WHO GAVE ME AMPLE REASONS
TO FOCUS ON MY CAREER
SO THAT I COULD ESCAPE FROM THEIR GRIP.

IT IS ALSO DEDICATED TO
THE *gracious* BOSSES
WHO ALLOWED ME TO MAKE MISTAKES
FROM WHICH I WAS ABLE TO LEARN
ABOUT FAILURE AND SUCCESS.

CONTENTS

part ONE

STATING YOUR POSITION

part TWO
FINDING YOUR DIRECTION

part THREE
DEVELOPING YOUR SKILLS

part FOUR
GETTING WHAT YOU WANT

part FIVE
HANDLING YOUR BOSS

sample CHAPTER
FROM 'HOW TO LOSE FRIENDS AND INFURIATE PEOPLE'

PART ONE

STATING *your* POSITION

Perception is virtual reality

CHAPTER 1

WHO'S THE BOSS?

BLOOD, SWEAT, AND FEARS

Too much of a good thing can't be bad,
and too much of a bad thing can't be good

I F A REPUTABLE ORGANISATION offered you a job that is similar to your current job, would you take it? If you decline the offer because you are happy with where you are, would you reconsider if the prospective employer offered to *double* your salary? You would not be alone if you jumped at the opportunity.

Now consider a different question. If you could design a job that fulfils your fantasies, what would that job entail? What would you say if someone offered to give you your dream-job, but said that you had to *halve* your current salary? For many people, income loses its importance when it is traded with job-satisfaction. Some respondents say that if their dream-job existed, they would try to find ways to reduce their living expenses so that they could focus less on their debts and more on their career. This type of question solicits varying responses based on age, maturity, and family commitments. Typically, those who have become disenchanted with the corporate treadmill are more likely to value job-satisfaction over wealth accumulation.

Many people do not have a clue about how to define their ideal job. Even some of the most senior of executives who are running large organisations have not paused to contemplate what they *really* want. When someone asks them about what would make them happy, they are unable to articulate what their dream-job would look like. How can you find a dream-job if you do not know what you are looking for?

How can you find a dream-job if you do not know what you are looking for?

If you are not sure what you want from a job, this book will help you to build a clearer picture of your career.

If you *are* the boss, or if you desire to *become* the boss, this book will help you to understand which skills will be the most important in the future.

If you do *not* want to be the boss, this book will show you how to become a successful employee who sells services at a premium. It will also show you how you can negotiate better conditions so that you do not suffer the typical ailments of stress and pressure.

KILLER DISEASES

Collectively, we entered the twenty-first century carrying a doctor's certificate. It said, 'Suffering from stress. Light duties prescribed.' What does it mean to be 'stressed out'? What causes us to feel pressured, overworked, and underpaid?

Every ten years or so, we learn about a new wave of occupational hazards. Most recently, public liability has become so expensive that community events have had to be cancelled and small businesses have had to be closed. Exorbitant insurance premiums have been fuelled by our litigious society, whose members no longer take responsibility for their own actions — even when walking across a field.

In the 1990s, employers discovered how costly it could be to handle grievances and 'emotional damage' in relation to sexual harassment and unfair dismissal.

In the 1980s, employers refused to believe that 'repetitive strain injury' was a serious ailment; not until the courts awarded astronomical payouts to victims of soft-tissue injury. All of a sudden, 'ergonomics' entered the vernacular.

In the 1970s, employers and insurers were learning about back pain and whiplash. For private investigators, business boomed as they spied on unethical workers for whom 'compensation' was another word for 'get-rich-quick'. Lawyers convinced victims to try their luck, promising 'no win, no fees'.

Despite employers' best efforts to appease unions, to placate environmentalists, and to satisfy insurance companies, it seems that our places of work are more dangerous than ever. Stress is the new killer that affects workers' mental and physical health. It destroys both productivity and profitability.

Is it conceivable that, despite earnest attempts to improve occupational health and safety, we have entered an era in which the greatest threat to our workforce is an ill-defined intangible disease that emanates from work itself? Could it be that workers are more inclined to suffer from stress because they are uncertain about their future or because they are dispassionate about their work?

Although we can point to many factors that fuel stress, we must find out what triggers it. In my search to understand the essence of stress, I have come to disagree with popular medical definitions. I define occupational stress as a condition resulting from our inability to reconcile our capability with our authority. This means that stress is ignited when we can *see* a solution to a major problem, and we *know* that we are capable of fixing that problem, but we have no authority to do so. We are shackled by bureaucracy.

Work, rest, and play ought to be rolled into one lifestyle from which we can derive complete satisfaction

Stress leads to frustration, which in turn leads to a debilitating disease called 'depression'. I define depression as a condition resulting from our inability to reconcile our inadequacy with our responsibility. This means that depression consumes us when we realise that we are unable to do anything about our own problems. As a result, we believe that our problems will never go away.

STRESS TEST

I have devised a stress test called the 'elasticity of command'. It enables me to determine an individual's propensity to suffer from occupational stress. I draw on the analogy of giving employees a piece of elastic to measure the distance between them and the nearest colleague who can obstruct a project unnecessarily. Employees are then asked to compare that by measuring the distance between them and their commander (the boss) — whose responsibility it would be to facilitate a smooth transition for the project.

If the boss is reachable and responsive, the stress level is said to be minimal. If the boss is unreachable and unresponsive, the stress level is said to be extreme.

Stress becomes 'frustration' when those who can obstruct us are more powerful than our boss. In industries where everything is processed in real-time, we must be given the tools to make decisions in real-time.

Using 'elasticity of command', we can see that the person who is ultimately responsible for work-related stress is none other than the boss (whether it be our own boss, or someone further up the ladder). Bosses, too, can suffer from stress if their superiors are unreachable and unresponsive.

Trouble comes your way without any trouble at all

It would be convenient to blame 'globalisation' or 'politics' or a myriad of external factors for today's stressful work environments. Ultimately, it all boils down to the boss. If you are the boss, or aspire to become the boss, it is important to equip yourself with the skills that will be demanded of you in the future. Otherwise, you could perpetuate this problem into the next decade.

IMAGINE YOURSELF ON YOUR DEATHBED

It worries me when an audience nods in agreement with gurus who say, 'People on their deathbed will not look back and wish that they had spent more time at work.' I can safely say that those who show such contempt for their career are in the wrong job.

It would be a miserable existence if we could not be absorbed by our work. Work, rest, and play ought to be rolled into one lifestyle from which we can derive complete satisfaction. We would not know the meaning of 'passion' if we were not excited enough about our work to think about it on our deathbed.

Prosperity abounds. You just need to know how to claim your fair share.

If we enjoy our work, we will feel relaxed *and* super-charged, simultaneously. A successful career is a satisfying journey, not a series of daily pit-stops marked by a breather called 'the weekend'.

IT'S EASY, WHEN YOU KNOW HOW

The purpose of this book is to equip you to handle whatever comes hurtling your way. This is important because trouble comes your way without any trouble at all, so you had better know how to confront it and how to overcome it.

Prosperity abounds. You just need to know how to claim your fair share. This starts by learning how to lose friends and infuriate your boss so that you can live a zestful and enchanting life. **Q**

P.S. You are encouraged to review the Table of Contents and read the chapters that you find of immediate relevance or interest.

CHAPTER 2

HAVE *you* BEEN NAUGHTY OR NICE?

FROM PERFORMANCE APPRAISAL TO STAFF REPRISAL

It's important to know when you are right,
and imperative to know when you are wrong

PERFORMANCE APPRAISALS IMPACT and affect the majority of employees. They are often a waste of time because they are manipulative, stressful, counter-productive, and ineffective. Most organisations tell employees that reviews are necessary for personal development and salary adjustments, yet they use them for 'crowd control' or as a legal tool to oust non-performers or those whom they do not like. Interestingly, this tool has backfired on employers just as many times as it has been useful in court. As a result, modern review documents are drafted by lawyers, written by psychologists, then edited by personnel managers. By the time they reach employees, they are unbelievably convoluted, irrelevant, and downright impossible to implement because the measurement processes are nonsensical.

Regardless of the final scores, pay rises and bonuses are determined arbitrarily by those who control the purse strings. Their game reminds me of magicians who start with, 'Pick a number, any number . . . ' and then proceed to tell us what that number is. Managers often know who they want to reward, so the performance review becomes an academic exercise that is reverse-engineered to fit the pool of funds that has been allocated for certain bands of 'performers' — or dare one say 'cohorts'.

I have no objection to managers using subjective and discriminating means to distribute rewards by way of money, title, position, and power. Why go against human nature? No matter how a review mechanism is designed, and no matter how many computerised forms are filled in, managers will still have their own inexplicable justifications for who they like, who they appreciate, who they loath, and who they wish to promote. These intangible feelings cannot be specified on forms. After all, what mathematical reasoning process do *you* engage in when determining who you like or dislike? The complex emotional

and egotistical methods used to categorise friends is not something that a computer can cope with. It all boils down to
processes that cannot be measured. For more about human
behaviour, see Chapter 8, 'I'm not a racist, but . . . '

NUDGE NUDGE, WINK WINK

When I was eighteen years old, there was a young chain-
smoker not far from where I lived. We used to go for walks in
the night air. I cannot recall his name, but what sticks in my
mind is that he was honest about being stressed. I never knew
what troubled him, and I did not ask, but he would say something like, 'I'm so stressed out . . . I am under so much pressure.'
That would not normally captivate me, except that he had an
obvious twitch. As a youngster, I did not link the two. I had no
idea that stress could cause such visible side-effects — not until
I suffered the same problem a few years later.

One of my bosses had the nicest smile. She was petite,
attractive, and said very little. I automatically assumed that her
demeanour made her an agreeable person. But I was in for a
shock. Her intimidating ways left me with a twitch that I could
not shake off for eighteen months. I did not link the two until
she left the company. It is funny how a clear and present threat
can linger with us for ages. It can even go undetected until we
are far away from the situation to see the real cause. I was
unaware that her subtle, yet unrelenting intimidation had such
an effect on me. I reflected upon my neighbour. I had erroneously presumed that his twitch was a result of a mental disorder
from birth.

I was angry with myself for being so naïve and helpless in
my manager's presence. I always thought that I was tough and
resilient. Although at school I was able to take on bullies of all

sizes, I had no tactics to handle adults. Worse still, I was untrained to detect the kind of intimidation that led to my nervous twitch. Eventually, I became aware of such terrorisation, but only to a limited extent because I was caught out *again* with a new mechanism called the 'performance review'. Regardless of their intended purpose, and irrespective of how they are implemented, performance reviews are demeaning. The whole notion of bosses sitting employees down and grading them, like farmers grade their eggs, is humiliating. Who do they think they are?

Irreverent logic

For organisations that use performance reviews, it would be difficult to convince them to abandon their entrenched procedures. It would be problematic to engage in a discussion about this because of magnetic thinking — meaning that irreverent logic is used to argue a point about a practice whereby the intention is virtuous, but the execution is flawed.

Advocates of performance reviews could list dozens of benefits. The ultimate and most important one is *to improve the company's performance*. With that intention in mind, anyone who argues against reviews would seem to be arguing against improving the company's performance. This is what is meant by irreverent logic. Of course we should find ways to improve performance. In so doing, managers are warned against using noble intentions to fuel ignoble programs that infest organisations in the guise of excellence.

Over the years, performance assessment schemes have been modified, tweaked, re-cast, and re-designed; all to no avail. For years, performance reviews have attempted to embrace seventeen main areas. These are to: set standards; determine benchmarks; give feedback; coach staff; drive pay rises; determine promotions;

reward on merit; measure performance; document incidents; meet legal obligations; develop talent; outline training requirements; plan careers; highlight weaknesses; raise the alarm for bad employees; give warnings; and justify dismissals.

Any human-resources mechanism would be burdened if it were expected to administer more than one objective; let alone seventeen.

Performance appraisals are not, in themselves, harmful. But the unavoidable side-effects are intolerable. If a commercial medicine caused insufferable side-effects, it would be withdrawn from the market. If a headache tablet worked wonders to relieve pain, but caused hair loss, people would reject it. When the downsides are obvious, it is not hard to understand that an effective product can also be defective.

Performance appraisals are not, in themselves, harmful. But the unavoidable side-effects are intolerable.

The secondary objection to performance appraisals is that the side-effects are wide-ranging and counter-productive.

Promoted as tools that enable frank and open discussions between employers and employees, *performance reviews have become the batons that silence the victims*. Employees are more inclined to avoid conflict and to conceal problems for fear of provoking friction and staining their employment record.

In truth, people remember the good times, not the technicalities. Similarly, people remember the *bad* times, not the technicalities. Therefore, staff members who fight worthy battles are more likely to be remembered for 'stirring trouble' than for fighting the good fight. Many times I was harassed by my managers for supposedly upsetting people. Never was there an opportunity for me to prove that such complaints came from troublemakers. I was protecting the company, standing by the brand, living up to the motto, and doing what my manager should have had the backbone to do on my behalf. Instead, I was rapped over the knuckles and penalised at the review. How can employees argue with managers who hold the key to their next promotion? From that, it is easy to develop an uncaring attitude, born of the need for self-preservation amid contradictory management behaviour.

People remember the good times, not the technicalities

CONTRADICTION

Employees, like children, have an uncanny ability to detect incongruence between what is *said* and what is *done* by those in authority. Contradiction is unavoidable when managers encourage 'teamwork' with one breath and call for 'peer assessment' with another.

On the one hand, employees are expected to be comrades fighting a common battle against the competitor, while on the other hand, their formalised assessment of each other signals a police-state, whereby colleagues could impact each other's careers and weaken the framework of trust and solidarity.

Other contradictions include the mantras of 'empowerment' and 'ownership' that urge staff members to freely embrace the business as their own. Yet the performance review soon reminds them that they are under the control of a whimsical ladder-climber whose expertise does not match theirs, and whose tenure is so short that it practically renders the review meaningless. Promises made by the previous manager at the preceding review are dismissed with, 'Things have changed . . . and *I* did not make those promises . . . so there's no use debating them, but if you prove yourself to *me*, I'll see what I can do.' If you then dare to ask for subsequent promises to be put in writing, you would be asking for trouble.

360-DEGREES TAKES YOU NOWHERE

The current '360-degree feedback' fad is useless. Most people would not so much as write a letter of complaint to their council about an annoying dog in their neighbourhood, let alone dare to document their views about their colleagues. They are careful to never cast judgement on those who deserve to be sacked, because there could be repercussions. There is an old saying along the lines of, 'Never abuse people while you climb the corporate ladder because you might need their support on your way down.' In this case, 360-degree feedback sparks a new maxim along the lines of, 'Never say anything about incompetent colleagues because one day you might find yourself reporting to them.'

Never say anything about incompetent colleagues because one day you might find yourself reporting to them

If organisations were serious about the 360-degree mechanism, they would not ask employees to find six congenial colleagues to assess them. Instead, the company policy would allow absolutely *any* employee, customer, or supplier to submit formal feedback about *any* staff member or manager, whether invited or not. Those volunteering the feedback would have to identify themselves. After all investigations have been made, the forms would need to be destroyed so that retaliation would be impossible.

Current 360-degree processes are as weak as character references that are attached to résumés. People are not likely to attach references that would reflect badly on their character. Similarly, no-one is going to seek feedback from colleagues with whom they do not have a harmonious relationship, or on whom they cannot count for unwavering support — by hook or by crook.

It is important to have mechanisms for instant feedback. An easy way to solicit genuine feedback is through an intranet site that anyone can access. Simply log in, enter the name of the person about whom you wish to comment, and fire away. That would give each manager *instant* feedback about immediate problems or praiseworthy incidents. Under this scheme, it would be a sackable offence to betray confidence about those who volunteer feedback.

The 360-degree process could become known as 'Global Feedback'.

CORPORATE COURT

When internal squabbles brew, staff members have nowhere to go to fully challenge the troublemakers. For example, how can a victimised police constable complain about a corrupt sergeant?

In most work environments, people are afraid to speak up. They do not know who they can trust. So, it is likely that they will: suffer in silence; work to rule (whereby they do only what is required of them and nothing more); lose enthusiasm; feel let down; and eventually leave. Meanwhile the power-hungry manipulators move up to infest other areas of the organisation.

Corporate cancer can spread quietly and thoroughly, to the point where no-one can challenge the beasts who obstruct progress and promote injustice.

For this reason, each organisation is encouraged to set up an internal and/or external Corporate Court whose independence is similar to civil courts. This gives employees an avenue to seek justice for the sake of the organisation, without fear of retribution. It also strikes at the heart of the perpetrators who inflict misery on the rest of the staff, thinking that they have clever tricks to conceal their Machiavellian ways.

In the modern world, evil triumphs over good

Evildoers will always win if left to fight within their own domain, because in the modern world, evil triumphs over good. The worst elements will surface and smother the wholesome, because manipulators are prepared to stoop to levels that decent, ethical folk would never contemplate.

Complex organisations that do not have a Corporate Court are like cities that do not have civil courts. Organisations that truly desire corporate peace and harmony, and truly want their corrupt troublemakers to be ousted, will benefit from a Corporate Court. It is an effective way to treat the corporate cancer before it infects everyone in sight.

The reference to corruption not only relates to the 'legal' sense, but also to the moral, including intimidation and harassment. A Corporate Court would enable corporate citizens to challenge those who are destroying the corporate fibre.

Corporate performance (the primary objective that sparked the need for performance reviews) will improve when the manipulating hounds are removed. In the absence of these leeches, most people make excellent employees if they can be shown what is required, and if they can be supported in their endeavour to build an exciting workplace.

The moment that corporate cancer grips, everyone becomes entangled in soul-destroying activities. Even when there is a common enemy *and* a common goal, people can easily be distracted in the presence of greed and confusion. In the absence of leadership, self-destruction is inevitable.

> *In the absence of leadership, self-destruction is inevitable*

FOLLOW YOUR HEART, BUT WATCH YOUR BACK

A new senior manager joined the company that I was working for. He asked his secretary to make an appointment with some key executives so that he could do the rounds and make his presence felt. I had already seen his unimpressive performance at a management meeting, and I had received reports from his staff that he was out of touch. Given that he made an effort to solicit advice and support, I wanted to acquiesce, in the hope that he would not be led astray. I had seen dozens of new recruits go wayward after the enemy within took hold.

In the session with me, he looked at his well-ordered notes and asked me the first of a set of questions that he said he was posing to each of the executives. 'What advice would you give me as a new executive in this company?' he asked.

'There are only two things I can suggest,' I said. 'The first is that you search your heart and determine what it is you are here to do. Are you really here to do a great job and make this company, this industry, and your profession proud, or are you just here to climb the corporate ladder without regard for what you do along the way?'

He interrupted me and assured me that he was not 'that type of person'. He emphasised that he was keen to make a major contribution, and that he would never leave a post until he had made his mark professionally and ethically. 'So what is your second piece of advice?' he asked. (By the way, it is always a good strategy to tell people how many points you are going to make beforehand so that after interruptions and diversions, you can return to your list. If you happen to be in a meeting, hold your fingers up and say, 'I have three points to make'. Then you can keep your three fingers up in the air and count down as you get through your points. It is a useful tactic I invented for myself after many frustrating meetings wherein interjections distracted my line of thought.)

My second point was to give him advice that I wished I had been given years before. I said, 'Over the years, we have been brainwashed into thinking that when we take over a new division, we have to be tolerant with staff, and get to know them before we make any changes. In this company, and in this industry, if you hesitate to act on your intuition, you will be eaten alive. If you detect that you have to get rid of some of your staff, you are encouraged to do so without a single day's delay.' He accused me of speaking passionately, and asked me why I said that. 'I am telling you this because I know that in your division, there are three people who should have been fired ages ago. They are powerful and malicious, and they will stop at nothing to dominate you and your staff.' It was my unpleasant duty to forewarn him of the malevolent troublemakers in his camp.

I either make lifelong friends or instant enemies

'You are new here, and whatever you do now will be supported by your managers. The longer you wait, the less power you will have over these manipulators. They are promoted every year. They destroy everything in their way. You cannot take them on; you cannot beat them; but you must fire them the moment that your radar spots them,' I explained.

With that, he insisted that I tell him who they were. 'There are two reasons why I do not want to tell you,' I said. 'The first is that it's not fair that I burden you with my judgement, and second, they would be able to smell your suspicion and trip you up. I'm not asking you to believe me. I am just urging you to follow your heart when you catch them.'

His face went red as his pride got in the way. 'Look, I've been here for five weeks, and I'm astute enough to know that I don't have such people on my team. And furthermore, I take exception to you saying that kind of thing about my staff. You'd better put up or shut up!' With that outburst, he stood from his chair saying, 'I'll take this matter up with personnel and have you counselled. You're out of order speaking badly about my people,' he said patriotically.

I could have avoided the whole affair, but I thought that I was doing him a favour. I was hoping that he would join my efforts for a better company. Little did he know that innocent staff members in his division were going home crying. Literally. They would drip tears in front of me when they described their trauma. I knew all too well what was going on in his division. I was hoping that he would see it too and have the courage to do something about it.

Never cross nice people, because among them are the most dangerous

I either make lifelong friends or instant enemies. His biggest mistake was to presume that a mild-mannered operative like me was a pushover. As I have often said, never cross nice people, because among them are the most dangerous.

I was unimpressed with his threats, so I decided to prove

the point by telling him the names of the three people. I knew that he would rush to tell them. I knew that they would panic and swing into offensive action. I knew that they would have to act to protect themselves. The stupid fool had instigated a coup d'état. It took six months to find this high-flyer. It took only six weeks from our fateful meeting to lose him. The three muske-teers had flushed him out. The CEO dangled another post in front of him so as to save face because his appointment had been well publicised. He was relocated to another country. The whole affair smacked of a witness protection program.

The person who was then appointed to the vacant post was a friend of mine. She had ears to listen. She had been with the company for a long time. She knew the lie of the land. She knew about these deviates. (I had locked horns with them often enough for her to eventually see the truth about those three in particular. She had defended me on many occasions. She stood by me out of loyalty, but for a long time she did not understand the issues, because they covered their tracks well.) Despite her awareness, and despite her power as their new boss, and despite her genuine desire to contribute to the company, and despite her absolute intolerance to energy sappers, and despite her professionalism and extensive training, it took her twelve months to get rid of them.

'It took you long enough,' I said. 'I'm not impressed, but at least you finally managed to do in twelve months what I would have done in one day. Still, I can understand that it would have been a tough process; so congratulations. Now you can get on with your real job. Oh, by the way, how did they take it?' I asked, wondering how the battle ended, and how many casual-ties the insurgence claimed. 'They took it fine. They've now been promoted and they work at headquarters,' she told me gleefully.

'Are you mad? Don't you realise that now they will oppress even more people!' I exclaimed in disbelief. She let them escape unscathed to another division. She even supported their promotion. At that point in the conversation I could hear the words echoing in her head: 'I had no choice. I had to promote them, or stand to be butchered.'

If the company had a bullet-proof and impeccably confidential 360-degree feedback mechanism that enabled its employees to comment about such tyrants, we might not have had to suffer the degradation of missing opportunities, losing good staff, reducing market share, and diminishing profits.

Mind you, one of the three musketeers had started his life with the company as one of the lowest-ranking staff members. How is that for a runaway success! How is that for a review process that supposedly promotes on merit and weeds out the non-contributors! How is that for a system that was so comprehensive and all-encompassing that managers needed off-site full-day training courses just to be able to decipher the 'Supervisor's Instruction Manual' that to this day makes my eyes glaze over with its inexplicable diagrams and incomprehensible formulae! How is that as a testimony to the ineffectiveness of review systems that are supposed to aid in counselling and coaching! All the while, I was the one being counselled and coached. My managers were blind. Some would say they were smart because they knew how to keep their head down.

By the way, I once had a manager who also rose to hideous heights. When the company had engaged a prestigious research firm to survey all the staff about what they thought about their managers, I (and each of the other direct-reports in turn) was called into his office for a briefing. He closed the door and told me that when the time came for the survey to be circulated, he wanted all his subordinates to understand one thing: we were not to say anything that reflected badly on him as the manager.

The mediators assured every staff member that no witch-hunt would follow the completely anonymous survey containing 120 questions. I had been embroiled in a witch-hunt before, so I was alert to these desensitising lies. Sure enough, he called an off-site meeting to go through each question to pin the culprits via a process of elimination. Nasty business indeed.

I LOVE YOU 4.62 OUT OF 5

Can you work out what 4.62 means? How does it really compare with 3.86 out of 5? Despite the tedious scaling and ranking systems used to grade staff during a review process, a final *overall* rating is given. What a joke! Evidently the perpetrators cannot understand their own system, so they insist on a final number in order to deal with one score — one number, one rating, one ranking. Dead simple. Why not ask for that conclusive ranking at the *start* and save a lot of palaver? Alas, the ritual contributes to the ceremony that justifies the actions that in turn support the decision. The following story illustrates this point.

When I was in India, I walked past a small jewellery boutique and saw what looked like a large diamond. If it were a real diamond, the Pink Panther would have stolen it ages ago. I knew it was a fake.

When I asked the shop attendant for the price, he performed a ritual that every sales attendant would do well to copy. He looked at my suit, my watch, my tie, my shoes, and within one second decided to rank me in his head as a certain class of clientele. He greeted me most royally. He donned pristine white gloves, pulled out an intricate old-fashioned hand-held brass scale from a beautiful wooden box, opened his velvet-lined draw and selected one of several tongs, with which he gently lifted the stone from its stand and started an elaborate weighing procedure.

It was all a load of fuss and nonsense, but it allowed him to look me in the eyes and ask for US$100. In his terms, that was three-months' salary. Imagine paying three-months' salary for a piece of glass. That is all it was. We haggled, and he allowed me to beat him down to $10. The stone was not worth ten cents, but I enjoyed his performance. Even then, while he was wrapping it for me, he was incessantly lamenting this unfair deal lest I lose interest or feel that I should push my luck even further.

Can you imagine if the whole process were over and done with in two seconds? If he were quick to reply 'ten dollars', without all the paraphernalia, I would have kept walking. Instead, his luring ritual paid off.

Sometimes, a decision is devalued if it is not preceded by a laborious performance. Managers could easily send an e-mail to say, 'Hello, your annual review is due today, and I have given you an overall rating of 3.86.' Instead, employees have to suffer mind-bending exercises to answer fifty questions to determine where the pendulum stops on a scale between two extreme options that sound something like this:

The employee listens to internal and external customers and tries to satisfy them by first understanding their needs then anticipating their requirements and maintaining a positive attitude while not losing one's temper when frustrated thereby resulting in customers regularly praising the high standards of personal customer attention.	5 4 3 2 1	The employee does not listen to internal and external customers and neither tries to satisfy nor understand them or their needs thereby unable to anticipate their requirements resorting to a negative disposition that leads to loss of composure which results in frequent complaints about the low quality of service provided.

Any rating other than 5 would raise all manner of illogical arguments. For example, from the phrases given above (taken from a real review document from a multi-billion dollar organisation) try to justify exactly when an employee can be given a rating of 4, and when a 3 could be rationalised? How can you summarise twelve months' worth of hard work into such convoluted descriptions? If anyone scores 1 in any of these, I would wonder why it takes a whole year to highlight that kind of unacceptable behaviour.

If a staff member were hovering east of 3, I would summon the manager and ask for an explanation. How could such incompetence be allowed to sustain itself in my organisation? I would have doubts about the manager's capability, not the staff member's frailty.

If you desire certain levels of customer satisfaction to be met, the first step is to lead by example. The second is to sit with your staff members and show them what you require. Coach them, demonstrate what you mean, teach them the way to do it, create the environment, and show them the path to excellence.

What about managers who do not know what 'excellence' means? These days, all sorts of people are being promoted for a myriad of reasons. I have seen experts rip their hair out when their superiors genuinely did not have a clue about their division.

When a scale from 1 to 5 is shown, it would be understandable to presume that the organisation is promoting the attainment of excellence as described in the left box. I doubt that CEOs understand what it would take for employees to achieve a rating of 5. Most corporate cultures, by virtue of their greedy budgets and myopic missions, could not tolerate anyone seeking to deliver such excellence. Employees who try, are usually accused of being pedantic, slow, and obsessive perfectionists. In the absence of support, they would soon be badgered into the groove wherein mediocrity thrives.

WHO ARE YOU KIDDING?

There is a trick in the human-resources manual that outlines how to avoid dissention when salaries are reviewed. Almost every performance appraisal program urges managers to divorce the *performance* review from the *salary* review. The objective is to prevent staff members from arguing about their final performance rating. If ratings were linked to salaries, and if staff members were able to calculate that the financial difference between the ratings 3.86 and 4.62 equated to a handsome delta, each point would be defended more vehemently. Review sessions would grind to a halt as staff members rightly argue the illogical and irrational nuances between each of the fifty tongue-twisters. Instead, employees are told that salaries would be reviewed during a totally different lunar cycle when the waters have been quelled and all the wounds have been healed.

Who do they think they are kidding? What do they mean by separating the two? It is just adding insult to injury. Naturally, managers would argue that one's performance has no bearing on the pool of funds that is bestowed by the ivory tower after the financial results have been finalised. Experts suggest that performance review programs are designed to focus on 'staff development', not on 'staff rewards'. If that were true, staff members who bombed out on their performance rating would still have a chance to score healthy pay rises. Yet, we are told that it is ludicrous to suggest that a poor performer deserves a pay rise. Pray tell, does this not prove the point that performance *does* impact salary? How can they say that the two are separable?

Moreover, discontentment surfaces within the ranks of the high-achievers because ultimately a bell curve is required to accommodate the complex computer program that allocates certain funds for each band. What they do not tell you is that the ivory tower will insist on limiting the number of qualifiers per band. This means that if only fifty people can be graded as Band-A, then even if there are sixty good people, ten of them will have to miss out. How can those ten be told that they missed out on a huge bonus? Simply by not letting them achieve an overall rating of 4.62. In this case, managers will premeditate a review that lands on 4.61 — just under the Band-A cut-off.

This tactic explains why many managers delay the review ceremony. They wait for the final figures from treasury. Sometimes, the delay is due to laziness and inconsideration. This creates disgruntled employees who cannot understand why their manager can be so insensitive to their needs. The only time in the year that the employees really want something done, the managers pussyfoot around, oblivious to the psychological impact caused by such delays.

More alarming are the managers who abdicate their responsibilities and ask employees to conduct a self-assessment. In other words, the employees have to do the manager's dirty work, because the manager cannot be bothered. What kind of signal does that send? Managers often complain that performance reviews are resource-intensive. So, instead of fixing the problem, they delegate it. This is no different from a busy judge who asks the defendant to write the verdict.

WHAT'S THE SOLUTION?

The solution is simple. Abolish performance reviews and learn how to speak with subordinates using coherent complete sentences —

not numbers. Hire professionals who know what they are doing, or people who are willing to learn how to do it. Crush cockroaches without hesitation, and train your managers to inject life and energy into your organisation.

If you are an employee who cannot escape the corporate charade, seek an audience with your manager and try to understand what is expected of you. You are well within your rights to say, 'I'd like to perform well, and achieve my goals. Could you please help me to understand what you expect of me, and what my responsibilities and duties are. Also, please specify my level of authority and my budget, and tell me how my actions will be evaluated. What other information will you rely on when reviewing my performance, and which colleagues could impact my performance?'

Furthermore, seek an agreement about your attitude and what you can and cannot do in relation to the elements outlined in the performance review, such as how the company expects you to handle difficult customers or innovative opportunities. It is vital for you to seek an agreement that if any of the figures change beyond your control, these would be documented and taken into consideration at the time of the review. For example, it is common for managers to change sales targets and expense budgets without warning or consultation. Although you might have done everything within your power to attain your target, you automatically drop to fifty percent after the amendment. This would tarnish your performance. It is another demeaning trick played by all and sundry.

Some clever salespeople who are able to crack the formula know exactly when to close the books. They withhold orders and conceal opportunities because they would have worked out their rating to maximise their bonus. They purposely do not want to over-achieve their target because such an heroic deed would earn them an unwelcome increase in their targets for the following year — something every salesperson dreads. Instead, at the dawn of the new financial year, they open the bottom draw to submit pending orders that give them a galloping start.

Mind you, the converse of this game is also played whereby salespeople process orders for non-existent stock. They dispatch empty boxes to their clients so that they can meet their end-of-year quota — and help their clients spend unused funds that would otherwise have expired. Every single person within the chain of command, from both buyer and seller, knows about this practice. Everyone turns a blind eye, which makes me wonder why it all happens on a nod amid mock trepidation.

BEWARE THE JOB-DESCRIPTION

It is imperative that staff members reject 'job goals' and 'job descriptions' if they do not understand them or if they disagree with the content. Employees have to take responsibility for their actions. They are equally to blame if they sign job goals that they know are beyond their capability. We could rightly blame managers for their insipid practices, but somewhere along the line, workers have to speak up and respond appropriately.

A chairman, to whom I give advice, recently showed me a four-page job-description that a consultant had drafted at the CEO's request. The document was intended for a new senior branch manager. It required the recruit to outperform Superman, and take responsibility for everything and everyone. It categorically stated that he was not allowed to post a letter unless the CEO had approved it. The job-description outlined, in excruciating detail, how many times the manager had to check his e-mail, and exactly how he was to introduce himself to a client when shaking hands. I advised the chairman to:

replace the consultant; ask the CEO to apply that document to himself to see how he would like to be muzzled; and refuse to hire any candidate who agreed to sign the document on the basis that anyone who accepted the four-pages of diatribe must have a screw loose.

Employees are also urged to study the corporate confidentiality statement. Back in the 1980s, confidentiality statements sprang up and became mandatory for everyone who worked in the information-technology arena. Growth had mushroomed faster than anyone had anticipated, and all sorts of legal battles gripped the industry. One of the biggest problems was stopping staff members from leaving their employers to start their own competitive business. The whole industry thrived on this type of viral growth.

I recall the day when we all received a ten-page document that we were all 'obliged' to sign. It was intimated that anyone who did not sign it 'must have something to hide'. Employees were signing their life away through legalese that even my lawyer could not understand.

'Jonar, each of the 11 000 staff members around the world have signed this document. No-one has had any problems with it. So we really want you to sign it today because it has to be returned to headquarters in this afternoon's mailbag,' said my personnel manager, trying to smile and scold me at the same time for daring to question some of the clauses.

I did not object to the general nature of a confidentiality agreement. Of course the company's intellectual property (IP) must be protected. I took exception to several clauses that would have numbed my brain. As an author, I would not have been able to own anything whatsoever, no matter what industry it was in. For example, according to the contract, I would not have been allowed to produce or invent anything without the company owning the rights, even if my unrelated invention took place after I had left the company. After enduring unwelcome coercion, I asked my lawyer to re-draft the agreement, and I managed to negotiate my way through it. The personnel manager did not care about my needs. He was worried about how he was going to explain this to headquarters.

He assured me that the company supported my extracurricular activities, and that this document was not meant to hinder my creativity. A few months later, the legal eagles at headquarters had written to tell me that the company 'owned' my book (a book that I had been working on for four years). You can imagine how that made me feel. The legal department had assumed that I, like every other employee, was under its spell. They did not think to check if I had been so gullible as to sign my life away. Luckily, I escaped their grip after they realised that I was operating under a modified IP contract. You can imagine the directives that circulated thereafter.

Every time I joined a new company, my name became mud at its legal office because I had the audacity to re-draft their confidentiality and IP agreements. It was always the same intimidation and innuendoes, trying to make me feel guilty for a crime that I 'might be contemplating'.

Some employers are preoccupied with the legal aspects of hiring and firing. They are terrified about being accused of unfairly dismissing employees. Managers are advised to use each tool appropriately. The performance review must not be used as a legal tool with which to prise unwanted staff from the mothership. When I detect that some staff members are a burden to the organisation, I first examine their manager's capabilities, and wonder why the situation was allowed to get out of hand. Usually, you will find that it is the manager's fault for not ensuring that the employee has had sufficient training, coaching, direction, or discipline. If a recalcitrant employee needs to be apprehended, a formal counselling program must be established. This should be customised for the situation and the person involved. Such counselling requires a high degree of skill. With so many managers lacking these fundamental managerial skills, it is no wonder they resort to administrative processes that can be instigated at arm's length.

Managers ought to have the courage to handle the issues at their root, not burden everyone with copious policies. I once knew a manager who was well aware of what two people in the division were getting up to. Instead of apprehending the culprits, every few weeks he would devise new policies that everyone had to contend with. This made the workplace bureaucratic. He could have fixed the problems by speaking with the two renegades. He disliked confrontation, so he hid behind his desk and issued memos and e-mails in every direction. His cowardly methods stifled creativity and diminished autonomy. In effect, eighty people had to pay the price for his inability to confront two people.

THERE'S NO TIME LIKE THE PRESENT

If you are a manager who wants to engender excellence, you are encouraged to learn how to mould your department as a sculptor fashions a statue. Every crevasse and every curve has to be finished by hand. Sometimes the gentle touches work wonders. Other times, a sledgehammer does the job.

I recall my first day on the job at a large multinational in the days when an entire company owned only one fax machine. Rolls of heat-sensitive paper were the order of the day. When faxes arrived, they would curl and bounce about all over the place. Some fell behind the cabinet without a trace. Sometimes, an inexperienced employee would replenish the machine with a new roll that was put on back-to-front, resulting in dozens of faxes printing out as blank sheets because the heat-sensitive side was upside-down.

The only way to retrieve faxes was for every person to go and search the pile. Mates did not distribute each other's faxes for fear of being accused of seeing the content. Mind you, the sticky-beaks read the interesting faxes — especially those marked 'confidential'.

During my first week on the job, I pleaded with the mail-room supervisor to take responsibility for this messy system and to distribute the faxes with the internal mail. I was put in my place quick-smart!

I then suggested to the operations manager to relocate the fax machine next to the switchboard operator who could sort the faxes during quiet periods. That riled the operations manager, the personnel manager, and the switchboard operator.

I then asked the building services manager if I could have a dedicated fax machine installed in my department. That went down like a lead balloon with him, the IT manager, and the finance manager. They feared that if I secured my own unit, every other manager would want one.

That single machine was used to receive each and every order. We did not have e-commerce systems in those days. We were turning over millions of dollars each month, and relied on the fax machine for our livelihood. Furthermore, it was not uncommon for the telephones to run hot with angry customers wondering why their shipment had been delayed. Not surprisingly, we could not find the order. On top of all this, when the fax machine was being used to *send* documents, nothing could be *received*. Over the weekend, no-one bothered to check that a new roll was installed. It was common to come in on Mondays and see just a few sheets, and an error light flashing. Those models did not have a memory chip. Hence, nothing could be stored in the buffer.

Given the severity of the situation, I could not believe that such a pathetic system existed. I became entangled in the fax issue because a head-hunter had told me that a confidential résumé had been sent to me in response to a request I had made for additional managers to be sourced. The résumé disappeared — twice. Eventually, it was couriered to me. (There were fax thieves who commandeered any document that they found useful, whether it was a price list or someone else's affairs.)

This whole situation was a farce. If the company relied on that one and only fax machine for so much of its business, why were the managers disinterested in such obvious flaws in the process? Which performance review, for which manager, would have documented the lapse in responsibility? Upon investigation, I discovered that the chaotic system had been in place for two years — and no-one had done anything about it. I can tell you what the appraisal system *did* catch. It caught *me* being a troublemaker. I was told that I 'upset people'.

That afternoon in question, after each of my suggestions was blocked, I approached one of my product managers and asked that she appoint one of the junior assistants to the task of going to the central machine several times each day to retrieve all of our department's faxes, just until I sorted out the mess. Within minutes, my product manager reported back that the junior refused to undertake such an administrative function and suggested that I charge one of the secretaries with the 'menial task'. I asked the manager to follow me into her office. With both of us still standing, I explained that the junior's bad attitude had to be corrected immediately. I advised her about my intolerance to such a work ethic. She in turn spoke to the junior and explained why this task was so critical for the overall health of the business. All this took place in a matter of minutes. Over the years, both employees grew into strong advocates who became staunch supporters of mine, and I of them. I could have waited to raise this issue in their performance review. Instead, I acted immediately, and it paid off.

Incidentally, several months later, I broke every rule in the book and crashed through every policy. I went into the office one weekend with a telecommunications technician who drilled holes in walls, constructed shelves, and installed the fax machine that I had purchased using the company credit card. On Monday morning, the executives hit the roof. That 'inexcusable' behaviour on my part gave them weeks of gossip fodder. It also lost me a few points at my performance review. The bill came to $900. Apparently I had the authority to spend millions of dollars whichever way I saw fit, with ample opportunities to squander funds every which way, but I was not allowed to invest $900 on such capital expenditure. If I had hired another assistant at $50 000 per annum just to iron my faxes, no-one would have batted an eye.

It is fascinating how performance appraisals are sometimes great contributors to staff reprisals. **U**

CHAPTER 3

NETWORKING

YOU SCRATCH MY BACK, AND I'LL BE OFF

*Put off until tomorrow that which you can
because today is reserved for more important things*

MANY PEOPLE ASK ME WHY, on my business cards, 'Post-Tentative Virtual Surrealist' appears under my name. I usually joke that it is a diagnosis of a rare medical condition. Here is the real story of how I came up with the title.

At a corporate function, an irritating couple was working the room. It was obvious that they saw the gathering as an opportunity to develop business contacts. They were not at all shy about walking up to each small group, offering their business cards, making some small talk, extracting some information, and then moving on to the next cluster, saying, 'We'll call you next week. We have some very interesting things to tell you.'

It was obvious that they were *networking*. Eventually, they meandered to my corner to perform their ritual — a big smile, a firm handshake that could easily turn into a hug if one were not careful, and the ceremonious exchange of business cards. The four people in my circle obliged by surrendering their cards. The smooth operators read the cards, clarified each person's title, and made some overly friendly remark that bordered on sycophancy.

'Oh, hello Jonar. Good to see you here,' said the woman, gleaning my name from my name tag. She had already given me her card, but noticing that I had not given her mine, she offered another card in one hand and held out the other hand in the hope that it would prompt me to give her mine. I took her second card, but I did not reciprocate.

'So, Jonar, who do you work for?' she asked.

'I'm just here as a guest,' I said, unwilling to divulge any information to the nosy assailant.

'He's with IBM,' volunteered one of the people in my group, thinking that he was being helpful.

'Who do you report to?' she asked.

'Someone overseas. You wouldn't know him,' I said.

'What's your title?' she persisted.

That style of interrogation is not to my liking, so I said that I did not have a title. She refused to believe me. 'You *must* have a title!' she said.

Irritated, I replied: 'I'm a post-tentative virtual surrealist.'

'A what?' she demanded, while maintaining her fake smile.

Talk about a nuisance! Still, I have her to thank for my new job title, which I had just made up on the spot.

WHAT DO YOU DO FOR A LIVING?

You might have gathered that I dislike networking. Those who know me might be confused, because they think of me as a good networker. I would remind them that I have never called to take advantage of them. I have never asked them a personal question, or probed into their private life or work. Furthermore, at functions I never ask anyone about their work, their job title, or their family, unless they first volunteer that information.

Here is another little secret about me: I am quick to dismiss people who start a sentence with, 'What do you do for a living?' Mind you, these days, my work is rather public, so there is less of that. I now have to suffer a *new* set of repetitive questions.

Although such questions are used as innocent ice-breakers, they show signs of a weak capacity for stimulating conversation.

The fundamental rule when initiating a conversation is to ask yourself if what you are about to say to a total stranger is original enough to be interesting. If the stranger is well known, such as a celebrity or an industry figure, you would have to con-sider if what you are about to utter are words that the celebrity has not heard a thousand times before.

A rule of thumb when meeting someone for the first time is to observe the first question that pops into your head — and make a point of *not* asking it. Do not bore others by asking mundane or excruciating questions. You will know how boring this can be if you have ever had to wear a cast for a broken arm or leg. Remember how many people made it a topic of conversation by asking, 'What happened to you?' It is the same when you have just had a haircut. People say, 'You've had a haircut,' as if you did not know.

Therefore, consider *what* you say, and *to whom*. Allow people to be *who* they are, not *what* they are. When you meet people for the first time, do not ask them stock-standard questions that do nothing more than box them into a social set, while signalling that you are only interested in them if they lead an interesting life. Besides, people who lead an interesting life do not usually want to talk about it with total strangers. They could well be exhausted with the subject, modest or shy about it, or just be in need of some privacy. Successful people long to be accepted — but not for their connections, contacts, or fame.

> *Allow people to be who they are, not what they are*

DO ME A FAVOUR

Many people seem to think that networking is all about getting to know influential people with a view to securing advantages. The practice is so entrenched in business and in society that formal invitations often say something like, 'You are cordially invited to our annual celebration where you will have an opportunity to network . . .'

Networking is damaging not because it is harmful in itself, but because it sets up expectations that could disarm you. Do

43

not become a victim of networking by placing your confidence in people who could distract you and sap your energy.

Fundamentally, networking is a waste of time because your success needs to be built on solid foundations. Those who live in the hope that one day someone will discover their talent, will be disappointed unless they build their own infrastructure.

Do not rely on others to do things for you. If you meet people in positions of power, what you do not know is how they got there, and how long they will be there. Beware the manipulators who hold positions of power. Before you know it, they will be hyping up their life and lifestyle in the hope that you will become enamoured of their connections and capabilities. If you try to seek favours from them, you will be targeted and caught before you know it. While you are hoping that they will do something for you, the tables will turn and you will end up doing something for them.

IF LOVE IS BLIND, WHAT IS HOPE?

You have heard it said that *love is blind*. What many people do not realise is that *hope is deaf*. When what you desire to obtain depends on others, then you have just surrendered yourself to forces beyond your control. Confidence tricksters abound because they are kept in business by the gullible, the innocent, and the naïve.

> *You have heard it said that love is blind. What many people do not realise is that hope is deaf.*

One of the difficulties of networking is that it becomes addictive by necessity, because the desire to succeed, when fuelled by the belief that one's substance is weak, drives people to surrender to anyone who shows them a glimmer of hope. This is a disease that many gamblers contend with all their life. They desire to win, and are prepared to lose everything to achieve this. As with many intangible addictions, one gives away the very thing that one is trying to find. This means that what one owns (such as money) is seen as expendable fuel to be used to attain what one wants to win (also money). The money they already own is devalued, whereas the money they win is prized.

Those who observe gamblers are often baffled by why they keep pouring away all that they have in the hope that they might win that which they *already* have. Even more confusing is the behaviour of gamblers who have the occasional windfall. Why do they not just walk away from the table, or the poker machine, or the racetrack, and pocket their winnings? Addicted gamblers will re-inject their takings, leaving their family and friends aghast at their stupidity. What observers do not understand is that the term 'winning' is misleading. Addiction to gambling has nothing to do with wanting to become rich. Gamblers do aspire to a life of prosperity, but not so that they no longer have to gamble — they desire wealth so that they can feed their addiction in comfort and style. Winning money is no more the primary goal of gamblers than is putting on weight the primary goal of food addicts.

Of all the fascinating scientific processes within the universe, chain reactions are the most staggeringly simple, yet devastatingly powerful

Gamblers live in self-destructive hope. This is one of the chain reactions associated with gambling; as well as with taking drugs. Addictions are complex diseases. Of all the fascinating scientific processes within the universe, chain reactions are the most staggeringly simple, yet devastatingly powerful. Once triggered, they can disarm anyone or anything that gets in the way.

Networking can become a disease that distracts people from the real issues by generating baseless hope. The self-destructive nature of this type of hope leads networkers to believe that they can achieve their goals without having to sow the seeds. They want the shortcut to success. They want to short-circuit the usual processes so that they can get ahead more rapidly through the help of others.

Networkers know that solid foundations are important, so they promise themselves that they will work on their shortcomings *after* they have achieved their goal. This is as misguided as someone saying, 'I would swim better if I knew that I could win an Olympic gold medal. So why don't you give me the medal now, and I promise to take up a complete swimming regime that will get me up to the standard where I could own the medal with pride.'

THE DISEASE OF NETWORKING

Of course, some ethical networkers set out to *give* before they *take*. They foster groups of like-minded individuals so that they can eradicate abusers from their life. At its best, networking allows people to sift through the time-wasters so that they can share their experiences for the benefit of others. Although their cause is noble, I will reiterate that networking is a waste of time for those who engage in it in the hope of seeking favours from others.

To live an enchanting and zestful life requires that you live a wholesome life

Success cannot be secured by favour. Even if you meet up with wholesome networkers who have no desire to abuse you, there is the question of what they would be willing to do for you that you cannot do for yourself. For example, experts who hold positions of power would not jeopardise their reputation by giving you opportunities for which you are not suitably equipped. They would not give you authority that you cannot handle. They would not put you in positions of responsibility if you were not capable of performing such tasks. So, herein lie the root questions. If you are *not* capable of performing a certain task, why are you yearning to attain your position through favour, instead of trying to remove your weaknesses? If you do have talent, but are unable to reach your goal, what are you lacking that has prevented you from reaching your goal? You must fix the problems at their root.

Yes, there are people who hold positions undeservedly. Similarly, there are people who steal worldly possessions and are comfortable with their conscience. Such people lack substance, and they know it. To live an enchanting and zestful life requires that you live a wholesome life. The rewards attained from such an existence are immeasurable and are unattainable by any other means. People who do not aspire to this level of bliss (usually because they do not know that it exists) plod along in search of position, power,

Intolerance of time-wasters is the hallmark of successful people

and material wealth. They do not understand that a zestful and wholesome life is the key to a supreme power that can lead to wealth and happiness.

This chapter denounces networking and urges you to curb your appetite for things that only others can give you. You can tantalise yourself with the beauties of life, but remember that you can only reap what you sow. Hence, probe your current status and ask why you are at your current level. What have you done in the past to engineer your current position? What have you *not* done that has held you back? Which direction would you like to take, and what would be required to build a solid foundation to get there?

If you address these questions, you will be able to make it on your own. You will no longer be anxious to please others lest you upset them. You will no longer need to surrender to those who drive you mad and deplete your spirit as you compromise yourself to appease them. You will feel liberated as you start to understand that *you* are in control of your destiny. You will no longer feel that you have to prostitute yourself to gain the favour of those who play with your desires and abuse your good nature.

People, like products, have a brand identity, whether they like it or not. What is the first thing that people think of when they think about you?

The disease of networking is not in the *action*, but in the *lust*. I am referring to your deep-seated desire to have others take care of your career. You need to extinguish that flame. When you do, you will become the life of the party. People will want to be with you because you are truly relaxed and confident. When you no longer need to obtain success through others, no-one can waste your time. Intolerance of time-wasters is the hallmark of successful people.

FROM NETWORKING TO NETMARKING

Networking thrives on short-term gains, yet it offers little in the way of sustainable results. Successful people set about building a solid foundation based on what they can offer to others, not on what others can offer to them.

If you are interested in making a mark, and thereby sharing your gifts with others, forget about networking, and set about *netmarking* — a process whereby you make a *mark* for yourself that others will understand.

Netmarking starts with branding. Everyone understands the power of the brand. Fashion houses and large corporations invest millions to develop and to protect their brand. They try to position the brand and its values in their consumers' mind. The brand becomes the mark that is used to speak volumes about a product. Brands offer assurance and they engender confidence.

For example, if you were given an unlimited budget to buy the best and fastest sports car in the world, which brand would you choose? When this exercise is conducted with a group of people, many of them agree on what the fastest sports car would be, despite never having sat in one, let alone inspected the engine. They believe in the brand to the point where they would be willing to part with their money for a car that they know little about.

People, like products, have a brand identity, whether they like it or not. What is the first thing that people think of when they think about you? What is *your* brand identity? Would people say that you are good at what you do? Would they say that you are a reliable person who always delivers on time? Would they say that you are pleasant to have around, or would they brand you as a loose cannon?

The most important aspect of developing your personal brand is to be consistent. For example, if you are reliable most of the time, yet hopelessly unreliable after you have had a few drinks, you will damage your credibility. You cannot be well-composed at a formal

The wise abhor glib talkers

function, yet an embarrassment when you let your hair down at the annual office party. You will become known for your weakest and your worst elements. You will be judged by your substance, not by your veneer. This means that no matter how much you invest in your clothes, car, and accessories, you will not impress anyone if your manners and behaviour are not congruent with your exterior.

ON YOUR MARK

When you start to make your mark, you will be surprised at how easily success will come your way, because you will attract what you deserve. Experts like to work with knowledgeable people. Mature people like to work with those who are content. Happy operators like to be surrounded by people of substance. The powerful surround themselves with those who are capable. The wise abhor glib talkers. Visionaries are irritated by non-believers. Successful people repel those who lack substance. Generous souls disdain the selfish. Graceful spirits shun the obnoxious.

Do you think that it is possible to fake a wholesome existence? Many try, and they *always* fail. Not because they are flushed out of the system, but because they do not know when they are among people of substance. The very group that they desire to belong to is not one that they will recognise even when they are right in the middle of it. Here is a chain reaction in full swing: what they desire cannot be found through networking, so they engage in networking to find what they desire.

The moment that you deviate from your strengths, you will become known for your weaknesses

The leeches, too, truly desire a better life, but all that they know to say is, 'You scratch my back, and I'll be off.' They are in search of that which they can never find. This is the epitome of self-inflicted torment. Can there be anything worse?

In developing your career, you need to let people know what you stand for. Note that you cannot *make* others associate certain qualities with you. For example, if you want people to know that you are honest, you cannot send them an e-mail declaring that you posses this noble quality. If you want people to believe that you are trustworthy, no amount of pleading will convince them of your trustworthiness. If you want your colleagues to think that you are a lot of fun, you cannot persuade them of the fact until *they* feel that they are having fun in your presence.

It is imperative to decide what you want to offer as part of your package. What *strengths* would you like your friends to associate with you? What *skills* would you like employers to attribute to you? What *characteristics* would you like your colleagues to admire in you? These qualities will enable others to position you in their mind and their heart. If you do not specifically set out to hone your strengths, skills, and characteristics, how will others know what you have to offer? Furthermore, if you do not deliver on your promises, your efforts will be futile. The moment that you deviate from your strengths, you will become known for your weaknesses. For example, it takes hard work to earn a reputation as a trustworthy person, yet it takes no effort to destroy that reputation. All you have to do is betray someone's confidence or let someone down. Redeeming yourself from that kind of fall will take much more energy than it took to build your reputation in the first place. Sometimes, betrayal or non-performance is irreparable.

Deciding on what you want to become known for is not a simple task. The strengths, skills, and characteristics that you choose have to be selected carefully, based on your belief systems, values, deep-seated desires, capabilities, and the level of investment that you are prepared to make. There is no point in coming up with an ambitious list that you have no hope of attaining. Take your time in deciding what you want to offer, and then set about living a life that is aligned to your strengths, skills, and characteristics. In due course your brand will form, and people will have no choice but to form a good or bad opinion about you — one that they would be willing to bet on. You want your friends, family, and colleagues to have faith in your brand to the point where they will have no doubt about your intentions and capabilities.

It is not who you know, but what you do with what you know that matters most

When you can engender in others a high level of confidence in you, you would have developed a sustainable brand around your name. Ultimately, in every transaction in life, people pay for confidence. They pay for goods and services that they believe will deliver an advantage. If you can make people believe, without a shadow of a doubt, that you are true to your word and true to your brand, you will be able to make a mark for yourself, no matter what industry you choose to be in. You will then be able to achieve your goals without seeking favours from others. You will be able to succeed on the thrust of your efforts.

If you take a close look at any significant project, you will find that it contains a 'hierarchy of importance'. For example, if you were organising a major product launch, you would place certain aspects above others. You might decide that the food is more important than the venue, or that the availability of parking spaces for guests is more important than the entertainment you choose for the night. Despite the hundreds of elements that make up the event, they are each ranked in order of importance. The elements that rank highest on the list are those that will command most of your attention. They are also those things for which you would be prepared to pay extra.

The essence of the hierarchy of importance is that once something is deemed to be important, it can command more attention, time, or money. If we relate this back to your brand, and your strengths, skills, and characteristics, you would do well to offer elements that are usually deemed more important than others. The moment that you can offer important services to people who have confidence in you, you too will be able to command more attention, time, or money. You will no longer need others to do favours for you. It is not *who* you know, but *what you do with what you know* that matters most.

When you have a strong personal brand, you will no longer need to worry about how to make money. In fact, you will find that opportunities will come at you from every direction. Can there be anything better? **E**

CHAPTER 4

The early bird catches the bookworm

From university to adversity

Getting an education means becoming
conscious of what we don't know.
Getting a promotion means becoming
conscious of what others don't know.

FOR YEARS, I have been a critic of commercialised education, saying that studying at university is, more often than not, a waste of time for those who go there in the 'hope' that they might find a direction. Unless they have a specific purpose for obtaining particular qualifications, students are likely to regret their actions. This chapter outlines salient points about how education relates to personal development. It points the way to a satisfying and rewarding career — with or without the help of formal education.

The first step is to acknowledge that no level of qualification is useful for prospective students, until they know the direction that they want to take. Alas, most students approach this problem in reverse, attending a university to *find* a direction. Such a process is futile. Tertiary studies ought to fuel *existing* passions, not ignite new passions. Studying a subject merely to seek a qualification, so as to impress employers or peers, is not being true to oneself.

Any criticism levelled at education does not pertain to *learning*. Fostering an inquiring mind and learning how to develop (and later to feed) an insatiable appetite for knowledge ought to be the *second*-most urgent pursuit of the intelligent being.

> *An insatiable appetite for knowledge ought to be the <u>second</u>-most urgent pursuit of the intelligent being*

OUR UNEDUCATED PIONEERS

Many of the products and technologies that we use today were given to us by *uneducated* pioneers.

At your next social gathering, ask your friends this question: 'Think of the ten major inventions or developments of all time that you would deem to have been the most important for society's progress.' Perhaps each of the ten would have been given to us by pioneers who, if lined up today, would not pass a basic university entrance examination. In their day, they might not even have been respected citizens.

Imagine attending a concert where you are entertained by sixty leading musicians performing some of the most energising music you have heard. How would you react to being told that the composer does not read music? It seems impossible that such a person can compose breathtaking masterpieces for a sixty-piece orchestra! One such musician is Yanni.

Who says that Yanni has to read sheet music? Which came first, music notation or music composition? Surely notation and sheet music *reflect* what musicians do best so that the rest of the world can learn from their talent.

Beethoven composed music while completely deaf, yet many of us would expect that hearing is a prerequisite for composing and performing. We need to adjust our understanding of what it means to be an expert of our craft.

Leading-edge thinkers are years ahead of educators in institutions. Thinkers go about their business by innovating, devising, inventing, building, and paving the way so that other people can benefit from better products and improved processes.

Universities do not create brilliant people. They merely seek the knowledge that brilliant people possess, and re-package it in the form of information. The recent information-technology industry that has changed many aspects of our life (and kept the economy buoyant) was propelled by non-graduates. Universities could not keep up with what these innovators developed. School dropouts were innovative, so universities rushed to observe what was going on. Entire faculties were built to capture the fury of an emerging

Universities do not create brilliant people

industry. The innovators were the inspired and talented, not necessarily the university-educated.

Nowadays we are hearing more about the importance of 'knowledge'. The slogan 'knowledge is power' is misleading. Knowledge is not in itself power. Rather, power comes from the application of knowledge.

THE GRAND ILLUSION

Many students are under the grand illusion that they can 'become something', merely by undertaking the appropriate course. When they make a decision about the profession they want to pursue, they genuinely believe that all they have to do is get the right marks, apply to a university, and if they are lucky enough to be selected, they can be on their way to reaching their goal.

The slogan 'knowledge is power' is misleading. Knowledge is not in itself power. Rather, power comes from the application of knowledge.

We live in a world of 'instant gratification' whereby we want answers and pleasures immediately. We expect to see results straight away. We are impatient when we go in search of joy and ecstasy. We dislike waiting for medication to work, and we expect speedy recoveries. We want paint to dry instantly, and we want beauty products to enhance our features without delay. Yet, strangely enough, there are still some things for which we are prepared to wait. For example, many people are prepared to go through tiresome routines and long time-frames to attain a goal. Prepared to work hard all year at a job that they do not particularly like, they wait patiently for a holiday, thinking that eleven months of misery can be alleviated by four weeks away at a resort.

It is with the same perverse sense of delayed fulfilment that people are prepared to invest years into tertiary education, hoping that they will eventually find an excellent job. They also believe that the more they study, the more likely they will find employment in an exciting industry, working for an innovative company. This is the promise that many students want to believe in — just like we all want to believe in the perfect marriage and the blissful loving relationship. Unfortunately, the problem with following such a dream is that by the time we find out that we have been misled, it is often too late to reclaim our energy and our youth. Seeking job-satisfaction by undertaking tertiary education is often a gamble. Gambling life away with idealistic fantasies at education institutions that paint rosy pictures, is folly.

Interestingly, institutions espouse the benefits of education, yet they are not responsible for delivering on the promises they make. There are no guarantees. There is no recourse at the end if you find that you do not have an advantage after all.

THE MODERN RATIONALE FOR TERTIARY STUDIES

Students have many reasons for attending college, not dissimilar to the varied reasons why some people attend church. Their faith might draw them to worship with their community. Some attend for social reasons, others attend out of habit, or because their parents force them to go. Some might be there to steal a glimpse of their sweetheart. They might pursue their religious activities out of hope, fear, guilt, or custom. Some churchgoers attend for the sake of their partner or children; others attend with neither a sense of purpose, nor conviction, but through obligation or indifference.

University students do not all share the same reasons for

enrolling. Most of them harbour fantasies or ill-founded precon-
ceived notions about what university life could offer. After they
enrol and attend lectures, reality sets in whereby their decision to
complete their course is based upon a *modified* set of ideals or
pressures. Those who endure the course begrudgingly, do so to
avoid social humiliation or personal shame and defeat. Notwithstanding that there are students who have a balanced and healthy
perspective on the value of tertiary studies, such folk are rare.

Those of you who are tertiary students, or are hoping to
engage in tertiary studies, are urged to question and to understand why you want to pursue this direction. Do you know
what the essence of your desire is, and why you want to undertake such studies?

Some of the many and varied reasons that students attend
college or university are listed below. Why they are attracted in
the first place, or why they pursue their studies, says much
about their hopes, dreams, fears, and inadequacies.

a) To open the right doors

We have built a social infrastructure that demands specific academic qualifications that are integral to 'opening the right doors'.
Some industries have built fortresses to protect their professional
and financial interests. Without the approved tertiary studies, students would never be permitted to enrol in some associations,
such as those that protect the medical or legal networks. Those
who desire to become lawyers or doctors are in non-negotiable
situations where they must follow the academic path set out
before them. The respective fraternities would argue that their
strict policies are designed to protect people from would-be
'sharks' who would take advantage of consumers and deliver sub-
standard services. There is merit in this argument. Unfortunately,

the hoops through which lawyers and doctors have to jump have not produced the desired results. Unprofessional, unethical, incompetent, and unscrupulous practitioners abound.

If you are studying because you believe that a qualification will open a door, you had better know on whose door you are knocking

There are people, from all walks of life, who truly believe that doors would open for them if they were to obtain qualifications. Some employers are impressed with candidates who flaunt their degrees. Such employers are also likely to be easily distracted by a person's exclusive address, family name, perceived social connections, or good looks. People are impressionable. The question is, are you prepared to invest (or waste) three to seven years of your life to obtain a qualification with a view to satisfying an *unknown* future employer who might well salivate at your double major, but turn you away because you are the wrong gender?

If you are studying because you believe that a qualification will open a door, you had better know on whose door you are knocking, and what the decision-maker is likely to find impressive or unimpressive.

b) To impress friends

Some of us fantasise about being surrounded by friends who will approve of us. We think of those whom we would most dearly want as our friends, and then we start to imagine what we have to do to attract their attention or to win their favour. They become our mirror, and their approval becomes the most important prize to secure. To that end, we might change the colour of our hair or the clothes we wear. We might change our lifestyle, where we live, what we drive (whether we can afford it or not), and take up hobbies and activities that we hope will take us closer to them.

This fixation with pleasing others is common in all societies and for all age groups. The possession of tertiary qualifications sometimes falls into this category, and it is understandable that people presume that their studies might impress others. If that is your aim, be sure to weigh up your decision against the time and energy that your studies would require. Be certain that the person you wish to impress is interested in your academic standing.

> It is too high a price to pay to obtain qualifications as corporate accessories. Prestige is not universal. It is an intangible concept that carries weight only in the eye of the beholder.

You need to know that there are people who are not impressed by qualifications. Do not blind yourself by unsubstantiated perceptions. It is too high a price to pay to obtain qualifications as corporate accessories. Remember that prestige is not universal. It is an intangible concept that carries weight only in the eye of the beholder.

Some students are not out to impress others. They commit to a study program to set themselves a personal challenge; to obtain a degree is part of a personal mission to prove to themselves that they have the stamina and the discipline. This is understandable and commendable. While some choose the academic path, others undertake similar arduous endeavours such as sailing around the world, or running a marathon. Seen from this perspective, tertiary studies would make a reasonable alternative, so long as the journey does not become clouded by an unhealthy fixation on the end-point. A mature person would feel satisfied with the journey, while an immature person would seek accolades. A well-balanced person would feel invigorated by the experience, while a confused person would seek social rewards.

There is a considerable 'show-off' factor associated with acquiring letters after one's name. Some executives magnify what little advantage they have by framing their certificates and flaunting their college crest. Their business cards are reprinted to highlight the newly-acquired qualifications, and their e-mail sign-off boasts the many associations to which they belong.

Passing a course does not always prove intelligence, but demonstrates persistence

Academic qualifications are for biographies and résumés, yet many qualifications have no relation to people's current positions. A sales clerk of an automotive company whose business card reads 'John Smith BSc' says little of John Smith, or the relevance of his degree to his current job, or of his ability. At best, passing a course does not always prove intelligence, but demonstrates persistence.

c) To impress employers

In some countries and in some industries, there are employers who are more impressed with your *brand* than your degree — meaning that they want qualifications from those universities that boast a recognisable and prestigious crest.

Many employers stipulate tertiary qualifications, more so to impress their clients than to capitalise on your creativity. Take a look at their annual reports wherein they publicise the precise number of highly-qualified staff that they employ.

Those who lack self-esteem boast about external factors in the hope that others might deem them worthy. Yes, some employers do discriminate against those without tertiary qualifications. Job advertisements stipulate that only the degree-qualified should apply.

Students say that they want to secure qualifications lest they be excluded from employment opportunities. In these situations, all that a degree would do is allow the candidate to stand at the front door alongside every other hopeful applicant. Given that the number of qualified candidates is high, what then shall be the sifting point?

Do you want to work for an employer who believes that a dynamic team comprises not the best person for the job, but the best candidate who happened to attend college for a few years? That elitist approach is short-sighted.

A competent marketing manager at a large international hotel called me. She had been with the chain for seven years, and in the hospitality industry for more than twenty years. She was hoping to apply for the position of marketing director within her hotel. Despite her exceptional performance and enviable track record, she felt the need to enrol at a university to undertake further studies. 'I feel that management might overlook me for the promotion because I do not have tertiary qualifications in hospitality', she confided. It was a difficult task for me to convince her that her work history was infinitely more valuable than an academic qualification.

I discouraged her from undertaking further studies because she was prepared to take on six years of part-time studies to rectify her personal self-doubt, the result of a few conversations she had had with managers whose only excuse for looking to employ outsiders was that she did not possess academic qualifications. If twenty years of experience and a seven-year proven track record within

Life is so precious that one would be committing a crime to waste the years to remedy a non-existent problem

the hotel were no longer sufficient proof of her capabilities, what was amiss with her manager?

The woman's desire to enrol at a local university was not triggered by professional curiosity or a need to learn new skills. Had she expressed a desire to go in search of information or knowledge about a particular aspect of her profession or industry, or had she identified an area of weakness, I would have encouraged her in that pursuit. Instead, she wanted to surrender a large part of her time to appease others. Life is so precious that one would be committing a crime to waste the years to remedy a non-existent problem.

If this woman had identified areas of weakness in her work, what could she not have taught herself, or have managed to find out through personal investigation and self-paced studies?

d) To conduct research

There are professionals who enjoy the discipline of conducting research and learning through probing in the areas of science, industry, society, or the environment. The personal journey of discovery can be rewarding and fascinating, especially if it leads to profound improvements in human life.

The personal journey of discovery can be rewarding and fascinating, especially if it leads to profound improvements in human life

Before engaging in worthwhile investigative projects, students are better served by first gaining commercial experience in their chosen field of endeavour.

There can be no excitement in pursuing research without clearly identifying how the findings can be applied to industry or to society. Students who want to become researchers or pioneers often end up as technicians or administrators.

Many students who surrender to the romantic and noble ideologies of laboratory or field research, bow out after a few years when their patience can no longer support their dream. Research is a costly, time-consuming vocation that requires endless patience and an inquisitive mind. Those who seek instant gratification are often disappointed with this line of work.

e) To respond to pressure from parents and peers

Pressure from family and friends is often the main reason given by students as to why they attend university. Some parents sponsor tertiary studies either because *they* were not afforded that opportunity, or because they believe that the workforce discriminates against those who do not pursue tertiary studies.

> *The education system fails each and every time that students cannot look forward to their career with enthusiasm and delight*

A few parents endorse university life as a means of instilling more discipline into their offspring. Some parents offload their children to boarding colleges in the hope of domestic peace and quiet.

Many high-school students cannot articulate their plans. Lost and helpless, the burden on them is immense. Although they have years to contemplate their career, they do not take the matter seriously. All of a sudden, they are expected to find a path and to pursue a profession. This is a cruel situation. It would be fabulous if students could feel a sense of excitement about their career. More often than not, these young people see work as boring, and they see studies as laborious. Activity without a zestful purpose is mind-numbing and regrettable. The education system fails each and every time that students cannot look forward to their career with enthusiasm and delight.

When parents become distressed about their children's apparent lack of direction, they insist that a university course would hold their children in good stead. If the children cannot suggest a better option, they lose the argument, and are forced to enrol in the 'best' course that their marks will allow.

It is an indictment on our developed Western society that there is such a high suicide rate among modern youth despite belonging to the most privileged generation of all time

There are students who do not set their sights on a profession, but on a 'range of marks' that they feel capable of attaining. This is hardly a process that engenders excellence and excitement.

Some students want to escape domestic responsibilities, so they follow their friends to college. Together, they pursue a life of sports, social activities, and some studies.

There are times when children's dreams are not approved of by their parents, especially if they involve studies that are not considered to be mainstream. Conservative parents express concern about children who seek to further their studies in the area of sports, theatre, or entertainment. The typical argument ends with the parents shouting, 'Get yourself real qualifications so that you can get a real job.' They fear that life within the arts is reserved for the lucky few. A similar struggle was played out in the movie *Dead Poets' Society* wherein a student called Neil Perry is torn between his desires for a career in the theatre and his father's demands that he study to become a doctor. Neil finally sees the light and says, 'For the first time in my life, I know what I want to do!' Unfortunately, his overbearing father exerts too much authority, and Neil commits suicide.

It is an indictment on our developed Western society that there is such a high suicide rate among modern youth, despite belonging to the most privileged generation of all time. Our young people, dubbed 'Generation Y', are: better able to express themselves; free to travel farther and more frequently; in possession of more disposable income; able to access more credit; presented with broader-based career choices at a younger age; granted more opportunities to start their own business; less inclined to heed taboos or to become embroiled in social paranoia; and able to access technology, medicine, education, welfare, and a host of social support structures. Yet, they also belong to the generation that is: more dependent on illicit and prescription drugs; more depressed; least satisfied; least engaged in society; and more prone to commit suicide than in previous generations.

Allow children to follow their heart's desires. If a spark of interest exists, it should be fanned and encouraged.

Societal pressures about education and careers contribute to overwhelming personal anxiety. Parents need to allow children to follow their heart's desires. If a spark of interest exists, it should be fanned and encouraged.

Students rarely pursue a job within the area of their studies. Most economics students do not pursue a job within the sphere of economics, for instance. Therefore, it is pointless to argue about the field of studies. It is more important that young students learn how to nurture sparks of enthusiasm.

It is far more important for teenagers to learn how to follow a dream than to wait and hope for the right dream to unfold before them

Which would you rather? Students who are excited to wake up each morning and engage in a line of study that stimulates their heart and soul, or miserable children from whom youth is stolen in the name of speculative comfort?

Young people need to taste for themselves the wonders of life. It is far more important for teenagers to learn *how* to follow a dream than to wait and hope for the right dream to unfold before them.

f) To pursue a career with passion

There are students who know exactly what they want and where they are heading. They are highly focussed and single-minded about their foray into academia. They pursue tertiary courses purposefully while they prepare the foundations for a well-planned career. Such students display a healthy perspective about tertiary studies for career development.

Universities are not the only institutions that can offer the desired tuition. There are effective ways in which students can gain valuable knowledge from mentors, coaches, professionals, libraries, and specialist training courses. If students know what they need to learn, they can take charge of their learning program.

When people tell me that they wish to acquire an MBA or PhD, I ask them why they cannot go in search of the knowledge without the formalised structure. Invariably, there is an egotistical basis for their decision. By the time they realise their error, they find it difficult to pull out, for fear of being labelled a 'dropout' or a failure. Under such circumstances, students quickly re-adjust their priorities and concede that their main aim is now to 'complete' the course, not to expand their mind.

I have met many Masters students who cursed the arduous course. All of them graduated (whether they deserved to or not) because their universities could not justify taking thousands of dollars for a course that does not deliver that all-important piece of paper. After graduation, they reminisced about the learning curve, convincing themselves that the course was worthwhile. They probably learned important lessons about human interaction, human pecking order, group dynamics, time management, and research procedures. Unfortunately, they failed to grasp a superior knowledge about the subject matter that they initially sought.

g) To engage in a hobby

Tertiary studies have a lot to offer to those who want to find a mentally-engaging past-time. If treated as a hobby, it can be rewarding to delve into new and unfamiliar territories to stimulate the brain. Some people enjoy the challenge of 'studentship'.

Hobbies should not turn into a boring slog. There are examinations to pass. If you take your learning processes too casually, and you do not want to maintain the required discipline of completing assignments on time, you stand to be marked down and to be excluded from subsequent classes.

Take a close look at the entire course before you enrol, and investigate and compare other courses from other institutions before committing to formal training. A hobby should serve your needs, not the other way around.

CHECKMATE

Many high-school students lack direction and personal vision. They are more inclined to hang on to the education thread and go to university, hoping to work out later where they can go. If you are such a student, I can confidently say that if you cannot articulate your direction in your final year of high-school, you will be none the wiser in your final year of university. If you feel scared and lost now, you will feel more fearful when you graduate and realise that your degree or diploma has not illuminated your path.

If you cannot articulate your direction in your final year of high-school, you will be none the wiser in your final year of university

More disturbing, are students who hold a high opinion of their qualifications. This leads them to refuse any work that does not sound grand or does not offer above-average salaries. They might succumb and accept a job with an organisation on the basis that they are getting a foot in the door. The unchallenging nature of their work often leads them to feel that they need to retreat to university to undertake additional studies to obtain more qualifications. They do this in the hope that they might be taken more seriously the next time they enter the workforce. After another three years of studies, they begrudge the fact that the workforce does not seem to recognise their attainments. Employers do not want to pay large salaries to candidates who do not have practical experience.

Many students say that they are studying because they want to increase their skills and expand their knowledge. They insist that they are not interested in big-noting themselves with their qualifications. Then I ask them this telling question: 'If you were not allowed to tell your prospective employer about your academic achievements, would you go through the agony of obtaining a degree?' This question leaves them speechless. They had convinced themselves that their studies were for their own intellectual benefit. Yet, when asked to keep their academic qualifications a secret, they panic. Deep down, most students labour for years so that they can impress future employers. They rarely listen to the voice of sanity until they leave the academic nest and go in search of 'advantage' while waving their degree about the town. It is then that they feel the heavy burden of their misplaced youth. By this stage, time, money, patience, and dreams would have run out. They are far too old to run back to their parents for support, so they either seek welfare, or work part-time for ages. You can meet such people who are permanent part-time

If you were not allowed to tell your prospective employer about your academic achievements, would you go through the agony of obtaining a degree?

workers. They might work as restaurant waiters for three years, yet they cannot bring themselves to admit that this is their full-time employment. They see themselves as 'executives-in-waiting'.

No doubt, my helping students to ask the right questions will upset many academics. Institutions have been trying to create a perception that their courses add esoteric personal value. When certain qualifications proliferate in a society, the bar is raised higher so that graduates are lured back in search of more feathers for their cap. These actions are along similar lines to the ways in which credit and debit cards are promoted. At first, there was the green card, the gold card, and now there is the platinum card. Soon, black, red, and diamond smart-cards will be the rage. The issuers are keen to maintain the 'social' (not practical) status of each colour because they know that the features and benefits offered are not sufficiently different to justify the annual fee. A similar shifting game occurs with airlines that try to maintain a sense of exclusivity. Instead of offering superior service to *all* their clients, they discriminate against those who cannot keep up with the latest colour.

Universities and colleges, who assist students to learn, need not be concerned about my warnings. I do not have an issue with ethical institutions that create professionals. I am opposed to universities and colleges that prey on people's weaknesses and fears.

THE SPIDER WEB AND THE TRAIN TRACK

Many young people have the impression that their career must follow a socially-approved path whereby they first attain qualifications and then get a job. Of the dozens of successful people whose careers I have observed, I do not know of any whose success came about through following the linear (straight line) path set before them by the education system or by society.

Those who signal their desire to take a different path are smothered by limiting language like, 'You should wait your turn for a promotion,' or 'You are too young.' Often they are told to be patient and tolerant, and they are reminded that 'good things come to those who wait'. These maxims are misleading. Although it is prudent to learn when to be patient and tolerant, it is just as important to discern when and how to be *impatient* and *intolerant* by moving independently to create your own path.

Of all the successful people I admire, none of them developed their brilliant and exciting career through the linear approach. Going along the track laid out by the education system seems like a solid and sensible method. Unfortunately, you could miss opportunities that spring up from left field. Flexibility is a vital ingredient for career development.

The winners whom I have studied have followed what I call the 'spider web' approach to success. If you take a look at a spider's web, you would see intricate, strange, messy, yet brilliant paths that interconnect all sorts of junctions. If you can yield to your judgement and intuition, and if you can learn to identify opportunities, you will be able to duck and weave through the confusion of life as you set your sights on the beacons that will guide you on exquisite journeys.

Some of the decisions you make might end up at dead-ends; others might cause you a lot of heartache. So long as your foundations are solid, and your ethics and values are firm, you will always land on your feet as a stronger more enlightened explorer who is nimble, versatile, and free.

Think about famous inventors and pioneers. It is likely that they were people of average capabilities and average intelligence who were prepared to get off the track and start their journey on the intricate web of life.

For example, within the music industry you cannot ignore the work of a young dyslexic school 'dropout' by the name of Richard Branson. He founded the Virgin Group, and chose the name 'Virgin' to denote how inexperienced he was at business. As a young boy he used his pocket money to publish a simple magazine that he later turned into a mail-order music catalogue to sell discounted music. At that time, the British Government had deregulated the music industry, which meant that retailers could decide the price of records. None of the retailers discounted their music, so Branson seized an opportunity to sell discounted music through his magazine. This worked well, until a time when there was a postal strike that disrupted his mail-order business. So Branson opened a small store to sell his music. Later he scouted for talent and launched his own music label, pressing albums for some of the biggest names at the time. All of these twists and turns made Branson what he is today — thanks to a young entrepreneurial spirit. The Virgin Group, with its 200 companies, now employs more than 25 000 people. It is involved in planes, trains, finance, soft drinks, music, mobile phones, holidays, cars, wines, publishing, and bridal wear, to name just a few.

Sir Richard Branson is a perfect example of how someone can move about a web structure and grab opportunities amidst adversity and unbelievable obstacles.

Travelling through the web is not a matter of potluck. Careful calculation, hard work, perceptivity, and an eye for detail are vital ingredients. Such opportunities rarely present themselves along fixed tracks, but they abound on the web of life.

Look around and you will find many more fascinating stories. Oprah Winfrey has overcome tremendous challenges to reach her goals. The Apple computer was developed by two college 'dropouts' who followed their heart against all odds. Henry

Ford, a farm boy who left home at sixteen, worked two jobs for most of his life. He was broke and miserable at the age of forty. By the age of fifty he had successfully started the Ford Motor Company that reshaped the motorcar industry. Ford faced troubled times, year after year. Everything that could go wrong did go wrong. Yet he stuck to his dream. He set about to learn what he wanted to learn, when he was ready to learn it.

McDonald's has a similar story. Ray Kroc, a Czechoslovakian boy whose parents migrated to the USA, sold real-estate and played the piano in bars to earn some cash. At the age of fifty-two he was selling milkshake mixers to restaurants. He became curious about why a small hamburger restaurant (run by the McDonald brothers) was buying so many of his appliances. Kroc encouraged the brothers to expand their business, hoping that this would lead to additional orders for appliances. The brothers did not like the idea of expanding their business. So Kroc decided to franchise the restaurant. He agreed to pay the brothers thirty cents for every hundred dollars of profit. Today, McDonald's has more than 28 000 restaurants in 120 countries, serving forty-five million customers daily.

WHAT'S THE BOTTOM LINE?

Journalists ask me why I choose to be a business consultant when I often criticise business and management. I spend time with executives, not because I care about 'corporations', but because I care about 'people'. My desire for organisa-

It is often the minorities who make the most significant contributions to society

tions to improve comes from a deep concern about the ways in which humans suffer under the weight of mismanagement and organisational greed. I seek to give businesses what they want on the understanding that their improvements will lead to better conditions for employees. When asked how I propose to 'take on the world', I remind journalists that all I have to do is to serve 'minorities'. It is often the minorities who make the most significant contributions to society.

I am not trying to change the education system. This would be far too difficult. Instead, I want to assist individuals to foster an insatiable appetite for life-long learning, and to dissuade them from falling victim to pressure and misinformation about the supposed benefits of academic accessories.

THE HIGHEST PRIORITY

Earlier I said that fostering an inquiring mind and learning how to develop, and to later feed, an insatiable appetite for knowledge ought to be the *second*-most urgent pursuit of the intelligent being, no matter what profession or trade is pursued.

Such a statement begs the question, 'What is the *first* priority?' In my opinion, the first priority ought to be this: seek to understand the framework of *wisdom*. Although we can inherit knowledge, technology, money, or material goods, none of us can inherit wisdom. We are all born with a zero measure of wisdom. Learning how to construct it, so that we know when and how to apply it, ought to be our most urgent pursuit.

Wisdom is not something that can be bought. It cannot be read. It cannot be obtained. Nor can it be bequeathed or inherited. Wisdom can only be made fresh on the spot. When I urge people to go in search of wisdom, I am asking them to learn how to *make* wisdom. Wisdom

Although we can inherit knowledge, technology, money, or material goods, none of us can inherit wisdom. We are all born with a zero measure of wisdom.

is not like a sequence of mathematical formulae that can be memorised. It is not a recipe that can be handed down from one generation to the next.

My definition of wisdom is the ability to arrive at a decision that we know will not lead to regret. Of all the human burdens, regret is the most penetrating because it relates to decisions that *we* make. This means that we are unable to apportion blame to others. The sorrow that drips from regret cannot be abdicated. For more about abdication, see Chapter 7, 'Please cancel my disorder'.

Phrases and quotes that people like to share with each other are indeed words of wisdom, but they are also like photographs. A photo of yourself is not you. A snapshot is but a memory of what was. A quotable quote is only a frozen moment when wisdom was constructed for that particular moment. Just as there is no such thing as pre-packaged wisdom, there is no such thing as pre-packaged honesty. Honesty is not something that I can give you right now, unless it can be put in context. It cannot stand on its own in the way that a chair can stand on its own. Like wisdom, honesty can only be constructed when it is required. For honesty to mean anything, it has to duel with dishonesty. If I were unable to exercise my option to be dishonest with you, what I say cannot be deemed to be honest.

Wisdom is the ability to arrive at a decision that we know will not lead to regret

DECLARING MY HAND

I was educated in both private and public schools. I changed countries and schools regularly, and eventually left high-school at the age of fourteen. During that brief period, I missed out on three years of schooling so in effect, I had the education of an eleven-year-old.

English was not my native tongue. I was introduced to it at the age of eight, and took several years to learn the basics. As a result, I found myself in the 'E' class — one reserved for socially awkward children who had learning difficulties, in some cases owing to their brilliance or to their madness. In addition, I faced problems with disorientation until the age of eighteen, having lived in a war-torn country in my formative years.

If I were unable to exercise my option to be dishonest with you, what I say cannot be deemed to be honest

One of several reasons why I left at fourteen was that I became an 'A' student and I was no longer challenged. The schooling process was excruciatingly slow for me. I found full-time employment and pursued part-time studies that continued for six years, eventually leading me to university. That too was unsatisfying because I was able to compare my studies with my real work environment and I observed that the two were like chalk and cheese. I decided to bow out gracefully and take charge of my own education. I was labelled 'a college dropout', and I had to contend with explaining myself to prospective employers who were curious or pompous or discriminatory.

Over the years, my appetite for learning and my love for teaching have enabled me to teach business-related subjects to under-graduates and post-graduates. I have designed and delivered courses at various management institutes and technical education centres. To this day, I am a guest lecturer at universities internationally, and I am a director of Australia's largest private adult education institution.

I have shared this information with you so as to pre-empt countless e-mails that are likely to ask how I can justify this chapter. I have noticed that readers are eager to learn about the perspective from which an author writes.

There is no doubt that there will be many exceptions to my philosophies. I know a doctor friend of mine who lectures about the hazards of smoking. Invariably, he receives letters from people who disagree with him. They are eager to tell him that their 'ninety-year-old grandmother has been smoking since the age of ten, and she is still in fine health.' Granted, there are smokers who make a mockery of the warnings. Unfortunately, for every such grandmother, there are 3 000 000 people who die each year as a direct result of smoking. Similarly, for every successful, contented, intelligent, and happy academic, there are thousands of bookworms who just do not seem to make it. They are beaten by the early birds who are sometimes called entrepreneurs, geniuses, or dropouts. It has been my experience that the early birds beat the bookworms. **S**

PART TWO

FINDING *your* DIRECTION

You'll know a brilliant idea when you think of one

CHAPTER 5

YOU DESERVE WHAT *you* GET

SEARCHING FOR A BLACK SPIDER IN A DARK ROOM

There's no shortcut to perfection

I CAN NOW CONFIDENTLY PREDICT the top-ten questions that I would be asked after my public lectures. Invariably they include queries about the secrets of job-satisfaction and career development. People of all ages, and of all backgrounds, are finding it hard to understand how their work can complement their life. They admit that they do not have a vision for where they are heading. They say that they do not have a sense of purpose. They feel guilty for not engaging in passionate pursuits. They blame themselves for having lost their zest, and they accuse the company of losing the plot.

Even those in well-paid positions within booming industries feel vulnerable and insecure because they know that they are not adequately contributing to their organisation. All that they can do is wait helplessly for something to happen, yet they stagnate as the empty years slip away.

Employees become frightened about their future because they cannot set a direction, let alone see the vision. They think that their only strategy is to engage in further studies in the hope that additional qualifications might lead to a better career. They lose their confidence slowly, much like a punctured tyre loses air. Before they know it, they are depleted and helpless. Eventually, they lose their ability to negotiate, because they no longer believe in themselves. When they reach this point, they become averse to risk. Besides, they have already emptied their energy tank, giving their all to their employer. They have no fuel left to tend to their own nest, so they work doubly hard on the treadmill so that they cannot be accused of disloyalty. Some employees cannot see that they are disposable — until that unfathomable moment when they are dismissed, or retrenched, or eased out one way or another.

The only thing more disturbing than abusive employers is surrendered employees

No matter how abusive their boss might be, they become numb to the torture because they do not dare to show signs of displeasure. They cannot afford to bite the hand that feeds them. They become professional beggars for financial and emotional sustenance. Like hostages who grow sympathetic to their captor, they become dependent on the boss to stroke their ego, no matter how brutally. Mind you, the only thing more disturbing than abusive employers is surrendered employees. Those who concede defeat will reason that they got what they deserved. Eventually, they attribute their failure to the company and its management, or to fate, or karma, or numerology, or astrology — in fact, to any external force that can explain their demise.

WHAT DO YOU DESERVE?

There is an old maxim that says *you get what you deserve*. If only that were true. Do the famine-stricken deserve relentless pain and sorrow? Are the forty million children who live in abject poverty and slavery deserving of their plight?

Every child deserves a loving family. Every family deserves a happy environment. Every society deserves peace. Every nation deserves prosperity. And why not?

The law of reciprocity allows us to extract love when we inject affection

Do you deserve a better job? Do you deserve a prosperous life packed with fun and adventure? Of course you do. Everyone deserves wonderful moments to fill the short amount of time we have on this planet. And why not?

Who among us would not feel deserving of a fabulous job? Who would not yearn for an energy-charged career? Who would not desire luxuries to share with loved ones?

The world offers its beauty and invites us to partake in its generosity. All that is required of us is to reciprocate. The law of reciprocity allows us to extract love when we inject affection, to extract peace when we inject happiness, and to extract wealth when we inject value. When we give our best, we can claim the best.

MY BRILLIANT CAREER

Central to all of these riches is our career. It is the mechanism through which we toil lovingly so that we can be rewarded completely. Through our work, we can claim our worth. Through our labour, we can claim our rest. Through our craft, we can claim our position.

Our social structures have conditioned us to believe that our status in society hinges on a respectable career. A job is like a name tag that reveals our identity.

Through our work, we can claim our worth. Through our labour, we can claim our rest.

Are you really engaged in a labour of love, or are you merely an employee whose primary objective is to race through the day so that you can get home on time? Is leaving work your main focus when starting work? Is concluding a call your principal goal when answering the telephone? Is finishing a task the main aim when starting it?

When your actions are activities that merely pass the time in anticipation of a brighter future, you can be assured that you will not be granted an enchanting future. Those whose current job is not rewarding can be certain that their next job will not be rewarding. This means that if you are not happy at this moment, you will not be happy at a later moment because *time* and *place* do not govern happiness. The same goes for job-satisfaction; it has little to do with the job itself.

WHEN THE VISION IS BLURRED

If you are dissatisfied with your job, yet have a deep-seated desire to improve it, you might be wondering what you can do to find your path. You might be searching for something to grab your attention. You might even be willing to surrender your every waking moment to something that can excite you. Alas, you have racked your brain and are unable to find your passion. Nothing takes your fancy — well, nothing within your reach.

Careers cannot be found because they must be built

You are not alone in feeling that your career is non-existent. You might even still be a student, trying to find a way to embrace your course, without a clue about how your studies can help you to find a direction. Lacking vision (blindness) is one of the nine modern intangible diseases that are explained in Chapter 7, 'Please cancel my disorder'.

When people ask for help to find an exciting career, I remind them that careers cannot be *found* because they must be *built*. There are no shortcuts. Do not confuse 'position' with 'career'. Positions are irrelevant and are of no value. To assume that a position brings contentment is as erroneous as the assumption that living in a mansion yields a happy family.

LIVING IN AGONY

Having understood that careers must be built, the next common query is that people do not know what career they want. They do not know what they should be nurturing, because nothing takes their fancy. Herein lies the secret to the dilemma. Anyone who does not grasp the next point will continue to live in agony. We have been taught that successful outcomes hinge on setting goals. We have been told that with-out a target, it is impossible to achieve greatness. Although this is true, it does not apply to establishing a career. Many people fail at this stage because they try to set a target for themselves. Furthermore, they ask the wrong questions. They keep hitting a brick wall when they cannot find

If you want to change your career, you do not start by changing your job

something that will excite them. The point is that a career is not a *subset* of 'who you are'. A career is not an optional extra that hangs off your résumé. It is not like a hobby or an extracurricular activity. A career is not something you build on the side. *You are your career* — every move, every step, every breath, every thought, and every deed. Right now you have a career. Whether you like it or not, your career is in full swing. Speaking of your career is like speaking of your financial situation — they can both be measured, no matter what their status.

Your daily existence denotes your career. Therefore, you have to decide if 'what you are' is 'what you want to be'. You need to search your soul to decide what you are prepared to invest and what you are willing to sacrifice. It would be a mistake to assume that your 'job' is what determines your career. In fact, 'you' determine your career — who you are, and what you are.

This means that if you want to change your career, you do not start by changing your job. Once you have decided on the career you want, you need to change everything that is necessary. Meanwhile, beware that you do not presume that 'to change' means 'to switch'. Switching from one car to the next, or from one job to the next, does not constitute change. External changes are only superficial. To change your career means to change everything associated with your career (and therefore your life). If you determine that you need to 'change' your car, be careful that you do not misunderstand that to mean 'switch' your car. Selling your existing car and buying another model does not mean that you have changed your car. Your car has not changed at all. It was sold, and a new one was purchased. Nothing about your original car has changed — except that it now has a new owner.

With that, you can see that 'change' does not mean 'switch', nor does it mean 'discard'. I emphasise this because when I suggest that people need to change, they quickly set about switching things. They switch their investments, their house, their spouse, and their job.

Students switch from one course to the next in search of a suitable one. Students who take up communications, desire law. Those in law, cannot wait to try their hand at commerce.

Harbouring self-doubt is the heaviest burden of all

To change your career, you need to start now by changing whatever is necessary that relates to you and your disciplines, your tolerances, your knowledge, and your attitudes. This requires that you carefully assess what you allow into your life and what valuable energy you allow out.

The secret to kick-starting a career is to remember that it does not require a goal. So stop searching for one! A career is not one task or one project. You need to drop the burdens you have been carrying about 'setting a direction' or 'finding a vision'. Stop fretting about your next job and your 'destination'.

It is important that you let go of the anxiety that has been distracting you. Self-inflicted agony becomes relentless torture. Harbouring self-doubt is the heaviest burden of all. Goals and strategies come, after you get your life's framework right.

OKAY, BUT NOW WHAT?

Once you have let go of all the burdens associated with your career, you might be wondering how it all works. You want to know the secrets to success. You are curious about how successful people got to where they are.

The popular advice about becoming brilliant is generally misunderstood. The conventional wisdom says that 'brilliance takes time' and that 'achieving excellence takes time'. You have no doubt also heard that reaching a goal takes time.

These are damaging thoughts because they are misleading. Becoming brilliant does not take time. If you have ever seen a helicopter starting its engine, you would have noticed that the propeller overhead starts slowly at first, it picks up momentum, and then it rotates at full speed. It could be said that a helicopter's propeller takes time to reach its goal of full speed. Even so, at every step along the way, that motor was doing its best to increase the speed. Every turn is dependent on the one before. Not a single revolution could be allowed to exert anything but the utmost of effort.

Using this helicopter analogy, you can see that those who believe that success takes time, are confusing the zero position with the full-speed position. If people mistakenly believe that it takes time to achieve success, they sit patiently, allowing time to pass unproductively. They presume that they can try again later, or that they can slacken off at some points along the way.

There can be no hesitation during the starting phase. Every turn and every step requires concentration and effort. If you liken your career to the helicopter's propeller, you will understand that it is wrong to assume that it takes time to build a career. There can be no letting up of energy when starting that propeller. Every turn contributes to the next, and no turn can be slower than the previous one.

Make sure that you have enough fuel to undertake your mission. To abort midway is wasteful and damaging. The common problem that causes employees to ease off is the delusion that they are advancing in their career. Some executives boast about having eight different jobs within a space of six years, and all with the *same* employer. They have been tricked into thinking that they are advancing because every few seasons they get to print a new set of business cards. They have new job goals, a new telephone extension, a new location, and therefore they presume that they are moving onwards and upwards.

Switching jobs is not what polishing one's career is all about because this is draining and confusing. It does not lead to brilliance. If anything, it leads to disaster if people are promoted to positions beyond their capabilities. To survive, they begin to bluff. They have to tread water merely to stay afloat.

NO TIME LIKE THE PRESENT

If you want to be brilliant, you have to do brilliant things. Brilliance is not the sole domain of geniuses. You can be brilliant by polishing your act and putting in a superior performance no matter what you are doing.

If you are not brilliant at everything you do *now*, you cannot be brilliant at anything you do in the next ten minutes. Every action is fuelled by the previous action. If you fancy yourself as a successful person in the future, your every move today needs to contribute to that momentum. Take a good look at what you did today. Were you brilliant at it? Never mind whether the customer you served deserved your attention or not. When you serve a customer to the best of your abilities, you are doing so for your own sake, not for the customer's. When you help your boss with a project, you need to do it as if your life depended on it. When you cooked your meal today, did you do it to perfection? When you wrote a letter, did you use your best handwriting? When you wrapped that gift, did you inject pride even in the way you folded every corner of the wrapping paper?

If you want to be brilliant, you have to do brilliant things

If you think that such attention to detail borders on being pedantic or fussy, or if you think that such actions would label you a 'perfectionist', you still do not understand what it takes to become brilliant. Remember, once your propeller is in full swing, everything you do will be done with ease. This is why successful people appear to be so relaxed. How do you expect to attain that level of ease and excellence? If you do not exert yourself, how can you reach a stage where you will be able to sail through the day effortlessly? These things do not happen of their own accord.

You have heard the expression, 'you get what you pay for.' As far as your career is concerned, 'you get what you *play* for.' So play hard in everything you do. If you refuse to apply yourself on the basis that you will do so only when you can see a vision for your future, you will fail because a vision cannot surface until you have perfected the art of injecting excellence in everything that you do. This little secret comes from 'the law of sequence', whereby things must be done in the right order. If you can learn to obey the laws of life, you will be able to get what you deserve. ∎

CHAPTER 6

LOOKING INTO THE SEEDS OF TIME

YOU CAN'T REAP WHAT YOU CAN'T SOW

What is fascinating is not so much that rip-off merchants abound, but that people can be so gullible

S HAKESPEARE WROTE, 'If you can look into the seeds of time and say which grain will grow and which will not, speak then to me . . . '

Can you look into your own situation and know where your future will take you? This is difficult. It is for this reason that you are better off focussing on planting the right seeds and nurturing them.

During some of my lectures, I hand out seeds and ask students to tell me what those seeds will produce. They could be holding seeds from which will grow the most intricate of flowers, or the most marvellous of vegetables. No-one is able to tell me because most seeds look the same. They are brown, hard, small, unattractive, and offer no clues whatsoever about what will spring from them. Even if cut in half, there is no way of seeing the miracles of creation. Deep within the cells reside incomprehensible codes that untangle to unite with the soil, sun, and rain to produce profound beauty. Each seed has an inbuilt reproductive system so complex that it can humble anyone who ponders the intricacy and miracle of life.

THE GARDEN OF EDEN

Each of us carries an assortment of seeds — whether inherited or acquired. All the seeds look the same, so the challenge is to know which to nurture and which to discard. These seeds are sometimes called opportunities, skills, talent, attitude, luck, or fortune. In the style of Vollenweider's poetry, I maintain that if we harbour seeds of doubt, we will grow vines of confusion.

If we harbour seeds of doubt, we will grow vines of confusion

If we endure seeds of tears, we will contend with leaves of loneliness. If we cultivate seeds of compassion, we will raise trees of love. If we develop seeds of understanding, we will produce fruits of forgiveness. If we foster seeds of tenderness, we will sprout flowers of laughter. If we nurture seeds of calmness, gardens of joy will flourish.

If you accept mediocrity, you can be certain of misfortune

So it is with our careers. What we sow today will determine what we can reap tomorrow. Therefore, those who are confused about their careers can easily determine what their future will bring, simply by looking at what they harbour, what they foster, and what they nurture. Take a close look at your life and observe what you tolerate and what you cherish. Observe what you find agreeable and what you find permissible. That which you allow into your life will set the foundation for your future. This means that if you allow energy-sappers into your life, you can be certain of a depleted future. If you accept mediocrity, you can be certain of misfortune. If selfishness is your disease, you will contend with emptiness.

MISSION IMPROBABLE; VISION IMPRACTICAL

Many people do not understand what it means to have a mission. A mission is a set of activities that you must accomplish if you are to reach your goal. So start by deciding what you want, then reverse engineer your strategy so that you can determine which seeds you need to accumulate. Never mind trying to dictate how the seeds will grow, because you cannot control the laws of nature. Do not tamper with nature. Instead, learn its laws. For example, if you inject hatred, you will see devastation. If you inject laziness, you will see death.

Your most urgent task is to focus on what you are doing *right now*. How well did you perform today? How hard did you work? How much love did you inject into your craft? Did you try to cheat anyone?

People fumble when they go in search of that which cannot be found, and when they seek to turn into that which they cannot become. For example, a chef who wants a cake does not set about to *become* the cake. Furthermore, the chef does not go in *search* of the cake. Instead, the chef sets about acquiring the right ingredients in order to bake a cake.

> *People fumble when they go in search of that which cannot be found, and when they seek to turn into that which they cannot become*

This means that when you can *see* what you want for yourself, you cannot attain it by looking for it because 'it' does not exist — you have to build it. This is what is meant by building your career. (By the way, what you 'see' becomes your *vision*, and what you must 'do' becomes your *mission*.)

The first step in any mission is to *acquire the appropriate ingredients*. These might include knowledge, awareness, attitude, and other soft and hard skills. The second step would be to *learn how to combine them*. The third step would be to build the stamina to be able to *physically unite them* in the right proportions so that they blend harmoniously.

This is not as easy as it sounds. In the case of baking a cake, almost every household has the ingredients, yet few would know how to mix them. Although their pantry contains flour, sugar, eggs, and butter, and even though they all have an oven, few are able to bake a mouth-watering chocolate gâteau. So it is with careers. Most people have the ingredients. Sadly, the possession of ingredients is not sufficient to cook up a storm. It requires knowledge and timing.

It is important to learn about the general ingredients you need for success. Set about acquiring them, and learn how to combine them, and build the stamina to be able to undertake any arduous task. Here you will need persistence and tenacity.

PRESS ON

The worst thing that disgruntled employees can do is to 'work to rule' (whereby they do only what is required of them and nothing more). Being on a 'go slow' is self-damaging. It would be like refusing to undertake your exercise program just because you do not like the gym instructor. Many resilient prisoners maintain their exercise regime while in captivity. If they refuse to train simply because they do not like the prison and its wardens, or because they feel that they were incarcerated unjustly, they would only be harming themselves.

You need to keep up your personal development program no matter what you think of your boss or the organisation. Whether your boss deserves it or not, you need to maintain your momentum so that you do not slow down. By the time you have built the right attitude, aptitude, and acuity, you will be in a comfortable position to design and build any career you choose — much like a chef can use handy ingredients to make different delicious four-course meals any night of the week. Combining talent and energy to create your own opportunities is more important than lusting over one job. It is better to learn how to cook, than to master one recipe.

Whether your boss deserves it or not, you need to maintain your momentum so that you do not slow down

Learning how to construct a rewarding career is infinitely more valuable than setting your heart on one particular job that you see in the distance. If the grass looks greener on the other side, causing you to desire greener pastures, it is better that you find ways to make *your* grass greener. If you do not build with substance, you will forever be chasing the distant and the unattainable.

THE CYCLE OF SUCCESS

Let us get back to the question of careers. There is no point in sitting around trying to find something to excite you. There is no point in trying to escape your current job. There is no point in undertaking further studies. This is not how it works.

> *If you do not build with substance, you will forever be chasing the distant and the unattainable*

The only way to develop your career is by understanding that *your career is you, not your job*. What you do here and now, and every minute of every day, will determine what type of winner or loser you will become.

For example, if you are a hairdresser, go to work determined to be the best hairdresser you can be. This includes how you dress, what you do for lunch, where you go after work, how you speak to customers, how you greet that beggar who interrupts you, how you respond when your boss drives you mad, and how you make it your business to learn about every product you use, and every client you meet.

Being the best is about being an eminent professional, a trusted friend, a passionate lover, a formidable fighter, a supportive colleague, a valuable employee, and the best person that you can be.

To build a solid career you need to engage inquisitively and invest (time, energy, and money) wisely in order to learn everything about your profession. This goes beyond the obvious, to explore everything associated with that line of work. For the hairdresser, this would include bookkeeping, government regula-tion, retailing principles, real estate, promotions, and consumer behaviour. Include your own personal development, and you are starting to complete the cycle of success that requires attention in three areas: 1) learn how to develop yourself; 2) learn how to work with others; and 3) understand the dynamics of your envi-ronment. The cycle of success that pertains to your job includes: 1) learn how to develop your skills; 2) learn how to work with your boss, your colleagues, and your clients; and 3) understand the dynamics of your organisation and its competitors.

I HATE MY JOB

Many people might argue that they do not feel it appropriate to inject so much energy into their craft because they do not like their job. They would prefer to find a new job before they spend any more effort. I have had doctors tell me that they can-not apply themselves passionately because they have lost the spark. They want to get out of the medical profession. If only they can understand this important point: to become the best at what you are doing now, does not mean that you have to stick with that profession. Unless you know *how* to be the best you can be at whatever you are doing *now*, you can be guaranteed that you will fail at your next step, no matter what it is. If you do not know how to apply yourself fully and completely *now*, you will not be able to apply yourself to anything else.

Some people say, 'When I open a café, I will apply myself,' or 'When I become the marketing director, I will do my best.' Impossible. If you are not good at what you are doing now, you will not be good at anything you do in the future because suc-cess must be ingrained into your whole being and it must envelop your existence.

If you can learn to absorb and engage now, you will start to build strength. This brings confidence, which in turn gives you audacity to claim your self-worth. When you can negotiate based on your expertise, you will find that doors will begin to be opened for you.

There is no other magic formula. This is the secret. Be the best you can be for *your* sake, not for your manager's sake. Learn everything you can about your profession and your industry and your customers and your competitors — even if this is not the industry that you seek to be in. It is the 'process' that you need to master. Learning how to become brilliant starts now, not when you acquire your ideal job. You cannot attain your ideal job any other way. If you accept mediocrity on the basis of dissatisfaction with your current job, then in no time you will suffer because mediocrity will become your area of expertise. The seed of mediocrity will develop thorns of blame.

The seed of mediocrity will develop thorns of blame

A WARNING TO STUDENTS

This advice applies equally to students. If you are at university or at college in the hope that a qualification will lead to a career, you have been misguided. You need to examine what you are doing at university. If you do not know what you are doing there, you had better conduct an emergency meeting with yourself to look into what you expect from your studies.

Your studies will not enhance your career unless you have already started to carve a path for yourself. You must get out of any system that brainwashes you and lulls you into a false sense of security. If you take action now to terminate wasteful studies, you can put that down to a bad experience and move on, having suffered a little bit of anger. If you pursue your studies without complete and clear objectives, your current seeds of anger will flourish into regret. Quit while you are ahead and take charge of your life. Only you can nurture your seeds. No institution or therapist can do that for you.

On the other hand, if you have determined that studying is vital, the main advice given in this chapter applies to you too. You need to become the best student you can be — not so that you attain good marks, but so that you can start practising what excellence means. Ignore the marks. They do not matter. What matters is your ability to engage in your studies. The day that you plough through your assignments merely to satisfy the minimum requirements, is the day that you fail your course. For more about how education relates to careers, see Chapter 4, 'The early bird catches the bookworm'.

SEE YOU AT THE TOP

There is an old maxim along the lines of, 'You will only acquire what you can attract'. Although this is true, take note that part two ought to be, 'No-one will give you anything that you cannot negotiate'. Additionally, you cannot negotiate anything that you cannot justify. Through your brilliance, you can justify your worth. Through your worth, you can justify your rewards. Through your rewards, you can justify your existence. Through your existence, you can justify your life. Once you can acquire all the riches of life, you will have reached a most desirable and enviable career. What you 'do' will no longer matter because if you choose to be a success, you will be a success at whatever you choose. ∎

You cannot negotiate anything that you cannot justify

CHAPTER 7

PLEASE CANCEL *my* DISORDER

THE NINE DEADLY INTANGIBLE DISEASES

*Don't say what you don't mean
because I'm likely to believe it*

IF ONLY IT WERE POSSIBLE to write a book called *First &* *Last* in which the author could list the very first and the very last of everything; and describe the event itself. For example, who was the first person to bite into a tomato? Who was the first person to see fire; and what did that person think or feel at the time? Which community was the first to experience the thunderous sound of an aircraft breaking the sound barrier? Who was the first person to be blinded by gazing at a solar eclipse?

Imagine how fascinating it would have been to follow the last dinosaur. Who outlived the group of people who personally knew King Henry VIII? What was occupying Galileo's mind during the last week of his life?

The initial concept of 'money' would have confounded many people. Can you imagine the discussion that would have taken place as a travelling trader visited the shores of the Nile in Egypt and said, 'Allah be with you. I like your vegetables. I'll take them, and in exchange, I'll give you this piece of stone we call money'. The seller's perplexity would have been precious to catch on camera.

We hear of things that happen once in a lifetime. Some comets appear in our solar system every 75 years or so. If we do not look heavenward at the right moment, we will have no other opportunity during our lifetime. Halley's comet last appeared in 1986, and will next appear in approximately 2061. What is more fascinating is not so much the concept of a 'once in a lifetime' experience, but the concept of a 'once-ever' event. There are some things that can never happen again. For example, your birth was a once-ever event.

Although these moments of history are locked away forever, we can rest assured that new marvels abound, including new problems, new solutions, and new sights and sounds that our ancestors could not have enjoyed.

WHAT AGE ARE WE IN?

If you were at a gathering and someone asked, 'What age are we in?' what would you say? Many people think that we are in the age of telecommunications. Other descriptions include: the age of consumption; the age of knowledge; the age of invention; the Internet age; and the space age. The majority believes that we are in the age of *technology*. I disagree. The technology that drives the world today has been around for decades. Most of the important advancements in the construction of social infrastructures took place long before the computer was invented.

I believe that we live in the age of *con-fusion*. I have hyphenated this word to emphasise more than one meaning. The first connotes the traditional use of 'confusion' to mean 'bewilderment'. The second meaning takes the word 'con' which means 'together' and the word 'fusion' which means 'to melt'. The implication is that we are in an age wherein we are fusing disciplines that had never before touched each other. The *primary* element is technology, whereby we fuse it with secondary elements such as medicine, finance, business, law, education, and farming.

The process of convergence is not as complex as con-fusion. The former merely brings elements together. The latter combines those elements to form a completely different substance.

We humans have been able to imitate nature in order to innovate. Unfortunately, the by-products have become the new burdens of our age. These include *tangible* consequences such as new waste and garbage, for which we have not yet developed adequate disposal methods. Also included are *intangibles* that complicate our world when we envelop them with regionally based ethics and values — meaning, what is considered acceptable within certain countries and customs.

Some intangible by-products are manufactured on purpose. For example, in the past, multinationals were accused of starting a new industry by inventing the perceived disease called 'body odour'. The multi-trillion dollar industry showers us with perfumes, body sprays, soaps, deodorants, and other products to make us smell more appealing. The modern equivalent is the perceived disease of computer illiteracy.

Other by-products that emerge from con-fusion include mental and social disorders that manifest tangibly (such as obesity) and intangibly (see those listed below) to grip nations and to torment people.

THE NINE DEADLY INTANGIBLE DISEASES

I have identified nine debilitating modern diseases that I think are responsible for personal failures and misery. Although these diseases are not new to the human race, they have now reached epidemic proportions. When counselling and coaching my clients and their staff members, I have been struck by the prevalence of these diseases. Below, I have summarised the results of my findings (listed in alphabetical order).

| MODERN DISEASE # 1 • ABDICATION |

The best technology is the one that is invisible and stable. The light bulb is an example of invisibility, in that it works without intervention on our part. The electricity station is so far away that most people will never get to see one in person. Television and radio are good examples of stability, in that they work every time we turn them on. The hard work that takes place behind the scenes to

The best technology is the one that is invisible and stable

produce the programs is not something with which we have to concern ourselves.

Invisibility and stability are the ideal states for fast-paced societies. Unfortunately, they are also the contributors to the disease of abdication, whereby we entrust the complexity of our world to someone else. For example, we have no idea how the electricity generator keeps working, nor do we doubt that it is being taken care of. At this level, dependability turns into dependency, while reliability becomes reliance.

Fears of dependency and reliance surfaced when the calculator was first allowed into the classroom. Educators fretted that students would lose their ability to perform basic arithmetic. Modernists argued that it did not matter, pointing to the fact that many services in modern life come to us without any intervention on our part, and that progress meant that we had to let go of the fundamentals. So much so, that some milk drinkers have never seen a real cow. There are also children who have never experienced the tears resulting from cutting an onion. Are they missing out on something? What about modern children for whom a box of matches is a novelty amid ignition gadgetry in their kitchen?

Problems arise when we confuse our rights with our responsibilities

There is nothing wrong with progress. There is no shame in dependency. The problems arise when we confuse our *rights* with our *responsibilities*. There are some things that cannot progress without our intervention. Right now, Radio Moscow is bouncing off this page; as is the BBC and the ABC. The only difficulty is that you cannot hear the radio waves because, in themselves, they are invisible and silent. Their existence is perfect, but their transformation depends upon another element, called a receiver. The radio receiver is not clever. It does not do much. It just has the capability to catch the radio waves and to convert the codes into something our ears can hear and our brains can comprehend. The wave and the receiver do not really need each other, in that they can exist on their own. When they combine, they create a transformation. The radio wave does not care to be de-coded. It has no need to be caught. The receiver has no need to catch the waves. It can sit there without doing anything. They each have their place, and they each have a purpose — without any pressure being applied either way.

The system breaks down when one element starts to dictate to the other or expects that the other will do the work for it. Can you imagine an obstinate radio sitting on your desk with its arms folded, refusing to convert the waves, and insisting that the waves had better arrive already converted so that it does not have to do any work? Not only would this be laziness, it would be impractical. The two elements do not depend upon each other per se, until they both agree to engage.

This analogy serves to show what the disease of abdication looks like. Humans sit with their arms folded and forget (or sometimes refuse) to play their part. So much so that if you observe the 'dissatisfied and disgruntled' among us, you would see that they abdicate their *welfare* to the government. They abdicate their *happiness* to their lover. They abdicate their *future* to a clairvoyant. They abdicate their *education* to a teacher. They abdicate their *health* to medicine. And, they abdicate their *wealth* to the lottery (or to the casino or to the stock market). Interestingly, the concept of 'insurance' smacks of this disease. For example, people insure their car, knowing that if it were to be stolen, they would be reimbursed. This is a way of pushing the problem onto someone else. I have heard people say that they do not care what happens to their car 'because it is insured'.

Abdication is classified as a disease because it grips, and will not let go. It leads to other troubles. It is one of those diseases that is rarely cured because inactivity is peaceful.

The world does not owe us anything. We can only reap what we sow. Others cannot harvest life's joys for us. No-one can drink on our behalf.

Do not abdicate your career to your boss

When it comes to building your future, be sure that you do not abdicate your *career* to your boss. Only *you* can take responsibility for your future and for your job-satisfaction. You need to identify your skills and the value that you can add, and set about learning how to negotiate the best price for your services. If you sit back and wait for someone to promote you, you could be waiting a long time.

| MODERN DISEASE # 2 • APATHY |

Apathy is a word used to mean 'without feeling'. It is associated with indifference, insensitivity, and a lack of interest.

Throughout the ages, we have had people who did not care about others. At least they made the decision after having understood the situation. Disregarding starving children presupposes that we are *aware* of their existence. Apathy is a condition worse than 'not caring' because it stops us from *knowing* about the children's plight.

In the good old days, apathy was defended, in part, by isolation and a lack of global communications. We tolerated apathy on the basis of distance — that which was far away seemed to be someone else's problem. These days, news bulletins come from every corner of the globe, so we can hardly claim that we do not know what is going on.

The disease of apathy is threatening because it goes deeper than indifference to the hardship of distant tribes. It even goes beyond trying to understand our neighbours down the street. Apathy strikes because we have honed our ability to ignore our *personal* problems. We presume that whatever threatens us can be cured by creams and lotions and pills and potions. We trust that the age of wonder-drugs will take care of our ailments: a tablet for this and an injection for that.

We presume that whatever threatens us can be cured by creams and lotions and pills and potions

While missionaries try to remove apathy on a global scale, I am trying to alert the world to the fact that apathy exists at the personal level. When you hear about those in need on the other side of the world, you might rationalise that 'someone' will take care of them. You might subscribe to the ideology of 'each to their own'. You might even presume that a charitable organisation has the situation covered. Notwithstanding, what do you call it when you do not care about your *own* problems? What kind of a disease is it that allows you to ignore your own needs?

Apathy is killing people because it muffles the cries for self-help. If our internal alarm systems are inoperative, how will we know when there is a problem? Our personal apathy is the result of our inability to feel what is happening in the 'middle ground' as we swing between happiness and sadness, or between pleasure and pain. It is further compounded by our inability to link feelings with actions. This means that if we finally managed to locate the fires, we would not know what started them. Extinguishing them is a draining exercise because they continue to be ignited by sparks that flash at us, without a trace of their origin. Worse still, when we do finally learn about the ignition points, we presume that we do not have to modify our behaviour, because a wonder-drug will take care of everything. We might even believe that 'time' will be the great healer, so we continue our self-destructive lifestyle.

Apathy strikes at fundamental levels. Observe the ways in which we are apathetic about the words we use to define our life. If our words are nothing more than alphabetical symbols, they are meaningless. Doubtless, most people who know what the word 'courage' means would not know what it *tastes* like? If a sentiment is merely a word, and a word is merely a symbol, we then lose the ability to feel. For example, the word 'fear' is one of the rare exceptions that can illustrate this point. This simple four-letter word is made known to us at childhood. When fear strikes, it consumes our whole body. Our entire physiology changes, our mouth dries up, our heart beats faster, our thinking becomes focussed, we perspire — and these are but the first stages of fear. Once it grips, fear devours the body *and* the mind.

The example about fear shows how one word (once applied as a concept) can overwhelm the whole body. How many of us experience such a total surrender to the word 'courage'? How many other words have such an effect on us? Both fear and courage are vital for survival. Unfortunately, many people do not have the ability to call on either one. Instead, one or the other controls them. The ideal state would be to call on *both* so that we can arrive at decisions with *conviction*.

No matter what you believe to be virtuous, you must seek to understand its opposite

No matter what you believe to be virtuous, you must seek to understand its opposite — not so that you can exercise it, but so that you can control it. For example, if you do not know the taste of courage, you cannot call upon it. You will become vulnerable.

The loss of control is devastating because it is demeaning for us as intelligent beings. Unlike other animals, we rarely act on instinct. Therefore, amid apathy, other animals have a higher chance of survival than we humans. Remember, apathy numbs our instincts. We become prisoners of our supposed virtues.

We can improve our chances of survival by starting to learn about the world of opposites. By this, I am not only referring to the Chinese concepts of ying and yang whereby balance is desired, but to learning to confront our world, so that we can move from a state of *balance* and achieve a level of *control*.

I have heard sages start with the question, 'Do you know what it is that you do not know?' This is a good question. A better one would be, 'Do you understand the opposites of all that you hold dear?' If you know what love feels like, do you know what hate feels like? If not, how will you know when it raises its ugly head? Ah, the dilemma of life. I have often pondered how we can train an army of elite soldiers in peacetime. How will they know how to kill if they have not had any practice? A disturbing thought indeed.

I have often pondered how we can train an army of elite soldiers in peacetime

If you want to build your career, you need to identify the virtues that you hold dear, and learn about their opposites. You then need to have the courage to do what has to be done. If you find that you are being held back by people who take advantage of your good nature and generosity, you need to learn how to stand up to them and to claim what is yours. Do you have colleagues and clients who abuse you? When are you going to stand up for yourself and tell them that you will no longer tolerate their abuse? They might abuse you by wasting your time, by not turning up to meetings, by not meeting their deadlines, by going back on their word, by not fulfilling their side of the bargain, or by not paying their bills on time.

I have had friends tell me that their largest clients have not paid their bills for more than three months. When I encouraged them to demand payment, they said that they were too afraid of upsetting their clients because they might not get any more work. How bizarre. What is the point of more work when the client does not pay? How many businesses have been badly burnt by large corporates that have withheld payment until they were insolvent, owing millions of dollars to innocent parties?

I know a company that has an unusual billing procedure. It charges its clients a fifty percent deposit on all work the moment that it is commissioned, and then it expects the remaining fifty percent a month prior to starting work. This means that the company gets paid *all* that it is owed, well in advance. In this way, it protects itself against bad debts.

You can break with tradition when you can show others that you can add value. If you can convince your boss that you are offering a professional service, you should be able to negotiate terms that suit you. If you sit back and wait for things to change in your favour, you will not be able to claim your worth. Do not be afraid to stand up for what you want, and do not hesitate to negotiate hard. Before you can do that, you need to know that you have a skill that you can sell. Start working on developing your skills, and do not be afraid to negotiate with those who need your services.

If your boss does not place too much value on your services, rectify the situation. You might need to upgrade your skills, or face the facts that you need to move to an organisation that does value what you have to offer. Either way, action is required. Sitting back apathetically will destroy your potential.

| MODERN DISEASE # 3 • BLINDNESS |

There is a word that successful people rub into the wounds of
the discontented. That word is 'vision'. Those who lack vision
become disheartened, but not devastated. They feel that their
deficiency is alarming, but not earth-shattering.

Lacking personal direction is problematic, but not an immediate threat. At worst, one stands still and masters the art of
inactivity. The danger is that the lack of vision manifests into
the disease of blindness whereby one traverses without an
understanding of the terrain and its hazards. When blindness
grips, all manner of absurdities flourish.

*If we are not careful,
celebrities
could dictate
our creativity,
while film stars
could dictate
our morality*

The changes in family and social structures, and our tendency to move about
from place to place and from job to job, has
inflicted us with a sense of aloneness and
loneliness. We lack companionship, we
lack camaraderie, and we lack mentors
who once were associates or members of
our extended family. In the absence of
guidance from local sages, we have to fend
for ourselves. This is why blindness affects us more than ever
before. The nearest substitute for guides and sages are celebrities
and sports stars to whom we turn for direction about permissible
conduct. If we are not careful, celebrities could dictate our creativity, while film stars could dictate our morality.

When blindness causes confusion and chaos, we are led to
believe that our problems could be solved if we were to acquire
a vision for our future.

Like many vital ingredients in life, 'vision' cannot be found
because it does not exist in its own right. It can only be constructed. The constituent parts that form personal vision are made

through fusing several elements. First, we must learn to fuse focus with awareness to arrive at *prudence*. We then need to fuse hindsight with foresight to arrive at *forethought*. When we fuse prudence with forethought, we arrive at *insight*. This, fused with creativity, enables us to form a picture of where we are heading. This picture is better known as 'vision'. A lack of vision eventually leads to blindness.

A lack of vision eventually leads to blindness

Blindness is compounded by a hectic lifestyle. With little time taken to reflect on what one is doing, and with little or no pride in one's craft, life becomes a series of hit-and-run affairs. Pride is rarely factored into the equation. The lack of pride in one's work, when mixed with blindness, leads to discontentment.

While those who lack vision are aware of their shortcomings, those who suffer blindness are unaware of their ailment. Blindness does not refer to being in the dark. It refers to making miscalculated moves whose consequences are not anticipated. The laws of complexity will take over, making it impossible to conduct an audit trail to trace the source of failure. When failure cannot be arrested, it cannot be thwarted.

The discontented are gripped by 'the law of momentum' that demands movement. A hazardous terrain is both inviting and welcoming, causing the disease carrier to move from one unmitigated disaster to the next. You have heard it said that 'desperate times call for desperate measures'. My advice for those in this predicament is that 'desperate times call for *tested* measures'. Cease the hyperactivity and re-assess the situation. When you are unaware of your surroundings, you become myopic. Myopia coupled with ignorance leads to disaster.

Those who are plagued by blindness can be heard saying things like, 'I had no idea. It just happened out of the blue. I was caught by surprise. If only I had checked it . . . '

When you are at your most confident, check everything. When you are at your fastest, ignore nothing. When you are at your most vulnerable, trust no-one. Despite your best efforts, one thing you cannot do is postpone the inevitable. If you can learn to pre-empt, you would be taking your first steps to seeing the light.

When you are at your most confident, check everything. When you are at your fastest, ignore nothing. When you are at your most vulnerable, trust no-one.

| MODERN DISEASE # 4 • DEPLETION |

Depletion is the act of draining vital resources for one purpose, without regard to other needs. There are seven categories worth observing:

a) Incapacitation

Sometimes, our excesses lead to incapacitation. This means that one action suppresses the opportunities for subsequent moves. We do this when we leave the car lights on and go shopping. By the time we return, the car battery has been drained. Of all the technological marvels in a modern car, the battery is the least sophisticated, yet without it, the vehicle is rendered inoperative. We need to be aware that what seems insignificant could be vital. Carelessness is the major contributor to this 'checkmate syndrome'. In life, we engage in incapacitation by making decisions to expend a resource (such as money) that is later needed to take the project to the next step. The inability to manage the flow of cash is one of the major contributors to business failures.

If you spend all that you earn, and are unable to save any money, you will become imprisoned to your work

If you spend all that you earn, and are unable to save any money, you will become imprisoned to your work. If you could save six months of your salary, you would be in a better position to negotiate with your boss about your work conditions. If you are always worried that you cannot meet the immediate bills, you will be forced to silence yourself for fear of losing your job.

Apart from money, look to see what else you deplete from your body and soul. How well do you manage your personal energy? Do you get enough rest? Do you maintain a healthy lifestyle? Or do you drain your concentration through excessive consumption of alcohol? You might have heard it said that everything is good in moderation. I say, only moderation is good in moderation. I do believe that we need to live to the maximum levels that life has to offer — but not if those limits are draining and depleting. Living to the maximum ought to mean maintaining maximum energy and full speed, not fumbling through life in a drowsy state of intellectual and emotional poverty — hungry for vital resources and fuel.

b) Misplacement

When we use the wrong tool, we are likely to deplete secondary vital resources. It would be like using the LCD screen on a battery-operated notebook computer to illuminate a room. The screen is not designed for that purpose, so after the battery has been drained, the computer can no longer be used.

Your body is a reservoir of resources. Do not let your boss

steal that away from you by forcing you to perform tasks that everyone knows will be futile. A friend told me that her boss used to ask her to stay back after work to prepare several more scenarios for a project, just so that her boss could cover his backside in case auditors should ever ask him if he had considered all the possible options. My friend knew that her boss was robbing her of her life and her energy. She had better things to do than stay back at the office until midnight for weeks on end. Her time was not something that she could replace. Such a misplacement of energy was not only draining her, it was tearing her away from the opportunity to expand her knowledge, to build her career, and to foster relationships with friends and family. Eventually she stood up to him and told him that if he felt that the plans were so important, he would have to cut down on other priorities so that she could do these during normal working hours. She did not mind working hard, but not when it was a futile exercise that added no value, and misplaced her limited energy. Her contract with him was for eight hours per day. He was demanding eighteen. How would it be if the tables were turned and she charged him for eighteen hours per day and only turned up for eight? If such an equation is unthinkable for any boss, why should the converse be acceptable to any employee? Working hard is one thing, but allowing your boss to deviate from the contract to such a degree is abuse.

If extended work is of value to you personally, and you are learning something from it, there would be some justification in it. In the absence of any such benefit, you need to stand up for yourself.

c) Diminution

Our efforts become less effective or even totally ineffectual if we try to apply our energy while it is diminished. This is like trying to extinguish a blaze with a fire hose that is punctured. The correct volume of water is discharged from the pump, but the pressure at the nozzle is so weak that the hose becomes useless. We are like that when we are low in energy.

Do not spread yourself thinly. Whatever you do, do it well, and build a framework that allows you to work at full speed and with a complete set of tools. If your boss expects you to spend your energy preparing a project, only to have it cancelled mid-way, you will grow resentful and apathetic. I have seen executives undertake assignments, knowing that the budgets will be cut half way. Their entire work life becomes a series of half-hearted efforts. Their lack of enthusiasm contributes to a diminished sense of excitement, a diminished sense of ownership, and a diminished sense of purpose. Eventually, they cannot apply themselves to their job, and they become dull and blunt. You should take great offence when your work environment diminishes your power and creativity because once you lose your momentum, you can easily become disengaged and uninterested, to the point of losing your passion. In the end, you can suffer at the hands of indecisive managers. You need to take the matter personally, and feel a sense of betrayal. Many workers do not care if their boss keeps pulling the plug on their projects, They say, 'Oh well, I don't care.' I would care, because I am a professional, not a slave. You can have my energy, but not to squander it.

You can have my energy, but not to squander it

d) Haemorrhaging

There are times when we dissipate our energy involuntarily. When we see others doing this, we accuse them of 'flying off the handle'. When it happens to us, we justify our actions based on morality or duty. Here is a small military exercise used to train army officers. A group is given the following information: 'You are the captain of a fighting unit whose enemy is not far behind. You lose all your weapons and all your communications equipment. Your whole platoon comes to a wide river, infested with crocodiles. The tide is high and the current is fast. You do not have any ropes. You have five minutes to get 200 soldiers across or you all face certain death. What would you do?' Students undertaking this exercise ask all sorts of questions to determine the safest way across the river. The instructor then reminds everyone about duty and responsibility, and says that it is *not* the captain's responsibility to work out how to get the soldiers across. The correct procedure would be to turn to the sergeant and say, 'Sergeant, get those soldiers across to the other side.' The lesson here, although seemingly mischievous, is to limit your activities to the issues that you can handle, and that are within your area of responsibility.

As a member of a team, it is your job to focus on what you do well, and not pour out your time and energy into areas that are not yours to worry about. This is not to say that you should mind your own business and ignore the bigger picture, but more to caution you that you would be of no use to anyone if you dissipate your energy to the point where you can no longer be relied upon to uphold your side of the bargain.

e) Wastage

When your fortunes are favourable, take care not to deplete your resources through complacency. War veterans learn to become spendthrifts. They find it abhorrent that young people do not value what they have. This is like keeping a tap open unnecessarily or never turning the lights off. Wastage of water and electricity also leads to wastage of money. Once used, neither can be retrieved. Those who apply this level of wastage to their life will undoubtedly regret their behaviour. They will not know what they have lost until they lose it.

Do not waste an opportunity to learn. Do not waste energy on futile activities. Ask yourself what it is that you value most, and what it is that you cannot easily replenish. This does not mean that you should hold back and not use your resources. No-one is asking you to reduce your level of enjoyment or to stop having fun. By all means do whatever you like, but do not waste resources, time, energy, or effort when such expenditure produces a nil return. Wastage means expending without return. Learn to avoid such transgressions.

f) Forfeiture

'Use it or lose it' is the motto associated with this form of depletion. This refers to opportunities that are presented to us within a short timeframe. For example, water flowing from upstream could dry up unless it is stored or used when it is available. Such opportunities must be captured in accordance with the law of timing. Your readiness will determine your ability to harness these opportunities. The expression, 'there are plenty of fish in the sea' leads us to believe that if we miss an opportunity, another will come. This is not always true. The forfeiture of opportunities is akin to the forfeiture of fortune.

The forfeiture of opportunities is akin to the forfeiture of fortune

There are times when people forfeit an opportunity to impress the boss, or to win a client. This is also prevalent in deteriorating relationships where one partner passes up an opportunity to give affection or to prove loyalty. The moment that such an opportunity is forfeited, it cannot be redeemed later because one cannot be sure that a similar opportunity will recur. Any future favours would not compensate for the initial denial of affection or the denial to show acts of love that could have confirmed one's real intentions.

g) Excess

Expending excess energy in the name of expediency is similar to cracking a walnut with a sledgehammer. It gets the job done, but not necessarily to one's satisfaction. When expediency is the driving force, certain excesses are overlooked. Unfortunately, if this practice turns into a habit, it can become the standard. A divorced lady said that she should have left her husband years ago. She was asked, 'If you knew that it was not right, why did you stay with him for so long?' Her reply was that every time she was ready to leave her husband, he would buy for her a diamond ring or a fancy car. She was smothered with distracting excesses.

MORE ABOUT DEPLETION

Replenishment is not the remedy for depletion. Expending time and energy is fine, so long as we are using our resources to nurture our life, not to fuel our extravagances. There are times when depletion occurs without our consent, such as when we allow others to command our time, energy, and resources.

> *Replenishment is not the remedy for depletion*

When we use fuel for the wrong reason, we are being improvident. For example, if you had a box of matches, a can of petrol, and a pile of wood, in which order would you expend your resources? Obviously, each must be used in the right order, otherwise if you throw all the matches on the fire, you not only lose a vital ignition tool, you make little difference to your fire. Watch that you do not use your energy in the wrong order. Ranking your resources can maximise your stamina.

You might know of people who engage in all seven depletion processes simultaneously. Give them golden opportunities and untold wealth, and they will dissipate each and every chance to build on what they have. Conversely, those who know how to resist these energy-sappers can build empires.

| MODERN DISEASE # 5 • FOOLISHNESS |

When we think of *conflict*, we tend to presume that one of the combatants must come out the winner. Whether it is two animals duelling for territorial supremacy, or two nations fighting over sovereignty, we expect that one victor will emerge. The law of stamina governs battles of this nature, whereby those with better resources eventually win — not so much because they are strong, but because their opponent eventually becomes weak.

As humans, we have similar battles inside our head. We wrestle with our conscience all the time. Eventually, we succumb to the stronger force within us. When the stronger force protects us from repetitive discomfort, we call this 'maturity'. When it generates self-inflicted torture, we call this 'immaturity'. If we are mature, we will yield to our conscience. If we are immature, we will surrender to our indulgence. Mature people are those who can resist the path that leads to disappointment. Immature people are those who cannot resist

If we are mature, we will yield to our conscience. If we are immature, we will surrender to our indulgence

the path that provides a short-term gain, but that ultimately leads to failure.

While immature people understand 'the law of stamina', they are not so well acquainted with 'the law of opposition'. This law dictates that when two opposing forces are engaged, neither one shall win. This is a game that produces no winner. Opposition mixed with ego soon becomes obfuscation — where both parties relinquish their desire for victory. They do not mind losing, so long as their opponent does not win. This is no longer a matter of investing energy to defend, but of expending energy to destroy.

Fools are those who oppose themselves, and thereby destroy themselves. They truly desire an outcome, but they undertake a course that can never lead them to that desired destination. This is a draining process that leads to self-destruction. What fools do not realise is that what they *desire* and what they *pursue* annihilate each other.

The picture we paint of fools shows them as docile simpletons. This is not the case. Fools are not so easily spotted. They have superior intellect and exceptional talent. They do not lack dexterity, and they are not dim-witted. Their desire might be wholesome, and their path might be reasonable, but they lack the ability to understand the dynamic physics of annihilating forces. This means that fools will stand aghast, unable to comprehend why their efforts do not yield fruit. They inject copious amounts of energy, and they infuse bountiful resources. They are neither miserly nor inadequate.

Growth does not guarantee power; power does not guarantee supremacy; supremacy does not guarantee victory

What they lack is the acuity to understand that: preservation does not guarantee wealth; wealth does not guarantee abundance; abundance does not guarantee growth; growth does not guarantee power; power does not guarantee supremacy; supremacy does not guarantee victory. Here, the cycle re-starts because victory does not guarantee preservation. Although these are all vital ingredients, they can be destroyed.

Disrespect destroys preservation. Greed nullifies wealth. Discontent diminishes abundance. Recklessness thwarts growth. Indecision dissipates power. Cunning foils supremacy. Contempt steals victory.

Greed nullifies wealth. Discontent diminishes abundance. Recklessness thwarts growth. Indecision dissipates power. Cunning foils supremacy.

Foolishness is the disease that allows well-meaning individuals to destroy their own foundations. This might include the destruction of things that they treasure, including careers, relationships, businesses, and health. When they are warned that they harbour self-destructive qualities, fools are certain that they can quarantine each element. They seem to think that size can overcome danger. The tiniest of sparks can ignite a gas bottle, no matter how large the bottle is. In fact, the larger it is, the more spectacular the blast. When ignition causes combustion, size no longer matters.

If you desire a bright and happy career, be sure that your path will lead you there. Having the vision, and working with passion, does not lead to success if the path itself is carved to take you down a different way. A train, no matter how large and impressive, has no option but to go where the tracks lead it.

There are not many people who can articulate, with conviction, their dreams and their desires. Fewer still can translate their desires into a set of actions. Of those who know what they want and where they can get it, hardly any of them choose the right path. What they desire and what they do, do not match. It is like having electricity plugs that do not fit into each other. Is it any wonder that so few people are runaway successes? Mind you, of the few who are unbelievably successful, they will each tell you that their success was not that hard to achieve. In fact, they cannot understand why so few people are high achievers.

Some people work day and night just to make ends meet, while high achievers do not seem to labour anywhere near as much. What is the secret? It all comes down to avoiding foolishness. Meaning, what you *desire* and what you *do* must link up. The links are not hard to find. The biggest challenge is understanding this concept and having the discipline and the maturity to identify foolish actions.

Here is an example. A friend was a good singer and wanted a stage career. When she started smoking, I warned her that it would not be good for her voice. She did not heed my warning and went down a path that led to failure. In her case, she was not so much foolish for smoking, but foolish for not understanding how her desires and her actions affected each other.

| MODERN DISEASE # 6 • INDECISION |

Anyone can make a decision. The most basic of human functions is the ability to pick one of two boxes. We can choose to go left instead of right. Given any two options, we can easily pick one. You might have heard the expression 'binary decision'. This refers to being given a choice of *two* things, such as the choice to say 'yes' or to say 'no'. These are basic cerebral challenges.

What can we do about decisions that require us to choose from a large number of options? What can we do about decisions that are interconnected, whereby one decision forces us to contend with uninvited consequences? This is often referred to as 'opening a can of worms'. And how about decisions that lead to dead-ends and limit future decisions?

The pain of not winning the lottery does not compare with the trauma of having picked the winning numbers but not having lodged the lottery ticket

Making a decision that leads to hardship is regrettable. More lamentable is avoiding a decision that later proves to have had the potential to be profitable. For example, the pain of not winning the lottery does not compare with the trauma of having picked the winning numbers but not having lodged the lottery ticket. This is known as the 'if only' syndrome.

Decision-making can become the most complex of human endeavours. Apart from the options on offer, we have to contemplate the consequences. These are further compounded by the presence (or absence) of virtues, morals, taboos, traditions, and ethics.

More complex is the process of *indecision*. There is a big difference between 'not making a decision' and 'being indecisive'. The former comes through choice whereby we choose not to engage — or we decide not to take action. The latter does not come from choice. Normally that would not matter, except that we have the ability to reason. Indecision is akin to helplessness. Watching your loved one drown while you are unable to help can leave additional mental scars that go beyond regret and grief.

As humans, we have the capacity to observe, to compute, to reason, and to analyse. When we are obliged to take part in undesirable situations, or when we are forced to stand back and watch horrific outcomes that we know could have been avoided, we drain our spirit. A drained spirit leads to renunciation — meaning that we relinquish everything physically and mentally. The crude term for this is 'becoming a vegetable'.

Those who allow feelings of helplessness to envelop them, run the risk of suffering a nervous breakdown.

Indecision starts when every step of every process emits unpleasant signals. It infests organisations when signals become electric prods felt at each and every step. It would be like standing in a huge maze, and no matter which way you go, you are zapped. The inevitable outcome is to freeze. Inactivity becomes the least painful option. This taming process saps people of their energy, removes their zest for life, exhausts their enthusiasm, and torments them as they try to work out why their ability to act is rendered useless.

Some organisations have electrified every fence after suffering a relentless series of bad decisions. They started to put 'systems' and 'procedures' in place to check on the managers. Each person started to check on every other person. This meant that blame could be shared. This gave rise to 'over caution', which resulted in no-one owning the project, and no-one seeing the bigger picture. Each person started to rely on the other to check for errors. People would say, 'If there is a problem, someone else down the line will spot it. Besides, there is no point in wasting my time on this because it's bound to be changed. I never get my way. I just don't care anymore.'

Collective decision-making, coupled with collective blame-sharing, led to witch-hunts. We are good panel-beaters. We bash and mould the witches like a panel-beater shapes metal. We then contradict ourselves by suggesting that we want to celebrate each other's differences. We espouse hideous mantras like, 'There's no "I" in team'. This never fails to raise my blood pressure. I am embarrassed for those who utter such nonsense.

Organisational indecision is a like a phantom because the location of the central nervous system is never obvious. Bewilderment surfaces when we realise that we are part of the beast, and there is nothing we can do to tame it. If you try to forge ahead with your plans, your comrades will surround you with stun-guns. They will use every means available to them to either put you back in your place, or to expel you from their system. Mind you, the latter is the preferred option — so perhaps we have found the solution. Protest most strongly until you are expelled. The view from outside the electric fence will bring you closer to understanding the meaning of insanity. Indecision and insanity go well together.

Indecision and insanity go well together

In such cases, you cannot take on the establishment. Therefore, do not waste your energy trying to convince your colleagues of the error of their ways. The only way out is out. The decision to leave will be the hardest, yet the most liberating.

| MODERN DISEASE # 7 • SELFISHNESS |

Selfishness combines two powerful forces. The first is *annihilation*. The second is *chain-reaction*. Let us deal with annihilation first.

When opposites are fused, we arrive at a third element. For example, when fear fuses with courage, we arrive at *conviction;* meaning that neither fear nor courage dominates. When we act with conviction, we can take the path that suits us best, not the one that our virtues dictate. Lopsided virtues are not noble; they are captivating, in that they captivate and imprison us to act involuntarily, not consciously.

The first book is this series is called *How to Lose Friends and Infuriate People*. The title advocates the opposite of what we have been taught for years. That book emphasises the need to learn the opposites of our indoctrinated virtues so that we can become thinkers who respond, instead of robots who react.

We must be aware that some elements, once combined, do not fuse, but annihilate each other. They cancel each other out. The process of annihilation is draining because the energy from both sources dissipates. Selfishness is a disease that annihilates whatever it comes into contact with. This means that selfish people who seek material wealth, end up spiritually poor. Selfishness destroys wholesomeness and demolishes talent.

The second factor is that selfishness is another of the diseases that causes devastating chain-reactions. The act of selfishness creates the very thing that selfish people are trying to discard or to run away from. The problem that they do not want, manufactures the problem that they do not want, and that in turn manufactures more of what they least need . . . and so the cycle feeds itself.

This is not unlike the cycle that smokers endure. Regardless of why they started smoking in the first place, they enjoy it because it makes them feel good. Alas, the act of smoking creates nervous tension. To alleviate that discomfort, they smoke. That cycle is never-ending. Their addiction to smoking causes an ailment that they try to fix by smoking. How this type of human logic can survive is a mystery that is explained by the deceptive 'law of distance'.

Someone once told me that a goldfish loses its memory every time it circles inside its bowl. By the time it comes back to its starting position, everything around it looks new again. If that were true, the goldfish would enjoy a life of constant variety and surprises. Mind you, humans suffer from the same problem. They cannot link one activity with the next, especially if there is a distance of time between the two. I have often said that if smokers felt excruciating pain the instant that they inhaled, the statistics would change. Thanks to the law of distance, smokers are prepared to continue in their destructive path, which will eventually lead some people to suffer years of lung disease, breathlessness, coughing, and hospitalisation — all the while unable to connect the intense discomfort with their actions. This disconnectivity illustrates why selfish people cannot see the errors of their ways. They cannot link the *cause* and the *effect*.

Selfish people have real desires. Like anyone else, they want love, happiness, wealth, and prosperity. Their desires are normal and reasonable. Their downfall is that they set about trying to acquire these riches in a devastating way. They smother anything they get their hands on. The disease of selfishness torments both the infected and the affected.

Selfishness shows itself via greed and destroys itself via impatience

Selfishness is not solely focussed on the process of acquisition. The toxic nature of this disease is that it damages instead of nurtures. For example, give magic lanterns to selfish people, and they would be delighted. Tell them that the genie in the lantern can grant them one wish every day, but warn them never to ask for *two* wishes in one day. Highlight the fact that if they break that rule, the genie would grant their two wishes, but never grant them anything else thereafter. A selfish person could not help but tempt fate and ask for two wishes. They would rather double their winnings now than wait until tomorrow. Selfishness shows itself via greed and destroys itself via impatience. It smothers through inconsideration. It is like a moth lured by the deadly bright light. It goes to the light not in search of death, but in search of heat. Unfortunately, the heat from modern lights causes death. Who will tell the moth to resist the temptation? I heard

this fascinating saying: 'Some people are able to resist everything except temptation.'

Selfish people feel affection. They
mean no harm to others. They are not
selfish because they want more than
anyone else. In fact, they do not care
what others get or do not get. They
would not begrudge abundance to oth-

*Some people are able
to resist everything
except temptation*

ers, but they do not assist anyone to attain abundance — not
because they are mean, but because their priority is to attend to
their own needs. Given that their needs are insatiable, they
never get around to assisting anyone else. Ask them for help, and
they will wholeheartedly promise to lend a hand when they
have a spare moment. That moment never comes because their
needs are never-ending. Selfishness is not the same as meanness.

I once worked with a lady who is today a multimillionaire.
Her personal motto was 'never be seen with any staff member
who is below your rank'. I recall the many occasions I asked her to
lend me a hand. She always promised, and then disappeared. I
could read her like a book. She premeditated every move. She
would never go to lunch with those below her rank; unless she
wanted something from them. By all accounts, she is now a successful businesswoman at the peak of her profession. I pity her.
Her cup is indeed full. She does not realise that her cup is so small.

When selfishness consumes well-meaning people, it suffocates those around them to the point where valued friends bow
out of the relationship. Selfish people do not realise that their
strategy is a vicious cycle that continues to repel success.

At first, selfishness has many rewards because loving
friends and family usually have a high measure of tolerance and
forgiveness. At this point, the parasite enjoys the riches, love,
and attention, unaware that their luck will soon run out. There

is a blissful period when the sky's the limit. This vindicates that selfishness works. When they start to sink, their sorrow and loss triggers a thought that they had better look after 'Number One'. And so the merry-go-round continues.

I often wonder what it would be like if the first stage of taking drugs produced the horrible symptoms that eventually grip the addicted. I wonder how many people would indulge if they had to endure the process in *reverse* — meaning that only after ten years of agony, would they start to enjoy the euphoric sensation as the drug starts to kick in. How many smokers would sacrifice a lifetime of ill health before they could enjoy the pleasures of a cigarette? Absurd notions such as these illustrate the truth about success. Success comes after an investment, not before it. Mercifully, the fruits of success are long-lasting, whereas the euphoria of drugs is short-lived. After the stages of addiction have run their course, users inject the drug merely to ward off pain, not to ignite ecstasy.

If you desire love, and are preoccupied with your own feelings, you are being selfish. Love is not concerned with how you feel, but with how you make your partner feel. If you seek wealth, and are engrossed with what you receive, you are being selfish. Wealth is not concerned with what you take, but with what you give. If you desire success and are concerned with what you accumulate, you are being selfish. Success is not concerned with what you amass, but with what you discard.

Consideration is the cornerstone of love. Generosity is the hallmark of wealth. Simplicity is the basis of success.

Consideration is the cornerstone of love. Generosity is the hallmark of wealth. Simplicity is the basis of success. None of these can survive in the presence of selfishness.

| MODERN DISEASE # 8 • SIMPLICITY |

There are some words that sound cute and fluffy. Simplicity is one of them. It implies ease and comfort. Sadly, simplicity is now a disease of the modern world because it corrodes mental stringency when its power is misunderstood.

In the fast-paced complex world, our mission is to avoid complication. We can do this by insisting on solid foundations and robust systems. The lethargic presume that promoting simplicity is the same as rejecting complications. Note that there are big differences between 'complexity' and 'complication'. The former denotes *intricacy*, while the latter denotes *difficulty*.

Albert Einstein once said, 'Everything should be made as simple as possible, but not simpler.' Perhaps he was frustrated by those whose short attention-span justified their indifference to perfection.

The game of chess is like the game of life. Both can be played at superficial levels whereby obligations can continue to be met, without the slightest thought about subsequent moves. Each fumbling step is justified on the basis of simplicity. Meanwhile, no strategy exists.

The way to overcome the difficulties caused by simplicity is to learn to link your decisions with your actions, and your actions with your outcomes. This is a difficult process because most outcomes are separated from their original decision by time and complexity.

Beware that you do not indulge in simplicity without understanding the law of complexity. Simplicity ought to be enjoyed

The game of chess is like the game of life. Both can be played at superficial levels whereby obligations can continue to be met, without the slightest thought about subsequent moves.

at the end of a project, not used at its input stages. When you work, be sure to support every act of simplicity with copious amounts of mental rigour. By all means make your job look simple, and make every process as smooth as possible. Resist the temptation to over-burden others with systems and procedures that do not add value to the end result. The message here is to become an employee who can take the most complex of elements and simplify them only when the backend processes have been thought through. Never present a simplified solution that you are unable to deconstruct.

Never present a simplified solution that you are unable to deconstruct

Mathematics teachers insist that each answer must include the 'working out', because teachers are just as concerned with *how* students arrived at the answer. Knowing how you arrive at simplicity is the trick to sustaining it. Never trade in simplicity if you cannot deconstruct and reconstruct the whole thing (whether it be an idea, a service, or a product). No-one in an organisation should be authorised to break rules or policies unless they know how they were constructed, why they were implemented, and what effect they have on every other rule.

| MODERN DISEASE # 9 • STUPIDITY |

Governments around the world are racing towards building a 'knowledge society' whose constituents would engage in a 'knowledge economy'. For the first time in decades, the intangible cerebral activity of 'thinking' might once more be revered. Intellect might no longer be associated with 'nerds' and 'dorks'. If it can be packaged and sold, intellectual property might become the new hot property. Unfortunately, it just might be a short-lived fad.

Of the nations that are starting to publish their blueprint for success, it is easy to spot the impostors. Those who do not understand what the knowledge economy is all about, exude sufficient clues within the first three paragraphs of their manifestos. They are likely to use impressive buzzwords to describe grandiose concepts about selling intangibles in a world where raw materials have become plentiful, and primary production has become competitive. To them, human capital and ideas are the new 'bread and butter'. They describe nations as 'heads' or 'bodies' meaning that *head* nations use their intellect to generate wealth via innovation and design, whereas *body* nations use their labourers to generate income via manufacturing and farming.

Ill-informed advocates of the new economy believe that selling information is the smart way to generate wealth. If Colonel Sanders were to listen to them, he might have succumbed to selling his secret recipe to the highest bidder. At sixty-five years of age, what chance would a penniless, unemployed Kentucky man have had? New economists would have advised him to sell his intellectual property to enable him to retire with dignity. Instead, the man travelled the country to franchise his business. He did not sell his knowledge. He used it! The secret to success in the knowledge economy is to *use* information, not to *sell* information.

This advice augurs well for the old economy too. For example, if ten of the world's most impressive thinkers gathered to design a country of their choice, what would they specify? If they had the ability to build a country from the ground up, what would they ask for in terms of climate range, natural resources, water ways, and land mass? I suspect that the design would resemble an existing land mass called Australia — a country that has everything anyone could ask for. Sadly, Australian business leaders complain that their rich minerals and raw material are insufficient. As you can see from this example, Australians cannot triumph with their raw material because they think that they have to *sell* their material, not *use* it. They do not know how to add value to the raw material, and so long as that is the case, their assets become commodities that enjoy no differentiation.

Those who do not know how to succeed in the old economy will undoubtedly fail in the new economy

Those who do not know how to succeed in the old economy will undoubtedly fail in the new economy, because the law of economics applies to both the old and new worlds. Simply put, do not sell the goose that lays the golden eggs. Furthermore, do not sell the golden eggs! Learn to transform them into products that can yield better returns. This requires ingenuity, innovation, and investment.

This example highlights how the disease of stupidity follows us from one era to the next. The concept of shedding a new leaf does not work when stupidity latches on. Stupidity is defined as *knowing something, but not acting on what you know*.

If nations do not deal with the issues that threatened their productivity and competitiveness in the old economy, they will find it just as difficult to adjust to the brave new world where taxes have become excruciating, bureaucracy has become agonising, and litigation has become rampant.

Stupidity also grips individuals who presume that their failings can be hushed up and left behind as they enter new doors and foster new beginnings. Letting go of the past, and letting bygones be bygones, presupposes that weaknesses have been dealt with.

A friend once asked me if I subscribe to the idea that people ought to let go of the past and start afresh with a clean slate. I said that such ideals verge on stupidity. Ignoring the errors of the past, and moving on to new environments and new lifestyles, cannot work unless all weaknesses have been rectified. When it is least expected, old habits will regain their prominence because people will be catapulted back to their comfort zone; a place that is not at all comfortable. Perhaps it is better described as the 'hostage zone' wherein people are shackled and are forced into a familiar lifestyle. The predictability of

When pain can be anticipated, it is less threatening. When joy can be pre-empted, it is less wonderful.

the hostage zone is comforting because people are able to brace themselves for both the joys and pains. When pain can be anticipated, it is less threatening. When joy can be pre-empted, it is less wonderful. When failure can be predicted, it is less devastating.

The push to turn information into knowledge is a curious one within societies that have more information and more knowledge than they can cope with. The hard part is not amassing knowledge, but acting upon it.

The test for you is to compare what you know, with what you do. Are you acting on what you know, or is something stopping you from doing what you know ought to be done? Stupidity is not the opposite of 'not knowing'. It is one's decision to act in a way that ignores existing knowledge.

Governments, corporations, and individuals are not lacking knowledge, but lacking conviction. I have not yet come across an organisation that does not know what it needs to do to attain excellence. I have not yet come across a business whose junior staff did not have the answers. I have not worked with anyone who has not been able to arrive at a solution if given the right environment to engage in mental rigour. Seek, and you will find.

Mind you, how many organisations do you know that have shunned good decisions for the sake of expediency? How many have blinded themselves with short-term needs? How many times have you seen monumental bungles that could have been avoided? People know what has to be done. They just do not do it.

If you have assessed areas in your life and your career that need to be dealt with, it would amount to stupidity if you do not do what you know has to be done. If you are lacking certain peripheral skills, you need to plot a course of action and a program of education to help you to overcome the hurdles that are stopping you. If you continue to shy away from your responsibilities, you will eventually shoulder the burden of self-blame. ◘

PART THREE

DEVELOPING *your* SKILLS

Critics are the thieves of time

CHAPTER 8

I'M *not* A RACIST, BUT . . .

PRIDE AND PREJUDICE IN THE WORKPLACE

*The trick is to turn your stumbling blocks
into stepping stones*

D O YOU BELIEVE that you have been denied work opportunities because your boss does not like something about you? This chapter explains how racism and discrimination work, and what you can do to minimise their effect on you.

At its essence, racism describes a preference for one group over another and the belief that one's own 'race' is superior to another 'race'. Regardless, I doubt that we operate at that level. At school, at work, and within our community, people are not concerned with the pure issues of race. They contend with its constituent parts that include discrimination, inequality, sexism, chauvinism, favouritism, nepotism, bias, preference, fear, and intolerance.

If you are trying to fight racism, forget it. By locking horns with fundamental human emotions, you will lose. Racism is not the enemy. It is not something that you can identify as an external foe, because it exists within each of us — not because we are all racists, but because we all harbour the basic ingredients that could easily ignite to form inexplicable feelings about others.

Although I do not condone racism, I believe that the many complaints about it are misdirected because people are being persecuted or disadvantaged based on *other* human factors, not on their race.

I'M GUILTY, BUT NOT OF RACISM

Although I do not know many racists, I do know many people who discriminate against others based not on 'race' but on 'human' factors. I must admit to being guilty of that myself — meaning that I find some people attractive and some people unattractive in their attitudes, their way of life, their physical appearance, their personality, and their intellectual and spiritual expression.

Could you have a physical and intimate relationship with *anyone*, regardless of hygiene, looks, habits, odour, general appearance, age, and beliefs? Marriages end because one partner could not cope with the other's table manners. Friends part because they could not tolerate each other's personal habits. Even those who meet the person of their dreams could be easily repulsed by peculiar personal preferences.

I must also admit to exercising that degree of discrimination at the business level — meaning that I prefer not to work with people whose business conduct and social graces are not to my liking. The dubious ethical standards of some professionals are disgusting, whereby I become uneasy about transacting with them. I can detect con-artists from afar, and I want nothing to do with such manipulators and liars. I prefer to avoid people whose negative or destructive views grate on my spirit. I would not want to work with people whose morals and principles are contrary to what I can cope with. That type of feeling is not one that I can always justify to my colleagues in 'words'. Do you call that racism? I call it human nature.

CATALOGUING THE WORLD

When meeting people for the first time, our brain goes into overdrive as we unintentionally categorise them. Some ignorant people do make erroneous judgements based on nationality or skin colour. Although this cannot be condoned, it is understandable. Society superficially operates on the basis of 'image'. The concept of 'branding' works by positioning the qualities of a brand in the consumer's mind. Consumers could, over time, be led to believe that certain brand names do represent certain qualities. If you were asked to identify the best brands in the world, you would probably mention some that you respect, but have never had any association with. Similarly, you are likely to have pre-conceived notions about cultures that you have never come into contact with.

Countries, too, have brand qualities. Regardless of fact, some people form opinions about products, depending upon the country of manufacture. Here is a simple test for which there are no right or wrong answers, merely 'perceptions' that you might have formed over the years. Answer these questions based on which of the two countries would offer the better product in your opinion: 1) Chocolate from Belgium or Switzerland; 2) Whisky from Scotland or Ireland; 3) Cheese from Australia or New Zealand; 4) Stereo systems from Japan or Korea; 5) Perfume from France or Norway; 6) Fast cars from Germany or Italy; 7) Computers from Taiwan or the USA. There are also perceived origins for different types of food such as curry, pasta, pizza, and noodle dishes.

Consider the judgements we make about professions. At gatherings, people react differently towards those who say that their occupations are astronauts, surgeons, car salespeople, judges, shop assistants, undertakers, students, accountants, psychiatrists, film producers, or street-sweepers. The unemployed could receive an altogether different reception.

Long tradition gives 'colours' superstitious attributes. Some people would never drive a red car. Some insist that purple is the colour that offers good fortune. In some countries, yellow represents bad luck. These are compounded by the inexplicable, yet popular beliefs, that certain numbers represent good luck. People move to a house whose street number adds up to a 'preferred' integer or they buy a car whose registration number plate includes the digit '3' or excludes the number '666'. Other people would not work on the fourth or thirteenth floors of a building, and some buildings do not have such floors. There is no explaining how these things are rationalised. In addition, there are fundamentalists, fanatics, extremists, and those who subscribe to astrology, numerology, and a dozen other mystical cults. So as you can see, racism is hardly the major obstacle to human harmony.

If the brain can make judgements about brands, why can it not make judgements about people? If people can be misled about brands, why can they not be misled about other aspects such as cultures, nationalities, countries, languages, gender, age groups, sexuality, and modes of dress — in fact, anything that is 'foreign' to them?

Tarred with the same brush

You might have heard a friend say, 'I would never again deal with XYZ Company because it's hopeless and it doesn't care about its customers.' It could well be that the company employs 300 000 people, yet your friend would be making a judgement based on what only *three* of its employees have done. That is a similar reaction to those who judge a whole race, country, or religion, based on what three people have done or said to them, or based on what they have seen on television. Foreign nationals have repeatedly objected to the images that the media portrays about their country and lifestyle. Some argue that travel advertisements showing natives in their national dress are misleading because such costumes are only worn at rare cultural events. What we see about a country through television does not necessarily portray the real day-to-day environment.

It is neither fair nor sensible to form unsubstantiated opinions about people and cultures. Unfortunately, that is how the human brain works when it is stirred with a cocktail of emotions and irrationalities.

Discrimination extends to social bigotry that forces some people to change suburbs merely to avoid the stigma associated with an 'unfashionable' address. Many colour their hair or undergo plastic surgery, believing that they will appease their social group or believing that they will look younger. Some even go to the trouble of changing their name to blend into their new community.

BREAKING THROUGH THE GLASS CEILING

In the work environment, it is important to be aware of some of your personal aspects that could detract from your capabilities. Although you do not want people to categorise you based on inexplicable predispositions, there is no point in trying to change human nature. To form small clubs to recruit plenty of 'us' to fight all of 'them' is counterproductive. Organisations are advised against forming groups for only men or only women — a practice that has become rife. Gender-based groups endorse the unhealthy 'them-and-us'

Fighting years of male domination cannot be won by creating female domination

attitude, where each group tries to reinforce its own position at the expense of the opposite sex. That approach is like combating terrorism with terrorism — alienating the innocent and fair-minded employees who cannot understand why such divisions exist. Fighting years of male domination cannot be won by creating female domination. The preferred solution would be to teach executives about reducing, not inflaming, chauvinism. This means that we need to educate or to stop the perpetrators, not encourage the underdog to adopt unpleasant means with which to combat the problems, because that course of action creates *new* struggles.

Employees who complain that they have hit a glass ceiling 'based on gender' are right in that the ceiling does exist. It is not always true to say that they have been disadvantaged only because of their gender. Rather, they have been disadvantaged because they have to deal with discriminating, small-minded executives. The problems do not lie within a person's gender, but within the chauvinists themselves who are discriminators, full stop.

Among those I have counselled are men and women who have *insisted* that they were passed up for promotion because of their gender. Others cry that they were ignored because of their *race*. As I was developing my career, some employers had a hang-up about my *age*, and for a while, I internalised the problem. They would tell me that I was too young for the positions I wanted (in the days when age discrimination was not illegal). Perhaps they did not like the colour of my eyes, but they could not bring themselves to explain that, so they used my age as an excuse. Who knows? It would be impossible to prove. Some people say it is gender, the young say it is age, the short say it is height, and the list goes on — each internalising the problem, yet all the while, the problem exists within the perpetrator, *not* the victim. The result is just as painful for all the victims — each one thinking that it is for a different reason, whereas each person was discriminated against for the *same* reason. That reason is the close-minded manager who does not know any better. Having said that, each person could have triggered discrimination for a *different* reason. Some employees are disadvantaged because of their mode of dress, the way they speak, their work ethic, their personality, or any of a hundred-and-one other things, but to suggest that it is simply gender or race would be a mistake.

I would dismiss any manager who believes that women are less intelligent than men

I would dismiss any manager who believes that women are less intelligent than men; or that skin colour is a reason to hinder someone's advancement. Mind you, I have heard women say words to the effect of, 'We have had it so bad for so long, I don't see why men can't suffer a little now.' I have also heard feminists say, 'No-one helped me to climb the corporate ladder, so why should I help her?' They too would be dismissed from my organisation.

Men and women are not born thinking that they are better than each other. No-one is born feeling that a particular race is better than any other. Unfortunately, those who do hold such beliefs are the victims of cultural conditioning. Managers who do not promote the opposite sex are guilty of blatant disregard for equality in the workplace.

It is all very well to say that in this country or in that country, members of a minority race feel aggrieved. Try going to the aggrieved person's country and see if the citizens will not discriminate against you. I used to hear stories that, in some countries, people of my race were not allowed into restaurants. In 2000 I happened to be a business foreigner, visiting what could be described as one of the most advanced nations, where I was physically refused entry into two high-class restaurants because I was an Aussie! There were signs on the door that read 'No Westerners'. If I had not experienced it for myself, I could not have believed it to be anything other than an exaggerated story. My fancy charge-card meant nothing there. The welcome sign on the door was not for me. I am not complaining. I am just saying that it happens both ways, and

You cannot change what cannot be changed

it is appalling that it should ever happen. If you want to do something constructive, you need to understand some of the issues that affect you personally, and deal with those yourself, without trying to change human nature. You cannot change what cannot be changed.

To aggrieved employees I want to say that I agree that they are sometimes disadvantaged, but I urge them to find out the real reasons. To think that it is gender-based is another form of social brainwashing. Those who forewarn young people about gender imbalance would be just as guilty as those who brainwash their tribe into thinking that one race is better than another. Young people grow up feeling powerless, always on the lookout for a problem that does not really exist in the way that they have been warned about it. Furthermore, if workers are too quick to attribute their hurdles to gender, they would be doing themselves a disservice by not delving into the real issues that cause conflict or disharmony between themselves and their boss.

EQUALITY FOR ALL?

Although the noble would say that we are all created equal, I am not sure that we *are* equal. In what way are we equal? In social terms? In our looks? In our strengths? In our capabilities? In our knowledge? In our tolerances? In our maturity? In our preferences? In our fantasies? In our pleasures? I have not met two people who are alike. So how equal are we, apart from the fact that we all bleed, hurt, and love?

The initial step in minimising the effect of discrimination on you is to become aware of what it is about you that others could misunderstand, misjudge, dislike, or fear. Frequently we are blinded by our own peculiarities because we are automatically conditioned to *ignore* the prevalent and obvious. For example, if a small stone hits your car's windscreen and chips a small piece of glass in front of your line of sight, you are likely to be distracted by the damage. Initially, the irritating speck causes focussing difficulties. Then, when you least expect it, you are distracted by something else and you forget about the chip in the windscreen. Your eyes compensate for it because you are conditioned to ignore the problem. These are mechanisms of survival. The mind and body are brilliantly designed in this respect. We are able to adjust to some things to the point where we are no longer aware of their existence. The downside is that we find it difficult to understand what it is that we do that irritates others.

We are able to adjust to some things to the point where we are no longer aware of their existence

THE BIGGEST OBSTACLE OF ALL

What would you say is the single biggest obstacle that triggers the highest incidence of workplace discrimination? What is the biggest factor that retards a person's career in the corporate environment? Since 1995, Logictivity, my consulting company, has been working to identify the major contributor to racially-based discrimination for employees. We have conducted numerous tests and focus groups to examine how people react to each other on the basis of: perceived power; skin colour; country of origin; mode of dress; wealth; level of education and qualifications; social position; personal appearance; and native tongue.

The predictable results from these nine categories did not answer the question: what is the single biggest obstacle that triggers the highest incidence of discrimination? The answer was 'none of the above'. It was a tenth factor that no-one in our workgroups had been able to guess. Are you able to guess the most important factor that causes the most problems for individuals in the workplace? It is also the factor that inhibits career advancement. The most significant obstacle is a person's *accent!*

There are three categories of accents. The first is the 'pleasant accent' that included 'cute', 'amusing', and 'romantic'. These ranked highly on the social front, but did not score so well on the serious business front — meaning that those with pleasant accents were well liked as friends, but found it difficult to be taken seriously in their job because their accent was distracting. Such colleagues were considered to be too playful for the high-powered jobs.

The second category is called the 'unpleasant accent' that included 'irritating' and 'annoying' as well as 'affected' and 'strained'. These accents carried more baggage than just their sound or their 'song'. They irritated people on the basis of the accent's political stigma and its nationalistic association. The interesting thing is that while some of the pleasant accents delighted people, their delight factor was less than half the converse reaction — meaning that those who were annoyed by certain accents were supremely annoyed to such a degree that their blood pressure seemed to rise and they spoke of a 'nauseating' effect. In audio experiments with news commentators of various 'unpleasant accents', listeners said that they could not tolerate the radio, and they had to switch it off. They were extremely agitated. It was not uncommon for members of the focus groups to fidget and turn in their chair, and to mouth-off the accent in mockery while pulling a face to express their displeasure.

The third category is the 'simpleton accent'. This is an unkind description given to accents that seem to indicate that the person is 'unintelligent' and 'not one of us'. The accent was projected by people for whom English was not their first language. For some, their vocabulary was limited and their pronunciation was imperfect. Regardless of their education level or their professional capability, these people were discriminated against based on a superficial aspect that inhibited them from being able to mix well with their peers.

We took this research one step further and decided to find out how a 'simpleton accent' can affect career advancement. We surveyed some of the leading organisations in the English-speaking world and found that fewer than half of one percent of senior managers had a 'simpleton accent' — meaning that those who exhibit this type of accent, no matter how bright they are, are not promoted into senior positions.

The lesson for you here is to consider what kind of effect your accent has on your colleagues. What would you sound like at an interview if you were applying for a job with a manager who does not know about your real capabilities, but might be distracted by your accent? I once knew a manager whose English was good, but whose accent was shocking. I convinced him to see a speech therapist. His public image eventually improved. I plucked up enough courage to advise him because he once drove me mad by telling me not to employ a man because his eyes were too close together. He judged people based on their facial features (not an uncommon thing to do in his culture). I told him that if he held such beliefs, he should then understand that some people would not be comfortable with his accent. At least he had the maturity to take advice.

I have always tried to encourage clients to modify their accent or speech impediment. Some sport lazy speech that does not do their social standing any favours. If you can accept that 'learning the language' is important, then please accept that an accent is an important part of the communication process.

I met a young chap who was referred to me by one of my clients on the basis that he needed career guidance. I said to the young man, 'If I had to give you one piece of advice that would change the course of your life, it is that you should go and fix your speech impediment'. He did not know what I was talking about. All his life, no-one had been kind enough to tell him about his poor speech. All his family members had the impediment. I set up meetings for him with two speech therapists. Unfortunately, his father was not in favour of my recommendations, so he badgered his son into a state of inaction. Sometimes you just cannot help some people because they either cannot see or they cannot understand what you are talking about. The deadly combination is when they can neither see nor understand.

The next chapter lists seven *additional* aspects that can hold you back from advancing your career. **N**

CHAPTER 9

THE *enemy* WITHIN

FIRST IMPRESSIONS LAST

*Being cool is not about what you do,
but where you end up after you've done it*

IN THE PREVIOUS CHAPTER, it was pointed out that it is natural for humans to discriminate against each other. Rather than fight the forces of nature, we would do well to understand how racism and discrimination work so that we do not trigger emotions in others that might cause them to distance themselves from us.

In the work environment, what we do and what we say, and how we interact and communicate, all contribute to how others might judge us. Below are seven aspects to reflect upon. The list focuses on some of the factors that contribute to discrimination during the early stages of meeting people.

1) Vocabulary

After you have grasped the language and polished your accent to suit the local market, consider the extent of your vocabulary. Those with a limited vocabulary reduce their chances of a promotion, not because people in power want to hear impressive words, but because they want to hear impressive ideas. If you are unable to vocalise your thoughts, how can you show your level of understanding of a subject? An expanded vocabulary is not meant to equip you with a 'social tool', but with a 'thinking tool'.

Those with a limited vocabulary reduce their chances of a promotion, not because people in power want to hear impressive words, but because they want to hear impressive ideas

Other than vocabulary, grammar and spelling are important. It is harder to keep climbing the corporate ladder if you lack competency in these areas. A weak handle on these presupposes deficiency of intellect and education. For example, there is a group of professionals who cringe at people who say 'haitch' when referring to the eighth letter of the alphabet. They also discriminate against those who say things like 'everythink' instead of 'everything'.

Regardless of how competent you might be at your profession, you are judged and ranked by what people can see, hear, and read. These are the external factors that help to paint a picture about you.

If you do not take care of your written and spoken skills, and improve these if required, you might not be given a second chance to prove your capabilities.

2) Public speaking

Ranked as one of the most uncomfortable things that an executive has to do, public speaking is seen as a terrifying obligation. Public speaking also refers to general presentations that are made to the media, staff, shareholders, and the members of the public via seminars or television.

The most successful of industry leaders are those who can stand behind a microphone and project their personality with confidence. It is not a skill that can be honed *after* one reaches an office of power. Rather, it is rare to reach an office of power without it.

Do not think that public speaking is reserved for high-flyers. To be able to present well to large and small groups is one of the most important personal qualities that an employee needs. Remember that the purpose is to get your message across without unnecessary interruptions and distractions. Those who cannot present their ideas confidently and succinctly are holding themselves back. It is difficult to rally support if you cannot communicate your ideas.

Presentation skills include how you present your ideas and how you use the tools to do so. Computers, microphones, lighting, projection systems, and other devices, form part of the picture. For example, a presenter who thumps the lectern with every sentence might not realise that the microphone is amplifying those thumps into irritating noises that fill the room and distract the audience.

Anyone who gets up to present and is nervous behind a microphone must immediately work to overcome that anxiety. I have often heard executives say, 'I'm hopeless at it, I just can't do it.' Unless they deal with this, it would be like saying 'I can't play the piano'. If playing the piano is an important part of your profession, and you never take lessons, you will look a fool when someone forces you on stage and asks you to perform. Imagine being asked to play an instrument that you know nothing about. Imagine being introduced by an enthusiastic master of ceremonies who builds you up as the next presenter and says, 'Now, would you please put your hands together and welcome our next speaker!' What would you do? I can tell you what ninety-nine percent of executives do. They walk on stage to take the microphone and they proceed painfully through their unrehearsed performance, using equipment that is out of tune, with no showmanship whatsoever, no content, and a dry presentation that would bore the socks off anyone. You would not contemplate a piano recital if you could not play the piano, so why would you ever get up to present if you are ill-prepared?

There is no point in ignoring your weaknesses. Do something constructive to overcome these difficulties. There is no escaping that requirement. If you lack the ability to present, you will find yourself in awkward positions where your future employers will feel uncomfortable about you. That is not a feeling you want to trigger in them. Mind you, there are many presenters who *think* that they do a good job. Do not fall into that trap. Wherever possible, record yourself so that you can scrutinise your performance.

3) *Written presentations*

Remember that anything about you that 'speaks for you' can influence how people see you, and can therefore lead them to form impressions about you. Your behaviour, your telephone manner, and your dress can be the source of a positive or negative effect.

Communicating through written means is far more prevalent and informal nowadays than in the last century. Take care to understand what signals you send when you submit your written presentations to people who do not know you well. Everything about your work must be to a standard that would avoid distractions.

Not everything you send out has to be on the finest paper, but it must be suitable for the reader. For that reason, every effort has to be made to impress the person with whom you are communicating. Do not try to use a word-processor to submit a job-application if you are not proficient at using the software, or if you are unfamiliar with what constitutes 'good layout'. There are ample courses that you can take to assist you in this regard. Do not overlook typography, layout, colour, and written presentation skills if you wish to communicate clearly. Look at design as being parallel to music. If you did not know how to compose a symphony, you would not contemplate recording one. Written presentations are like symphonies. To the trained observer, they can be inappropriate or pleasing. To make your mark, engage professionals to guide you as to how to present yourself.

Imagine an employer receiving 200 job-applications. Poorly presented ones might be overlooked. Those that look like the rest would not stand out. Those that stand out in an inappropriate way are probably mocked. The balance would be those that make an impression and cause the reviewer to read parts of the applications.

It would be rare for anyone to read a whole document. The important elements should be alluring so that your messages are clear and come across without distracting the reader. It is for this reason that I have always refused to send my résumé by e-mail or by facsimile. The facsimile might be convenient, but it offers no chance for the candidate to excite the recipient, especially if it is the first contact. The appearance of e-mails is unpredictable because fonts and layout sometimes drop out, and the overall effect can be lost. Sending an important document through e-mail is like sending music down a telephone line. There is no excitement and it loses its dynamics. When sending important presentations by post or by courier, always put a backing board so that the document does not become bent or crushed in transit. All these finer details reduce the risk of someone defacing your document.

Your handwriting is also a vital part of your presentation. I am not suggesting that there are spooky clues about your personality within your handwriting, although your handwriting and signature, if distracting, could raise some questions about your capability. People will discriminate against those whose handwriting is unappealing, messy, indecipherable, or hard to comprehend. It is interesting that people presume that their handwriting is as much a part of their 'being' as the colour of their eyes. This is not true. Handwriting must be honed, refined, and practised.

In the same way that irritating accents can create difficulties for people, irritating handwriting can also work against you — whereby the reader can make all sorts of inaccurate, but real, assumptions about your level of intelligence or education, and your level of excitement about an application. Employers who ask for hand-written applications, or who ask for 'creative' applications, might be interested in the level of enthusiasm that you project, more so than the content of the material.

4) Peripheral dress

The young do not understand the old, and the old do not understand the young. This division is called 'the generation gap'.

Once upon a time, board members were more than fifty years of age. Now professionals as young as twenty hold senior posts. In days of old, if you met two colleagues, you could have assumed that the older one was the boss — but not these days. More so than ever before, the young and old are working side by side.

The major stumbling stone for the young was their youthful looks. Back then, it was not unusual for young executives to ask their hairdresser to make them look older by colouring their hair grey to exhibit an air of maturity. These days, the converse is true with older people colouring their hair to *hide* the grey streaks.

When young and old meet each other, they are no longer concerned with the potential conflict of 'youth versus wisdom', but with 'hip versus dorky'. In other words, despite the popular misconception about age discrimination, I believe that age no longer matters. It is now more important that colleagues are on the same wavelength.

We are quick to rely on visual clues to make unhealthy generalisations. For that reason, modes of dress and the use of other accessories tend to paint a picture about a person's 'type'. If you want to cross the line into a work environment that is predominantly held by one generation or another, you need to become aware of the visual signals you send by what you are wearing, including your peripheral dress. These might include tattoos, earrings, body-piercing, and body decoration. Hair colours and hair styles, as well as the formality or otherwise of the clothes, give clues about the 'era' to which each person belongs. Footwear and jewellery contribute to giving the game away at the first job interview.

For those whose antenna is finely tuned, they observe every detail, such as the length of a skirt or whether the handbag matches the shoes. For men, the gentry would look to see if the belt matches the shoes, or if the socks match the trousers, or if the tie is fashioned using the Windsor knot. The length of the cuffs gives clues about a person's breeding.

There are many conventions that give clues about an applicant's understanding of the terms and conditions of the 'clique'.

The advice here is twofold. First, do not try to blend into a group unless you know the rules, because you are likely to be caught out by omitting some simple detail. For example, there is a fraternity of businessmen who would expect that anyone wearing a vest to leave the bottom button undone. It is insignificant for some, and a major signal for others. Second, if you choose to wear any accessory that is considered out of fashion, you risk being alienated.

I have often told young people that they can pierce any part of their body they like, but they cannot enter certain professions and hope to go unnoticed. Their mode of dress, although modern and 'normal' puts the potential employer in a spot of bother because tension could arise about how the employer's colleagues, customers, and suppliers might cope. Just remember that what you might find acceptable could work against you.

First impressions do count. You do not want to distract someone at a job interview. Learn to speak the language and to dress appropriately. It is often easy to notice a young man wearing a suit for the *first* time. His awkwardness becomes evident. In the same way that you might think it reasonable to rehearse a part for a stage play, you need to practise wearing the 'uniform'.

Many young folk object to the notion that they have to modify their peripheral accessories. They feel that they are betraying their clan if they remove their earring or cover their tattoo. The bottom line is that they need to understand that a job interview is not the place to be flaunting their beliefs. That is distracting and unnecessary.

Deportment is also an important consideration. Whether you like it or not, people do make judgements about you, based on what they see and hear in the first sixty seconds of a meeting. This could be by your confidence, articulation, stance, the way you shake hands, how you hand out a business card, how you carry yourself, how well you listen, and where your eyes gaze. Your level of comfort can be easily seen by experienced observers. At the end of such an encounter, people might use an obscure reason as to why you were not selected, when in fact, they might not have been comfortable with your personality. They will not write a letter saying that you were not chosen because you lacked certain social graces. They are more likely to say, 'We will keep your application on file and let you know if a suitable position comes up.'

Some people send their résumés to friends and family, asking for a critical assessment about its contents and layout. What they ought to be doing is dressing up for a few mock interviews and visiting established professionals who could comment about decorum, deportment, presentation, and facial expression.

Discrimination is alive and well at every level. It is used by people to protect their territory from 'aliens'. Make sure that you are not alienating yourself. If you have had to suffer inexplicable discrimination, try to understand its origins, rather than to fight what cannot be tamed.

5) Know your stuff

Once you have refined the external issues, such as your language, accent, deportment, presentation skills, dress, handwriting, and similar factors that could cause people to pre-judge you, focus on the 'content'. This mean, know what you are talking about. If you are not proficient in your job, this will become obvious to experts who fear anyone who could jeopardise the success of their project.

In most cases, experts are kind to those who are willing to learn, so take advantage of their knowledge. They generally enjoy teaching others, and they love to talk about their craft or their industry. Experts take pride in doing a good job, and they become excited with a successful outcome.

Take extra care not to bluff your way through important meetings. Those who know better could easily pick up on your weaknesses. They might never confront you with them. Instead, they might find reasons to exclude you from their circle. Experts enjoy working with experts. You stand a much greater chance of success if you build your career on solid foundations. In other words, know your stuff.

Although this seems like simple advice, let me add another layer to it. By learning more about your craft or your area of interest, you also need to learn about your competitors. To this day I still see advertisements that try to lure customers away from competitors. When I telephone the company in question, I explain that I was using its competitor's product or service for fifteen years, and that I would be willing to switch over if they could tell me the differences between their offer and my current package. Their answer, every single time, has been, 'We don't know anything about your current supplier, we can only tell you what we offer.' The moment that I hear that ever-so-common phrase, I switch off and lose interest. It tells me that the company will fail in the market. A fundamental rule of sales and marketing is to know what you are up against. If you can-not speak in terms that a customer can understand, and if you cannot provide useful comparisons, failure is a certainty.

An employer would expect that you not only know about the products and services of the company, but also about the competitive landscape. Before any job interview, scour every source you can to find out as much information as possible about the company *and* its competitors.

After you secure the job, read industry magazines, attend conferences, go to seminars, speak with people, join associations — all with the purpose of learning about your industry. When you know your landscape, it would be difficult for anyone to trip you up.

When you know your landscape, it would be difficult for anyone to trip you up

You must understand as much as you can about your customers and products, and about your competitors' customers and products. It is also vital that you understand the legal aspects of your industry. Know its history, its players, its current issues, the international forces that could affect you, and learn about everyone within your distribution channel. There are managers who fail because they have never met anyone within the retail chain on whom their success relies. There are senior managers who have never met any of their customers yet they make vital decisions about pricing, delivery, services, and other policies that affect everyone in the chain. When things do not work, they blame anything from the election, to the fluctuations in currency, or the economy, or the market. It is frightening to see organisations whose employees do not have a clue about the business they are in. Is it any wonder they fail?

If you want to be the best in your profession, learn everything you can. It might sound like hard work, but once you start, you will find that it is relatively easy to keep your finger on the pulse.

Finally, of the people with whom you feel you must argue, never press a point unless you are sure of what you are saying. Even then, do not force your knowledge onto those who are unwilling to listen and to learn.

Do not force your knowledge onto those who are unwilling to listen and to learn

6) Do not boast

What is the psychological intention behind the process of boasting? There are two basic aspects to consider. The first is the unintentional expression of ideas by those who are so enthusiastic and energetic that they do not stop to consider that others might not be interested in what they have to say. They try to support their conversation with what they think is proof of truth. They feel that their conversation would carry added credibility if they could tell everyone about what they know and how they came to know it.

The other type of 'show-offs' are people who try hard to impress others in the hope of gaining their approval. They feel that if they can make their colleagues or friends aware of their fortunes or capabilities, they might be liked or accepted. Often, the root cause is a deep-seated dissatisfaction with their life.

Regardless of the reasons, the primary outcome is that show-offs are trying to amplify a message. They are trying to use actions to speak the words. For example, they know that it would be difficult to say, 'Please like me, I am cool'. Therefore, they waste a lot of money buying a fancy car in the hope that the car would speak on their behalf. When that does not work, they try other things, while burning bridges along the way, or creating other misunderstandings that they had not intended. Their generosity could be mistaken for bribes, or their liveliness could be mistaken for inconsideration. Often those who show-off do care about what others think about them. That is the problem. They care so much, that they want to gain the approval of others, and they want to be accepted.

The most unfortunate aspect is the one that gives the impression, 'I am better than you.' An expression of supremacy is rarely the aim. They are not really trying to say 'I am better than you.' They are hoping that other people would acknowledge them as worthy peers whose presence is wanted and whose friendship is valued.

Beware that you do not boast. You might not realise it, but your vibes will be felt by others. Transmitting only a few seconds of uncomfortable vibes can be enough to turn people off. Human interactions are often hindered by feelings that people form within *seconds* of a meeting.

Humility is an intangible tool that complements social graces. It is not important to let others know what you know. Use your knowledge to produce results. Refrain from expressing your opinion when it is not sought. Timing is a crucial part of any human exchange. You can be heard best if you speak when you are invited. In life, only students who are ready to learn can be taught. Only exchange information with those who are willing participants. Anything else would cause friction that you cannot afford to create so early in the encounter.

Humility is an intangible tool that complements social graces

After you have built up your credibility, you can get away with deviations from that advice. Until you have established yourself, be aware of what impression you are making. You cannot force someone to accept what you are trying to project. Enthusiasm must be tempered with timing.

7) Don't put people down

These days I study humour, just as most people set about studying any other subject. I have realised that comedy is not a process of making one laugh, but of making one think. Many a truth can be uttered in the guise of humour. What many people do not realise is that humour and controversy are related, meaning that they can both do exactly

> Comedy
> is not a process of
> making one laugh, but
> of making one think

the same thing — they operate on the premise of revealing truths. Humour touches on personal, revealing subjects, but manages to ignite laughter because it deflects off a person, microseconds before it hits a raw nerve. Controversy does exactly the same thing, except that at the last moment, instead of opening the relief valve, it hits the nerve, causing embarrassment, anger, or other unpleasant emotions. Humour allows us to laugh at someone else's situation (to which we can relate), while controversy makes us uneasy about our own situation.

If you observe much of television's cheap comedy, the basis for its humour is the abuse of others — how people put each other down or tease one another. As a result of this social conditioning, people have come to speak with each other in short, sharp phrases, accompanied by misplaced wit. The personal jibes are usually meant as terms of endearment, like the way young boys play 'rough and tumble' in the hope that they could develop a stronger friendship. It is socially awkward for two boys to admit that they like each other, so they engage in a friendly fight to express their mutual admiration.

Unfortunately, using put-downs or snide remarks is potentially a volatile way to interact. What you might express with good intentions could easily ignite discomfort and lead to defensive behaviour. It is hard enough trying to say to people, 'Please like me, I want to be your friend', without risking an internal and secret abhorrence to your incessant quips that could cause others to say, 'That person keeps on embarrassing me and making me feel uncomfortable.'

You might never know what it is that others find offensive. Some people do not have a problem with their public image, and they might enjoy hearing new and funny jokes about an aspect of their appearance or behaviour. Others might appear to laugh at such jokes, but could secretly find them tasteless and demeaning. Avoid commenting on physical or behavioural aspects about which people can do nothing. Do not tease people for being different. You would not be the first person to give them the third degree about their choices in life. Give it a rest. For example, it is no-one's business as to why some people do not drink alcohol. Alcoholism, preference, or religious belief could motivate abstinence. It is a personal matter that should not be questioned by the inquisitive at gatherings. Learn to be sensitive about other people's differences.

In the process of trying to build ourselves, we sometimes tread on others, thereby putting them down. That is a definite way to fail in trying to make a good first impression. More information about social graces is presented in Chapter 11, 'Would a hit man ring the doorbell?'

IGNITING FIRES

When we speak about human nature, we have to realise that our intellect and our advancements pale into insignificance when we pit ourselves against natural forces. One of those forces is our human make-up. Humans are fundamentally the same, although no two are alike. We are all ruled by the same types of emotions and cultural or personal limitations.

In the same way that we cannot fight fire with fire, I suspect that we cannot fight racism with anti-racism. Riddle me this: what is the difference between racists, and those who restrain them? I think that the former are acting out of *ignorance*, while the latter are acting out of *arrogance*. When anti-racists refuse to engage with racists, they are adopting the same discriminatory processes that they are trying to expunge. This cannot be progressive for the human soul. Some anti-racists seem to think that it is permissible for them to discriminate against the discriminators. Who is right? Who is wrong?

The 'tolerant humanitarian righteous' might remind us that both the victims and the perpetrators need to learn to tolerate each other. I would be more inclined to say that it is difficult to get everyone to agree. We need to learn as much as we can about ourselves and others, forgetting about trying to get others to understand us. When we can equip ourselves with sufficient awareness and understanding, we can sharpen our insight into human nature, so that we can use what we know to advance our career and to improve the quality of our life. That would have to be the first priority if we were to work towards making this world a better place. By learning to make our life better, we can later help others. Otherwise, we will be fighting a losing battle that will surely drag us down to the lowest common denominator because when natural forces are left to their own devices, the most evil or destructive forces win.

You cannot force people to hear what you want them to hear. You cannot force them to see what you want them to see.

This chapter has outlined how you communicate silently and unintentionally. Many messages about you are sent out long before you can put your case forward. Take care that you refine your signals so that others do not judge you based on information that you did not mean to submit. You cannot force people to hear what you want them to hear. You cannot force them to see what you want them to see.

Once you have made an impression, it is almost impossible to reverse it. Remember that 'first impressions last!'

Once you have made an impression, it is almost impossible to reverse it

Apart from messy legislation, I am not sure that we can do anything about racists and discriminators, but I do believe that we can do something to build a better world whereby people do not dislike each other unnecessarily. Notice that I said 'unnecessarily', meaning that likes and dislikes cannot be regulated. They are part of our genetic make-up. Our ability to like and dislike cannot be removed. What we can do is make sure that *our* preferences are not the result of ignorance or arrogance. We can make sure that what we project is what we mean to project. Beyond that, we cannot do anything to change our fundamental constitution. ◼A

CHAPTER 10

WANTED: THE BOSS OF THE FUTURE

THE SKILLS YOU'LL NEED FOR YOUR NEXT PROMOTION

Only extremists can see the edge,
but only radicals can get there

S UCCESSFUL PEOPLE are those who can pre-empt future needs. They build personal skills that will be useful and valuable for their career.

What will employers of the future be looking for? Here are the top-fifteen *current* requests from employers when looking to appoint managers. Following each of the requirements listed below are the skills that I believe the boss of the *future* would need to offer. Take a look at these and try to identify what you need to do to prepare yourself for your next promotion.

1
Current skill: Be a team player
Future skill: Be a troublemaker

Politicians are expected to be schizophrenic team players, in that they are required to appease voters, sponsors, journalists, and power brokers. Under these circumstances, politicians are expected to possess the qualities of a chameleon. No wonder some of them become dispassionate and disengaged. As Sir Humphrey in *Yes, Minister* observed, he served eleven governments in thirty years, so if he had believed in all their policies, he would have ended up a stark, staring, raving loony!

We are told that to be a team player in the general work environment, we need to be a good listener who subscribes to consensus management. We are expected to be amiable, friendly, tolerant, and not inclined to upset others. Take a look at recruitment advertisements, or read job-specifications drafted by head-hunters. They all seem to want a 'hard-working, hands-on, visionary leader who is a results-oriented team player with bottom-line responsibility who can take the company into the next decade while over-achieving the monthly targets, reducing expenses, and motivating a team of professionals'. These are contradictory requirements.

In the future, managers will need to be decisive, action-oriented, and influential operators who do not suffer fools. Managers need not bother with the diplomatic game of team-work. Instead, they should focus on constructing *teams that work*. Further-more, if you study all the significant developments of the past, you will find that somewhere in there was a person who was neither a team player nor a hero, but a *troublemaker*.

Give me troublemakers any day over timid diplomats

Future success will rely less on exec-utives who can appease teams and get along with people, and more on those who can make things happen. Give me troublemakers any day over timid diplomats, for it is the former who shape our world. The challenge is to guide their energy in a positive direction.

2
Current skill: Turn managers into leaders
Future skill: Reinvigorate the role of managers

There is a new trend buzzing around corporate boardrooms, born from a popular notion that progressive organisations hire 'leaders', while stagnating ones employ 'managers'. The general inference is that leaders are superior to managers.

Board members might believe that their current 'managers' are incapable of taking the troops into the fierce future, saying that managers are only administrators, whereas 'leaders' are the visionary saviours. This is naïve. Are doctors better than dentists?

Are plumbers better than bricklayers? Surely it is horses for courses. Each has a role in society. In business, one mustn't assume that leaders are better than managers. This would be an insult to both professions. And yes, being a leader is as much a profession as any other.

The difficulties emerge because, over the years, the word 'leader' has amassed magnificent brand value. If the word were a trademark, it would stand alongside the biggest of brand names — revered and respected. Regardless, being a leader is not something to be coveted. Yet, despite the fact that we all know that there are just as many bad leaders as there are good, it is still considered a compliment to call someone a leader.

A leader is simply someone who is engaging in a job — performing a function, and carrying out a task. Being a leader requires specialised skills and it needs to be done well. Yet, being a leader is no more important than any other function.

There is a huge difference between 'being a leader' and 'engaging in leadership'. (This topic is covered in *How to Lose Friends and Infuriate People*.) Until one can grasp this, the subject of leaders, managers, and leadership remains muddy and emotionally charged. It conjures up all sorts of irrational opposition from petty players who just want to be called leaders, regardless of what it means. Just ask teenagers whether it matters to them that their favourite brand of running shoes is not worth a fraction of the price they paid. Price and function have nothing to do with image.

If one understands the differences between being a leader and engaging in leadership, one can begin to understand that it would be misguided to replace managers with leaders.

Whatever the case, the general health of corporations is in a sorry state. Managers have been stripped of their authority. They have been demoralised by the hideous matrix-management structure that baffles them to the point of inactivity. They have been tormented by those to whom they report — junior school-yard bullies with split personalities who purport to be autonomous business leaders, when in fact they are puppets of the almighty headquarters (and those at headquarters are puppets of the stock market). At the end of all the rhetoric and nonsense about the 'vision' and 'mission' statements, nothing matters to them. Not even customers. Ah yes, remember the customers? No, what matters most to them is the end-of-month results.

It used to be that we measured things quarter by quarter. Before that, it was what we did during a twelve-month period that mattered. And prior to that, we all had to think about our three-year plan, and work towards that. Now you are lucky if you can finish your lunch before some goon in a silk tie asks, 'Why have you only achieved forty-five percent of the monthly target with only two weeks to go until the end of the month?' Oh no, drop everything! Drop your lunch, forget about tomorrow, just do what has to be done *now* to get the numbers *now*. Never mind about what your long-standing customers might want, and do not worry about following up on that last complaint. No-one cares. If you do not make your monthly figures, you will not even be there to care. So, who cares?

Amid all that childish, money-hungry, Wall-Street madness, board members want leaders. What they should do is to vacate their chair and give someone else a go. Someone for whom a $13 million salary is considered satisfactory. Not someone who lives and breathes the stock markets, and has a ticker-tape running across the Internet browser showing the fluctuations by the second. They do not want to hire leaders in the true sense. Such leaders would tell them where to go.

3

Current skill: Be an expert at time management
Future skill: Be an expert at attention management

Those who can manage their time are seen as efficient workers who do not waste valuable resources. Almost all job-descriptions stipulate this requirement, because it is believed that many managers fail when they do not know how to manage their time.

In the future, there will be another good reason why many managers will fail. It relates to an emerging crisis that most people have not yet come to grips with because they do not understand it or its impact. I am referring to what I call the Attention Bandwidth Crisis (ABC).

ABC describes the demands placed on us to pay attention to so many areas of our life. We are finding that the scarcest resource is no longer time or money, but *attention*. As such, we have to graduate from the school of time management, and learn about attention management.

Executives today are starved of attention. They are working longer hours, and taking work home. They are cramming more activity into a week than ever before, with family and friends being squeezed into whatever time remains. Some people feel disconnected if they do not take their mobile phone to the bathroom with them. They have structured a life that demands that they check their e-mails day and night.

We can no longer compartmentalise our life. We have to be available to everyone all the time. In addition to constantly being on-call, we have to cope with information and misinformation at our fingertips.

One thousand years ago, university libraries contained fewer books than will be found in an average household today.

Daily newspapers today contain more factual information than all the factual information that was available to the public back then.

Consider the rate of progress. It took more than 30 000 years for humans to turn a rock into a sharp axe. In the nineteenth century, technological progress was equal to the combined efforts of the ten centuries that preceded it. Advancements from 1900 to 1920 matched the entire previous 100 years. This level of acceleration and development means that major changes are taking place from one year to the next, not from one generation to the next. One hundred years ago, it was possible for a student to grasp the combined knowledge of almost all the fields of science or art. Today, one would be lucky to master a single strand of a single field of study.

There are millions of Web pages created each year, in addition to the 300 000 books, 150 000 magazines, and 350 000 journals published each year. Add the increasing number of databases, radio and TV programs, and feature films, and we can see how it would be easy to drown in information.

Consumers are inundated with choices of products and services. They have to fight their way through supermarkets that offer twenty-five brands of tomato paste and fifty brands of toothpaste.

The world is not short of money. It is not short of communications equipment or technology. We used to differentiate people on the basis of those who were time-rich and those who were time-poor. Successful employers of the future will be those who can recruit the attention-rich and quarantine those who are attention-poor. Attention poverty leads to attention bankruptcy, and that leads to serious personal illnesses as a result of relentless and overwhelming pressures to cope with endless demands on one's faculties.

Organisations are spending up to ten times more money than their net profit on trying to attract people's attention. Individuals are spending more money than ever before on delegating tasks and duties. They try to cope with the demands not by reducing them, but by finding ways to offload what they can, to make room for more attention-sapping activities. For example, people are outsourcing their washing, cleaning, ironing, babysitting, lawn-mowing, driving, shopping, cooking and any other domestic chore they can, leaving themselves with little or no disposable income, just so that they can maintain a job to afford to pay their helpers. The vicious cycle is leading to bizarre effects on people. While some become gripped by the never-ending loop, others spot the insanity and refuse to play the game, causing heartache for employers who have to decide how to respond to those whose work ethic does not support the unquenchable needs of the organisation. These liberated workers are labelled as the new generation. Some call them 'Generation Y'.

When a commodity becomes scarce, it often becomes expensive. Sometimes it becomes a currency in its own right — like gold in affluent societies and cigarettes in poverty-stricken societies. Although money can be used to create more money, attention cannot be used to create more attention. Instead, it creates an atmosphere whereby magnetic attention becomes expedient (meaning that people will do things without thinking about what they are doing and why). Historically, magnetic attention was expedient because of a lack of information (meaning that people had little choice, so they focussed on what was at hand). Today, magnetic attention is expedient due to *too much* information (because we have far too much to choose from, and things can become confusing). For example, although in the days of Mozart there were many competent composers, he stole the limelight. Suggesting that Mozart was the only great composer of his day would be like suggesting that the Beatles were the only pop band around in the 1960s. Interestingly, despite the endless array of artists and musicians around the world, it seems that only a few celebrities are able to grab our attention. The same can be said of politicians. Of the hundreds of active politicians, it seems that only a handful manage to dominate the media, despite the abundance of media outlets. It seems that during an Attention Bandwidth Crisis, the populace creates the popular so that it can have a common point of reference. This means that while attention cannot create attention, those in the limelight can *command* attention more easily than anyone else. If they know how to play the PR game, they can sustain an unfair advantage. I would modify one of Shakespeare's quotes by saying, 'All the world's a stage . . . but you need to know where the spotlight is.'

*All the world's
a stage . . .
but you need to know
where the spotlight is*

As employers seek those who are not affected by the Attention Bandwidth Crisis, they will also be looking for managers who can shift the hyphen so that they are not only good time-managers, but also *good-time* managers.

4

Current skill: Have good ideas
Future skill: Recognise good ideas

Industry does not need any more *information*. It is not the lack of information that is causing corporate collapses. Society would not suffer if it stopped amassing *knowledge*. Our current woes are not due to insufficient knowledge. The world is not in need of any more *ideas*. It is not the lack of ideas that is stifling progress. Rather, it is the apparent inability to *recognise* what a good idea looks like. Furthermore, the real stumbling block is the inability to *execute* projects skilfully. 'Execution' was the skill that bosses of the past possessed, but which they lost when matrix management raised its ugly head. Note that the word 'executive' comes from the root 'to execute'.

Future success will rely less on coming up with good ideas, and more on executing decisions with speed, precision, and skill. Organisations that want to survive the tumultuous times ahead must construct frameworks for accountability and autonomy.

5
Current skill: Have depth of experience
Future skill: Navigate uncharted territories

For missionaries, there is a maxim that says it is better to teach primitive peoples how to farm or fish, than to make them dependent on handouts. In the 1970s, the maxim was: managers must have *qualifications*. In the 1990s, the emphasis shifted to *experience*. This has now come under scrutiny because even those with a depth of experience are failing to survive in the modern, networked, digital world. There is no doubt that experience will continue to reign supreme over academic qualifications. The type and nature of the experience will change from industry experience to an ability to *navigate and survive uncharted territories*.

Future success will rely less on executives who exhibit a wealth of knowledge about any one field, and more on those who can cope with the dark portals that lead to new waters and new territories that will demand an ability to invent new solutions to new challenges.

6

Current skill: Be imaginative
Future skill: Create the blueprint

For decades, organisations have relied on those who could see the big picture. Those who could imagine a better future were entrusted to greet it. Imaginative managers were asked to articulate what they could see, and this exercise often led to the definition of the organisation's vision. It was certainly true that those working towards a vision stood a better chance of survival.

It is much easier to suggest that one needs to construct a new and more useful machine, than it is to create the blueprint for it. For that reason, future success will rely less on executives who can look into the future, and more on those who can draw the maps and plans, and be able to specify the materials and resources required to build the solutions.

7

Current skill: Be conservative
Future skill: Be innovative

In business, extremes are easy to maintain — for instance, it is easy to freeze all spending, and just as easy to overspend on all projects.

> *Inactivity and activity resemble each other in that, once started, they can be maintained either manually or automatically*

Inactivity and activity resemble each other in that, once started, they can be maintained either manually or automatically. They tend to snowball, so that inactivity breeds inactivity, and activity breeds activity. Similarly, conservative managers have a huge impact on their business because they can halt progress, all in the name of conserving energy or resources. In a world often depleted of vital resources, conservation seems to be greeted with respect. Unfortunately, conservation suffocates the very skill that managers of the future will need — *innovation*.

Future success will rely less on executives who can preserve tools and resources, and more on those who can apportion the vital resources in appropriate doses so as to feed innovation. Innovation is all about creativity — the art of creating that which did not exist before. It is difficult to justify expenditure for a project that is likely to create new paths, because it is easy to argue that the tried and tested old path at least offers certainty. Conservative people seek certainty, whereas innovators seek vitality. Certainty leads to stagnation, which leads to deterioration. Vitality leads to growth, which leads to strength.

> *Conservative people seek certainty, whereas innovators seek vitality*

Innovators know the importance of power and control. They might be accused of being power-mad or control freaks. Once, when I was accused of this myself, I exclaimed, 'Yes I am a control freak. But only when I don't know who is in control!' Power is required because it enables innovators to facilitate their creativity. Power could be tools, money, resources, influence, or know-how. The world is full of obstacles. Without power, innovators would only be able to dream, not construct.

8

Current skill: Be prudent
Future skill: Be a risk-taker

Those who are prudent are careful, sensible, and calculating. Unfortunately, they lack an important skill that every manager of the future will need to master: *risk-taking*. Managers are not taught how to calculate 'risk of loss' and 'risk of exposure', except in limited ways pertaining to auditing and finance. In the same way that every manager has had to understand the function of marketing and the impact of technology, there will be a need to comprehend the parameters that govern risk. Taking risks is easy. In fact, it is the ease with which risks can be taken that jeopardises most organisations. Hence, all the more reason why managers will need to understand how to calculate the risks of taking action, and of *inaction*. Also, they will need the skills to assess what would happen if their competitors beat them to a project. Organisations will be set apart by the speed with which they can make the right decisions.

It is the ease with which risks can be taken that jeopardises most organisations

Future success will rely less on executives who exercise caution, and more on those who can calculate both the tangible and intangible benefits and costs associated with long-term and short-term decisions that they might take, or that their competitors might take. Sometimes the calculation has to be made for imaginary competitors who do not yet exist. Trying to predict and calculate the impact of a non-existent competitor's behaviour requires exceptional forecasting capabilities and scenario planning. For example, the traditional 'white paper' is no longer good enough. In the networked world, an organisation that seriously wants to consider its position in relation to a business risk, needs to submit *three* white papers. The first would outline the investment proposition and give the reasons why an activity should be undertaken. The second would outline what could happen if the organisation *did not* undertake the investment.

The third would outline what could happen if a competitor (whether known or unknown) were to beat them to it.

Almost everything has a level of risk associated with it. A challenge of the networked world is that decisions need to be made instantly. Careful deliberation seems to be a luxury that few can afford. Time is often a pressing factor that leads many organisations to make hasty decisions. Yet those who do not respond quickly enough, run the risk of missing out altogether.

The pace and rate of change have forced organisations to operate at unsafe speeds

The pace and rate of change have forced organisations to operate at unsafe speeds. They hire people far too quickly. Their training programs have to take place in a shorter time frame, if at all. Their product development cycles are dictated by the competitive market, not by what is feasible or economical, and not in response to consumer needs.

When operating at such speeds, the risks are far too high. Errors are often tolerated because the books can be manipulated to reflect success, even when everyone knows that the foundations are being eroded.

Successful managers will be those who can keep the pace of change in perspective, knowing that they might suffer in the short term while they build solid foundations for a stable, prosperous, and self-sustaining future. Incidentally, solid foundations will be useless without an understanding of the meaning, action, and deeds associated with the words 'nimble', 'quick', 'accelerating', 'decisive', 'autonomous', and 'creative'. These qualities, in turn, will be useless in the absence of expertise. Are you and your colleagues experts at what you do? Are you all skilled in your respective professions? If not, you run the risk of *accelerated destruction.* For more information about the personal qualities that entrepreneurs need, see Chapter 17, 'Heads or Tails?'

9
Current skill: Understand international trade
Future skill: Possess cultural literacy

These days, there is nothing that one cannot find out about transacting in foreign countries. We have learned many lessons about: coping with different channels; working within disparate infrastructures; tolerating unfathomable taboos; embracing unusual practices; transacting within unfamiliar procedures; and surviving unorthodox business cultures. These challenges are the price one has to pay for pursuing international trade.

Foreign traders are not hindered by a lack of understanding about national and international protocols. Rather, they stumble over the *cultural* aspects of making deals. Executives of the future will need to possess *cultural literacy* between people, not just between nations. They will need to respect and be considerate of those differences in their dealings with all their business partners. Cultural literacy extends to each and every person, because the cultural cringe affects not only distant associates but also close affiliates.

Trade does not take place between countries, but between people

Future success will rely less on executives who can speak different languages, and more on those who are sensitive to other people's needs in relation to religious, social, political, and cultural differences. These could relate to dress code, etiquette, and protocol, including a person's mannerisms and idiosyncrasies. Cultural literacy will extend to every colleague, whether based locally or internationally. Trade does not take place between countries, but between people. Culture exists within people, not within groups of people.

10
Current skill: Form an opinion
Future skill: Possess discernment

Job-descriptions tend to emphasise the need for executives to possess analytical skills that can be used to develop action plans. This translates to being able to arrive at recommendations through the formation of opinions. I have a motto that I sometimes place at the bottom of media releases: 'Give me a microphone, and I'll give you an opinion.' This attention-grabber appeals to radio producers who want quick grabs for their radio show. They call me in the early hours of the morning, looking for someone brave enough to stick their neck out and give an opinion about a controversial topic. Most people can freely express an opinion, so long as they are not muffled by political considerations. That is why talkback radio works so well. Everyone can join in, even if the person at the centre of the attention refuses to comment. In democratic societies, expressing opinions has become a pastime.

Discernment creates order out of chaos

In the future, employers will need more than those with opinions. They will look for executives who can *discern* between the multitude of opinions and options, and arrive at the most appropriate one. This is not an easy task in the face of pressure from dozens of constituents, who each have a vested interest in skewing the outcome to suit their own needs.

Future success will rely less on executives who can arrive at a plausible opinion, and more on those who can search, observe, probe, analyse, sort, study, and recommend a firm course of action, untainted by personal bias. Discernment creates order out of chaos and then sifts the bad from the good.

11
Current skill: Be a good decision-maker
Future skill: Be a maker of good decisions

Making decisions is easy. In fact, it is impossible to escape from it, because even when you avoid making a decision, you have still made the decision *not* to make a decision. In an interconnected and interrelated world, your indecision automatically triggers a chain of events, whether you like it or not. The speed with which you secure your position is just as important as the decision itself. Unfortunately, taking action merely to lock out others from having the opportunity to secure an advantage might not be a wise move. This is the basis on which the psychology of auctions works. It is also the secret behind the power of tenders. Many corporations seek to win a tender, not because they want the work at such a low profit margin, but because they want to prevent their competitors from securing the tender, lest it give some sort of advantage, momentum, cash flow, sustenance, or prestige to the competitor. Such decision-making will no longer be rewarded in the future, because longer-term considerations will enter the domain of sensible management.

Future success will rely less on executives who are good decision-makers, and more on those who are makers of good decisions

Future success will rely less on executives who are good decision-makers, and more on those who are *makers of good decisions*. Unfortunately, the tenure of executives is so short, or their reward structures are based on such short-term results, that they are often forced to make expedient or convenient decisions, not far-sighted ones. As organisations adjust their measurement processes, makers of good decisions will once again be heard.

12

Current skill: Be an entrepreneur

Future skill: Remain an entrepreneur

In life, those who are content are the richest of all. In business, those who are content are sitting ducks. They are usually successful business operators who have worked hard to build their enterprise and now want to take it easy and enjoy the fruits of their labour. Ask them about 'growth' and they shy away from it because it usually means change, and change spells discomfort and more hard work.

> *In life,*
> *those who are content*
> *are the richest of all.*
> *In business,*
> *those who are content*
> *are sitting ducks.*

Unfortunately, there is no such thing as standing still. You either move forward and grow, or you automatically go backwards.

In the good old days, you could monitor your competitors, because they were not far away. These days, your competitors could be on the other side of the world. Even worse, your fiercest competitors could be those who have not yet decided to compete with you, so neither you nor they know who they are. So, how can any business be happy with the status quo?

The secret to growth does not lie in setting goals and making plans. Growth and success have nothing to do with writing business plans and white papers. Beware the business plan syndrome. If growth, to you, starts out as a figure on a piece of paper, your heart is not in it.

The most successful entrepreneurs are those who love what they are doing. If they bake bread, they are out to bake the best bread. They think, breathe, and live their craft, and are totally absorbed by what they do. This level of interest in a business makes them shine, and growth comes automatically.

These days, you have to lead, follow, add value, or perish

Who in your organisation is living and breathing your products or services? If you have lost the zest for it all, that is okay. Groom someone else. But do not smother them with all the reasons why things cannot be done. These days, you have to lead, follow, add value, or perish. Who is leading the way in your organisation? Entrepreneurs of the future will be those who are prepared to give up everything they possess, in order to follow their own dream.

Future success will rely less on executives who can use other people's assets, and more on those who can earn the respect of the business community by risking their own money, time, and resources to follow their dream. The underlying characteristic of future entrepreneurs will be their ability to attract (not seek) investors, and woo (not hunt) clients. Praiseworthy entrepreneurs are those who build assets and create opportunities for themselves and for others. Blameworthy entrepreneurs are those who sap energies and shift resources (they might fancy themselves as reverse Robin Hoods, who take from the poor and give to the rich).

13
Current skill: Understand how to use technology
Future skill: Understand the impact of technology

For many years, professionals who understood the complexities of technology were able to command large salaries. This might have been because there was sufficient mystery surrounding the various components of technology to make everyone else's eyes glaze over.

Notwithstanding the importance of technical skills, there are two things that will matter more in the future. The first is the ability to *apply* technological devices to everyday business challenges. The concept of 'application' requires an intimate understanding of the business and the market. The second factor is the ability to pre-empt how the technology will impact businesses, governments, and society. This means that executives of the future will have to be able to assess what would happen to their organisation if: (a) they implemented the technology; (b) they did not implement it; (c) their competitor beat them to it; and (d) they did not implement it on time. When technology can be used to steal the march on the competitor, it needs to be relegated into the background so that it becomes an *invisible* tool. Alongside invisibility must be *stability*.

14
Current skill: Manage change
Future skill: Survive turmoil

Executives who possessed change-management skills were sometimes called change agents. They were the champions who dragged the diehards into the new world. Within a fast-moving environment, the change agents were seen as the saviours.

Future success will rely less on change agents, and more on executives who can *survive turmoil*. Those who are able to cope with contradictions, incongruence, and disorder will be the new heroes.

15

Current skill: Possess accounting skills
Future skill: Possess financial acumen

Once upon a time, chief executives were the founders of their company. Later, manufacturing and engineering experts took the helm, followed by externals (known as 'new blood') who came from political spheres and offered 'connections' to new markets. Then, the marketing supremos rose to the top because they knew how to speak with new types of consumers. Thereafter, the bean counters, who were entrusted with the coffers, took over as captains of industry. They spoke sensibly and acted cautiously to remedy the damage done by previous chief executives who had been led astray by their greedy directors.

Future success will rely less on accountants, and more on executives who possess *financial acumen*. Those who are able to understand the financial impact of risk, innovation, indecision, and growth will stand a greater chance of communicating with the various departments that comprise large and complex multinational organisations. Financial acumen is not the same as financial expertise. The boss must understand the issues of sound financial planning, not necessarily the ins and outs of accounting. Similarly, the bosses of the future must possess technological acumen, meaning that they must understand the impact of technology on business and society, even though they might not understand the latest Internet protocols or programming languages.

THE GOOD NEW DAYS

At an IT expo some time ago I saw a software company giving away small badges as a promotional tool. The badge read: 'Make trouble and something good might happen.' I liked its pithy, mischievous message. Perhaps one day, job-advertisements will read: 'Troublemakers wanted.' It might be the kind of company that is after my own heart. ∎

> *Make trouble and something good might happen*

CHAPTER 11

WOULD A HIT MAN *ring* THE DOORBELL?

LIVING DANGEROUSLY; LIVING GRACIOUSLY

Facts are not virtuous.
They might speak the truth,
but they do not speak justice.

A S A CHILD, I REMEMBER feeling my heart skip a beat whenever I heard a loud thumping on the front door. My mother and I would look at each other and wonder who it could be and what they might want. In time, we knew to appear as casual as possible on answering the door, so as not to give the impression of feeling intimidated. In the underground world of gangsters and ruffians, intimidation must be greeted nonchalantly if one is to start on a sure footing.

One day, when there was a disturbing knock at our door, I opened it to find three burly men towering over me.

'Is your father at home?' asked the one with a scruffy moustache.

My mother appeared in the corridor. 'No,' she said. 'But please come in.'

Her confident manner disguised her fear that the men could force their way in if they wanted to. There was little need for dialogue with the men, whose demeanour gave a clear indication about who they were and what they wanted.

Our visitors were obviously professional hit men. But even gangsters and mobsters have a code of conduct that they live by. Like other professionals, they tend to be good at what they do. What stands out is their discipline, their adherence to their word, and their dedication to their (albeit usually illegal) cause. I do not condone illegal activities, nor do I choose to associate with gangsters of any kind. Unfortunately, over the years, I have come across a number of them, and they have taught me two valuable lessons. The first is that their word is their bond. They would lay down their life before they would consider going back on their promise. This is a quality that, sadly, many people lack. I prefer to associate with people who say what they mean, and mean what they say. I am always sorely disappointed when people go back on their word or when they do not deliver on their promise.

The other lesson I learned was *grace*. Professional gangsters are usually able to balance their brutal nature with tolerance for what is known in the underworld as IPs (innocent parties). My mother and I were innocent parties. We knew that we had nothing to fear, so long as the IP factor could be established. From the moment we were identified as IPs, we were treated very well. I felt safe with these murderers. They treated me like a son. They treated my mother with respect and courtesy. They were remarkably and genuinely gentle. They had no axe to grind with us, so there was no need for them to intimidate us.

This story illustrates four personal characteristics that are important if you are to succeed in the work environment. They are:

1) *maintaining grace under pressure*
2) *protecting innocent parties*
3) *honouring promises*
4) *maintaining humility.*

The rest of this chapter explores each of these characteristics in more detail.

1) *Maintaining grace under pressure*

Immature people often are rude and inconsiderate towards those whom they dislike. They seem to think that it is acceptable for them to lower their standards of behaviour when dealing with irritating colleagues.

Living peacefully means not allowing others to upset your good nature

Conflict is a natural part of life. The world is full of opposing forces that tend either to annihilate each other or to clash constantly. At other times, opposing forces fuse to create a whole new set of problems or opportunities. The ideal state is one of *control*. The next-best state is one of *balance*. Although maintaining balance is relatively easy, achieving it in the first place can be a challenge. The third-best state is to learn to *co-exist* with opposing forces or with people you dislike. Such co-existence is known as peace. This means that you can operate peacefully without having to embrace undesirable elements. (The opposite of this is called co-dependence, where both parties become entangled in each other's unwholesome habits.)

Living *peacefully* means not allowing others to upset your good nature. Living *generously* means injecting energy into other people's lives. Living *mercifully* means allowing others to cope with their frailties. Living *gracefully* means not draining others of their emotional resources, and not expecting them to meet *your* standards.

Even amid conflict, it is important that you do not lose sight of the characteristics that define who you are. If you stoop to the level of your opponents, you could be guilty of displaying the characteristics that you were fighting to eradicate in the first place. By all means take on the battle, and fight the good fight, but do not play by the rules that triggered your disdain.

> *You can express your generosity through civility. You can express your mercy through clemency.*

Peace, generosity, mercy, and grace are not human qualities that can be applied selectively. They are either ever-present or non-existent. It is not possible to possess these qualities in half-measures, or only some of the time.

You can express your sense of peace through forgiveness. You can express your generosity through civility. You can express your mercy through clemency. And you can express your grace through courtesy.

Are you courteous? Are you pleasant to deal with? Are you sensitive to other people's needs? We spend so much of our time at work trying to enrich our own life, we sometimes lose sight of how our behaviour might impact others.

Remember that what you do and what you say reverberate in ways that you might never know. In view of the huge impact that people have on each other, it is important to live graciously so that we can be sure we are doing everything we can to enrich other people's lives. For example, you might like to consider how you express your gratitude towards your colleagues. When was the last time you sent handwritten notes of thanks to your workmates? Did you personally thank your boss the last time you were invited out to lunch with the group? Always make a point of recognising and appreciating the generosity of others.

Grace also means knowing how to listen. It means being sensitive to other people's presence. When you interact with junior staff, do you make them feel that you are interested in their well-being? When you are in a meeting, do you kowtow to the powerbroker and ignore the efforts of the meek?

When pain strikes, time seems to grind to a halt. Five minutes spent in agony feels like an eternity.

Children have an uncanny way of connecting with adults who genuinely enjoy their company. Colleagues, too, are able to detect someone's grace. They are comforted by it, and they feel safe in expressing themselves when among those who are accepting of their human frailties. Intimidators are like human panel-beaters: they knock others into shape, forcing them to put on a false demeanour so as to avoid criticism.

You might have read about military or corporate leaders whose followers would lay down their life in support of their efforts. Such leaders know how to make each person feel important to the overall mission. When your colleagues believe that you care about them, and they understand that you are prepared to let them be the person they are, you stand to win them over effortlessly. In whatever way you do this, your efforts must be genuine; false courtesies and sycophantic behaviour are easily detected and always mistrusted.

During times of tribulation, we often hear the maxim, 'If you have your health, nothing else matters.' Healthy people tend not to fully appreciate this sentiment. In the absence of pain and discomfort, it is difficult to fully heed the warnings about our health. As a result, we tend to live more dangerously than is good for our health. The poignancy of the maxim is driven home only after we suffer an ailment. When pain strikes, time seems to grind to a halt. Five minutes spent in agony feels like an eternity.

We tend to respect our health after we have already jeopardised it. In some ways, modern medicine has spared us much of the pain that previous generations endured. The older folk in our community would remember the unbearable pain of a toothache. Modern technology has all but eliminated dental torture.

I mention this because most of us would not want to think that we are contributing to other people's ill-health. Although it is not easy for us to make our colleagues feel physically sick, it might not take much for us to affect their mental or emotional health. The

When we put our head on the pillow each night, it is generally the intangibles of life (such as our emotions) that consume us

non-physical aspects of life can hurt just as much as the physical. By contributing to another's sense of intimidation, fear, hopelessness, despair, anguish, dejection, terror, misery, or depression, we are contributing to lowering their self-esteem and diminishing their sense of hope.

When we put our head on the pillow each night, it is generally the intangibles of life (such as our emotions) that consume us. In trying to cope with the intangibles in your own life, take care not to inflict undue suffering on others. Be aware that you might never know what might hurt your colleagues. A comment that seems frivolous or humorous to you, might be adding insult to another's injury.

2) Protecting innocent parties

I learned an important lesson from a boss whom I did not like. For many reasons, we did not see eye to eye, and it was clear that we would never become friends. One year, we were all encouraged to invite our friends and family to join us at the annual staff party. I dreaded introducing my boss to any of my friends, so I tried to keep them away from him. As luck would have it, we bumped into each other accidentally and we were forced to exchange pleasantries. He greeted my guests and engaged in some small talk. Innocently, one of my friends asked, 'What's Jonar like to have on your team?' My boss responded in a most positive and charming way. He was complimentary towards me, and made me feel important in front of my friends. He also made each of them feel welcome.

I was amazed that he should speak so highly of me. As I got to know him better, I realised that he had the grace to shelter innocent parties and to protect their feelings. He often said that staff members need never feel embarrassed in front of their friends and family. He was not trying to score points or make friends; he was simply living by the golden rule of sheltering innocent parties from fallout, and giving people like me the opportunity to 'save face'. 'Saving face' is an important concept in the Chinese culture, whereby people protect each other's feelings. Mature adults might agree that they dislike each other, but they would never embarrass each other in front of a third party, especially family and friends.

Having adopted this philosophy, I found it to be a valuable tool. Whenever any of my staff members had family or friends visit them at the office, I would make sure that the guests were treated well. We had a rule of courtesy which meant that none of us would ever embarrass each other in front of innocent third parties. We also went out of our way to extend a warm welcome to personal visitors, especially the children of staff members.

It is funny how things go around in circles. When it was my turn to be the boss, I had inherited an employee who proved to be quite a handful. We had a major event for which we had to prepare during a weekend. My difficult staff member, who was on the verge of being fired, brought her husband with her to the venue where we were all busy setting up. The moment that we saw her with her husband, we swallowed our misgivings and greeted them royally, and made him feel that his wife was an important member of the team. That small act of kindness helped to boost her confidence in front of her husband. We made a point of not burdening him with our battles. He was an innocent party, and she deserved to be treated with respect for the sake of her relationship with him.

It was obvious that our gesture touched her deeply. She left the event with her head held high, and in no time she became a supportive and co-operative employee. She was thrilled to be respected, and that made her realise that our differences were professional, not personal.

At that same function, one of the staging managers asked if she could bring her parents to see some of her creative work, including the pyrotechnics and floorshow that she had worked on. There were over a thousand invited guests, so I did not see any reason why her parents, who were visiting from overseas, could not join the party. During our briefing sessions, I made sure that everyone knew that her parents would be present. After the event, she told me that her parents had told her they had never been treated so well or made to feel so welcome.

It is important to protect people from your mood swings and your personal troubles. It is unfair to burden your colleagues with your personal issues (such as domestic unrest). In general terms, people are compassionate and caring when they can see that a fellow human is going through some tough times. It is not a bad idea to let your colleagues know that you are going through a rough period in your life and that you might need some support; but there is no need to go into any detail, especially if you feel uncomfortable speaking about your family affairs. A few colleagues might be insensitive, but the majority will give you some leeway to cope with your emotions. One manager I knew was going through a difficult divorce and asked a fellow manager to deputise for her. She told her employees that they should feel free to go to the deputy if they felt they were not receiving the level of attention or service that they needed to do their job.

Try not to judge other people's fears. For example, I knew a young man who was devastated when his wife became pregnant. This was his worst nightmare. Even after the child was born, he did not tell anyone about it. His colleagues had no idea what had brought on his change of behaviour, and many of them judged him harshly.

When you are instrumental in helping your colleagues to

save face, and when you take the time to shelter innocent parties, you are acting graciously.

3) Honouring promises

It is interesting that we have developed a legal system around the concept of signatures. When transacting with strangers in a marketplace marred by fraudsters, we use signatures to authenticate our intentions and to commit to our promises. When dealing with friends and colleagues, we use 'intangible signatures', which others interpret as our 'reputation', to express our commitment.

The word 'signature' comes from a Latin word that means 'sign', from which we also arrive at 'signal'. Each of us has a personal, intangible signature that we emit in the form of signals — the way we walk, the way we talk, and the way we react or respond to certain situations. What we say, what we give, what we expect, and how we communicate are elements of our personal trademark that emit signals that others interpret.

While some people might be conscious of the signals they emit, others are unaware of how their behaviour affects others and themselves. Think of those who wear the same brand of perfume every day. They become so accustomed to the scent, they can no longer smell it, no matter how much of it they splash on. Similarly, garlic lovers are usually unaware of the ever-present smell of garlic on their breath.

If you want people to value your promises, you need to take care to emit signals that are congruent with your words. Those who do not align what they *say* with what they *do* are called hypocrites.

Do not confuse 'reputation' with 'image'. Many people try to change their image by changing the way they dress or the people with whom they associate. Image refers to the exhibition of external factors, whereas reputation (signature) refers to the projection of one's internal nature.

There have been endless arguments about whether or not personal signatures are hardwired. Can we delve into our internal software and reprogram ourselves? This is part of that old chestnut about nature versus nurture. Is it in our nature to be who we are, or can we nurture ourselves away from our undesirable habits? Fundamentalists argue that a leopard cannot change its spots. Although we cannot be anything other than what we truly are, we can redesign some of our circuitry. Although we cannot be what we are not, we can become the person we desire to be.

Although we cannot be what we are not, we can become the person we desire to be

What are some of the important elements that *you* need to nurture, in order to build a successful career? What characteristics are you harbouring in the shadows? Do you know if your current 'signature' is holding you back from realising your potential?

Is your word your bond? Does it carry much weight? Do your colleagues believe that you will deliver on your promises? Do not be a glib talker who speaks volumes but does nothing. Ultimately, people will judge you based on your track record and on the congruence between your intentions and your actions.

Each time you go back on your word, you cause damage to your own reputation and to the person you have let down. Do not impose hardship on people in ways that might amount to abuse. Some time ago, I was flat broke. I had only $30 in the bank. A colleague of mine said that she would visit me over the weekend. I withdrew the $30 and purchased snacks and drinks from the delicatessen so that I could entertain her. I had everything ready, but she did not show up. She did not even call to cancel. Two hours later I called her, and she told me that she did not feel like going out. I did not let on about the trouble I had gone to — I was too proud to admit my financial situation to her — but I was annoyed enough not to want anything more to do with her.

Generally, people are not totally candid with each other. For that reason, you might never be told about your annoying habits or about the signals you emit. It is up to you to hone your sensitivities. The same principles apply in business. A friend of mine told me that she stopped going to a particular pharmacy because she found the staff to be indiscreet. She was embarrassed to approach the counter after her name was called out, and the somewhat personal medicine was waved about for everyone to see.

What we do and what we say can affect other people in ways that we might be unaware. Having grace is having the ability to be conscious of other people's hidden affairs, even if we do not know exactly what they are. It also means having the ability to scrutinise our intangible signatures, to ensure that we stop making promises that we cannot keep. It would be damaging for your career if people were inclined to dismiss what you say.

Having grace is having the ability to be conscious of other people's hidden affairs, even if we do not know exactly what they are

Perhaps it would be best to say little, until you are certain about your intention and your ability to fulfil your promises.

4) Maintaining humility

A friend of mine is a radio announcer. His favourite saying is, 'Tell people something about themselves, and you will always have an audience.' Although people are generally absorbed in their own affairs, they are also interested in others if the relationship is not draining, and if the interaction is uplifting.

In general terms, your friends and colleagues would be delighted to hear that you are successful. If you are arrogant about your success, they might be critical of your lack of humility. Although there is nothing wrong with promoting yourself and showcasing your talent, do not confuse self-promotion with self-importance. People can tolerate the famous and successful, but they frown upon those who presume to be 'better' people. There is nothing more odious than people who treat others with scorn.

Being humble means being proud of your achievements without presuming that your success ought to afford you greater privileges

Being humble means being proud of your achievements without presuming that your success ought to afford you greater privileges. Whatever your position or status, people will detest you if you refuse to help them when they need assistance. I once attended a conference whose organisers were running late in preparing the venue. I pitched in and did whatever I could to assist. Many of the crew had no idea that I was the keynote speaker. When they found out, they were amazed that I had helped them out. I was amazed that they were so surprised. Why would I not help out? I felt that they would have done the same for me.

Some executives seem to feel that it will not do their image any good if they are seen to be doing menial tasks. What they do not know is what people are saying behind their back. No-one likes a snob. No-one feels warm towards someone who uses other people's weaknesses as an opportunity to shine.

Some people believe that when playing golf with the boss, it is advisable to lose. They think that outshining the boss is a

CLM (career-limiting move). I know that sometimes there are entrenched protocols which, although acknowledged as rather silly, are still thought to be deadly serious. I disagree with such tactics. Your boss might enjoy a good challenge, so long as it is done sportingly. Professional managers enjoy working with employees who are switched on — so long as the managers are not put in embarrassing positions or made to feel inadequate.

The secret to humility is to realise that it is not only your demeanour that matters, but also the way that you respond to people. Different situations require different responses. Different people can cope with different aspects of your life and your beliefs. Therefore, do not burden them with situations or information with which they cannot cope. This also applies to unsolicited advice. I no longer give advice to those who do not seek it.

Humility requires a delicate balance between modesty and self-promotion

Humility requires a delicate balance between modesty and self-promotion, between reserve and expression, between timidity and confidence, and between meekness and valour.

What is intriguing about humility is that it is revered when self-administered, and despised when forced onto others (in the form of humiliation).

SIGN ON THE DOTTED LINE

There are differences between what is *preferred*, what is *expected*, and what is *required*. These are further complicated by cultural interpretations. Wherever you go and whatever you do, you are exuding signals that others will observe and interpret in their own way. Although you cannot control what other people think, you can take responsibility for ensuring that the signals you emit contain the messages you intended to broadcast.

Your reputation is not something you can vet or veto. It might belong to you, but you have no say about how it is perceived or received. For that reason, take extra care to reduce the likelihood of sending out contradictory messages. The marvellous thing about personal signals is that they cannot be switched off. Even in your states of silence and stillness, you are being assessed and judged. The best that you can do is to be true to yourself. Only when you are true to yourself can you be true to others. Only when you trust yourself can others begin to trust you. Do not try to impress others. Focus on building a set of values that you can pursue with conviction.

Your reputation is not something you can vet or veto. It might belong to you, but you have no say about how it is perceived or received.

When you can understand yourself, you will be in a position to live graciously. Until you do, the chances are that you will live recklessly. From there, it is only a few steps away from living dangerously. **L**

CHAPTER 12

WELCOME TO THE GOSSIP CLUB

MUM'S THE WORD

*We never seem to appreciate things
until their opposite is revealed*

THE MODERN WORK ENVIRONMENT comprises disparate divisions whose dislocated mobile workers tend to travel frequently, or they tend to work from their home or car. As a result, office cliques are not able to form so readily. This is why I encourage the formation of Gossip Clubs. Juicy gossip can make a gathering much more interesting when people can talk about who said what to whom, and why.

The Gossip Clubs that I form tend to produce life-long friendships linked by a common past. Members meet for lunch or dinner and go through some slapstick rituals just for fun. We exchange war stories and travel notes, and we discuss our industry, its people, and the funny things that happened to us on the way to the forum.

Regardless of how much we dislike someone, or how loyal we are to each other, we all know the two basic rules. The first stipulates that each meeting ought to foster uplifting experiences, and it must not deteriorate into a whinge session. We look at life in a bright and happy way, and we exchange useful or amusing information. Club members are discouraged from setting out to harm anyone's reputation or career. The second rule is that we are not allowed to discuss anything that was originally told to us in 'confidence' by a colleague or by our boss. Gossip must have limits within the confines of ethics.

Gossip must have limits within the confines of ethics

It is acceptable to have fun at work, but never at other people's expense. The golden rule is that confidential information must never be divulged. Employees must learn to treat private or confidential information as if it were sacred.

People who know that I can keep a secret come to me with, 'I shouldn't be telling you this, but I know I can trust you.' The

Never trust anyone who is prepared to betray another person's confidence

moment anyone says that to me, I react with, 'I don't want to know.' I remind them that they were told something in confidence by someone who thought that *they* could be trusted. Evidently not. It is amazing how people seem to think that secrets have an expiry date, usually triggered by an argument. For example, many would say, 'John told me this in confidence, but I want to tell you about it

because I had a fight with him and I don't like him any more.' Never trust anyone who is prepared to betray another person's confidence.

LEARN TO TAKE A HINT

A colleague of mine was writing a staff newsletter in which he was penning a creative but naughty poem about a girl called Mary-Lou. The poem was harmless, and it named a few members of staff, including the manager. What my colleague did not know was that the manager had recently told me of a new mistress he was seeing, called Mary-Lou. They had several clandestine meetings, and he was unsure how to handle the situation because he did not want his wife to find out about the affair. When I was proof-reading the newsletter I urged my colleague to select a different name. He would not listen. He said, 'If you don't tell me why I should change the name, I will keep it in.' The silly man was placing me in an impossible position. I could not stress the point too strongly, lest I spark suspicion. I could hardly tell him that the boss was having an affair. When the newsletter was published, the boss hit the roof. I explained that it was pure co-incidence and advised that he let the matter rest, but he, too, would not listen. The boss fired the writer, and in the process, the writer became aware of Mary-Lou's existence. Upon being fired, the writer felt that he had nothing more to lose, so he sent an e-mail to every employee, detailing why he was fired. The manager's little secret was out.

Learning to take a subtle hint is a worthwhile sensitivity to hone. Managers often speak to each other in code. Throughout my career, there have been a limited number of trusted colleagues with whom I would speak in code. We used our symbols, expressions, and hidden messages to warn each other about certain emerging dangers. We would protect each other fully, but we were also bound by our ethics as professionals who would not divulge secrets, not even to each other. So we would give each other certain friendly clues. When 'timing' was an important part of a battle, it was not uncommon for my colleague to say, 'I can't tell you what I know, but trust me, the climate is not right for you to raise your concerns at today's meeting.'

WHO WILL RID ME OF THIS MEDDLESOME PRIEST?

Late one afternoon, my CEO rushed into my office and asked me to travel interstate that evening. He wanted me to join him on an emergency dash to one of our interstate offices because a large contract was in jeopardy and he wanted to act quickly to rectify some staffing problems, including the dismissal of the state manager — something that I later talked him out of doing.

When we both returned to our office the next morning, rumours had already circulated that we had flown in to remove the manager. The state manager telephoned to question the rationale behind the previous night's emergency dash. I could not tell him that the CEO wanted to relieve him of his duties, and that I saved his career by convincing the CEO to give him another chance. Typical of this man's problems, he immediately circulated the rumours that *I* was trying to get him dismissed. His loyal supporters believed that I was the enemy. At no time could I convince them otherwise because that would have necessitated my betraying the CEO's confidence. To this day, that man is convinced that I was out to get him. He has no idea that I saved him. Injustices such as these abound.

Sometimes people in power cannot utter certain words for fear of retribution or for fear of compromising their position. As a result, they rely on their subordinates to take the hint and to act accordingly. There will be times when you need to execute a plan that might have been your manager's idea, but for which you have to take the fall if it back-fires.

Apart from maintaining your silence as a gesture of loyalty, it makes sense that you should not place your manager in the same predicament you land in, because you would be cutting off your only lifeline. I was once placed in a position wherein I was the fall guy. My manager wanted certain decisions to be executed, but was not in a position to undertake the job himself. He knew that he could trust me to get the job done. We only had one crack at getting it right. If it worked, he would be the hero. If it failed, I would be in trouble.

Fortunately, I managed to get the job done. The mission was accomplished, but not without some fallout from certain powerful factions who could have damaged my manager's career. I recall the very minute that the bloodthirsty opponents came barging through the security doors. Click-click, clack-clack went the doors as each heavy-footed assailant gained entry into our restricted area. At that moment, I happened to be chatting with my manager in one of the corridors. We looked at each other and froze. It would not have been appropriate to be seen together at that moment. We both hid behind the door of the stationery room and held our breath while the brigade charged past. He scurried back to his office while I remained in my position, waiting for them to return. All the while, they were calling out for someone to tell them who was responsible. Although we were in a high-tech high-rise tower, the scene resembled medieval England. I jumped out of the stationery room and said, 'I think you are looking for me.' Expletives echoed like the sounds of clashing metal swords in full battle. They had found their man, and they were hovering between feelings of victory and revenge.

At that moment, my manager feigned ignorance and came out of his office. 'What's all this about?' He asked. Upon being told of my actions, he looked at me and said, 'Jonar, who authorised you to do that?' He and I knew that it was all his idea, but I was not one to weaken under pressure. 'No-one authorised me . . . ' He cut me short and started to add his words of dismay.

Knowledge is for 'using' not 'flaunting'

At the court-marshal, my manager appeared to be the incensed executive who was bound to weigh up the evidence. The laws of jurisdiction gave my manager full rights in handing down any sentence. So long as his name was unblemished, he was able to pass judgement on me. Despite the pressure from others, he was able to protect me. I was given a token reprimand, and exonerated for what was an important deed that saved the jobs of several hundred employees.

If I had not protected my manager, he would not have been able to protect me. If I had refused to do his dirty work, he would have had to sacrifice his position. In this way, his reputation remained spotless and we all lived happily ever after.

KNOWLEDGE IS POWER. POWER IS DANGEROUS.

In a world espousing 'knowledge is power', people seem to think that the more knowledge they possess, the more beneficial it would be. Although it is important to know what is going on, be sure to understand that knowledge is for 'using' not 'flaunting'. Most people do not understand that sometimes it is important to feign ignorance.

Do what you have to do, but never tell the opponent what you are likely to do

Do not tease people with your information because that will scare them to the point where they could fear you, or plot against you. A mighty warrior fights by stealth whereby no-one knows the master-plan and no-one can anticipate which of the soldiers is leading the charge.

As tempting as it might be, never threaten anyone that you might divulge information about them. By all means do what you have to do, but never tell the opponent what you are *likely* to do, nor what you *are* doing. This only attracts unwelcome attacks on you.

It would not be in your interest to divulge what you know about the person who is in a position of power. Many a king has beheaded faithful servants — not for letting him down, but for knowing too much. Nervous leaders do not like to surround themselves with trusted allies who know more than they should. They fear potential betrayal by those who have all the information to topple the leader. If it is not fear of betrayal, it might be embarrassment for a turbulent past. A friend of mine once mused, 'I have nothing to hide, except my past.' As leaders climb the ladder, they like to think that they have earned their place by their maturity. If their old friends hang around, leaders would be reminded of their juvenile past. History is full of examples where once-powerful allies ended their friend-ships brutally.

I have nothing to hide, except my past

TURNING A BLIND EYE

At deportment colleges where private butlers are trained in the art of service and discretion, students are presented with scenarios about awkward moments that they might face. A typical question is, 'Supposing you walk into your master's chamber to deliver the newspaper one morning, only to find that he has a lady in bed with him — what would you do and where would you look?' The correct answer is 'nothing and nowhere'. Butlers are trained to divert their eyes. As tempting as it might be to look, the master's guest must be given the impression that she was not seen.

What would you do if you walked into your manager's office and witnessed a romantic interlude with another employee? Or, how would you react if you saw your boss in a compromising situation at the beach on the weekend? Many would delight in spreading the news. A mature person would turn a blind eye and say nothing. Indulging in juicy and idle gossip of this nature is not suitable for ethical employees. For more about interpersonal behaviour, see Chapter 11, 'Would a hit man ring the doorbell?'

Human frailty is something we all contend with, yet we seem to delight in watching others fumble with it

Human frailty is something we all contend with, yet we seem to delight in watching others fumble with it. Such a perverse sense of voyeurism is unhealthy. We would all do well to refrain from noxious activities because they drain our soul. Common decency requires that we give people their space and allow them their errors of judgement. It is not our business to sully our colleagues' reputation. **T**

PART FOUR

GETTING WHAT *you* WANT

*I'm very easily satisfied
when people give me what I want*

CHAPTER 13

MORE, PLEASE!

HAVING THE COURAGE TO ASK FOR A PAY RISE

The best time to stipulate your demands is when you are in demand

W HY IS IT THAT SOME PEOPLE earn a lot of money, while others have to struggle with a low wage — always remaining one pay packet away from poverty? Why is it that some employees cannot pluck up enough courage to confront their boss for a pay rise, while others are showered with bonuses? This chapter will outline some of the strategies that you could consider next time you feel deserving of more money.

The first question to you is, are you able to justify your *current* salary? This is a poignant question, because if you really assess what value you add to your employer, it might be revealed that someone else would be willing to do your job for less pay.

Very few employees can justify what they earn — not because they are not willing to do a good job, but because what they do for the company is not worth the wage and add-on costs. This is not to say that people do not want to work hard. As organisations grow, their structures often lead to diminishing productivity. The larger they become, the more cumbersome they are. Eventually, employees have no choice but to slow down and go at the pace of the organisation.

When employees realise that they are not earning their way (even if it is through no fault of their own), they make it their business to look busy. Often, they learn the art of 'fussing about' just so that others might assume that they are productive or useful. The manipulators know how to create drama so that they can distract everyone into believing that they are attending to important issues. In such organisations, everyone soon learns what was meant by 'much ado about nothing'.

We live in a world that is governed by the economic law of 'supply and demand' whereby people value products and services based on demand. For some commodities such as oil, the prices fluctuate daily. As far as salaries are concerned, they fluctuate less frequently, depending on the level of importance that society places on each profession. For example, computer programmers cannot charge what they like, because the law of supply and demand governs their hourly rates — which in the early days of computing were often higher than what lawyers were earning. More recently, with programmers being plentiful, they have not been able to command a high price except in times of crisis, such as when a serious computer virus hits cyberspace.

Notwithstanding such market forces, why is it that some people can attain a high income, while others sustain a low income? Is the person whose salary is ten times higher than yours actually ten times smarter or ten times faster or ten times better than you? This is rarely possible. For example, the winning horse that earns 100 times more prize-money than the horse that comes second, is not 100 times faster. If that were the case, it would have reached the finish line before the other horses could blink. In fact, the winner is neither 100 times faster nor *two* times faster. Sometimes the race is so close that a photo-finish is required to determine the champion. Life is sometimes like that. Those who earn a lot of money are not much better or smarter. They are merely able to get to the finish line first. They do this by thinking ahead, strategising, and then working methodically while making some sacrifices along the way.

THE RIGHT WHAT?

Open any book about personal development, and you can read about the importance of 'having the right attitude'. Although I have heard it all my life, no-one has been able to define that for me. It seems that the onus is always on employees to have an attitude that allows them to meet the demands of their employer.

A healthy attitude about work is one that is balanced. It delivers excellence and *demands* excellence. It shows flexibility and *demands* flexibility. It gives energy and *demands* energy. If someone has brainwashed you into believing that having the right attitude means that you have to dig into your good nature to give, give, give, then you are allowing yourself to be abused.

Yes, the first step to securing a prosperous career does start with the right attitude. That does not mean kowtowing to anyone, least of all to your boss. What is your attitude to your relationship with your boss? Are you employed because your employer needs *you* personally, or does your employer just need 'a person' who could just do the job?

Are you doing your boss a favour by getting the work done, or is your boss doing you a favour by employing you? How do you feel about the 'supply and demand' relationship with your boss?

When people are perplexed by this question, I pose this scenario to them; supposing that your boss wants you to work an extra hour per day, do you feel that you have the courage to ask how you would be compensated for that time? Regardless of the notion that a little give-and-take is desirable, do you feel that you have the *strength* and *conviction* to bargain? If not, you do *not* have the right attitude.

If you allow your boss to take up more of your time, that is fine if you feel that you are learning from the experience, and that your time is not being wasted. You have to think of your time as a vital resource. You need it to invest into other important areas such as in your future, education, or family. If, with every day that passes, you do not nurture your future, you will get stuck in a rut.

When a boss abuses an employee's time, many workers justify this by convincing themselves that they are showing flexibility, when in fact they do not have the courage to confront their boss with their real feelings. How on earth can that be a healthy attitude? Employees with the right attitude are those who *choose* their decisions. For example, if you are polite because you know of no other way, you are not being polite. If you tolerate someone because you have no other means available to you, you are not being tolerant. Rather, this makes you passive and helpless because you have no control over your emotions and your feelings, and no control over your actions. If you let your boss take up your time, and you have not *consciously* and completely decided to allow that to happen, you will forever permit others to chip away at your health and well-being.

In a healthy work environment, it should not be a problem to invest more energy into your job to assist the boss. The way to test if a scenario is enacted within a healthy environment, is to *reverse* the question and see if the same rules apply. In this case, what would your boss say if you announced that you plan to leave one hour earlier each day? How many bosses would tolerate that scenario?

When I was in corporate life, it was not uncommon to leave the office at 11:00 pm each night. This went on for years! My contract stated that I had a nine-to-five job. Sadly, most of us were expected to work an extra six hours per day, not counting the demands on weekends, and other travel requirements that often meant we could not see our family and friends for months on end. I once told my boss that I deserved a pay rise because I was putting in six extra hours every day. The response was, 'I didn't ask you to work back.' How ungrateful! In cases like these, employers have the audacity to say that employees 'choose' to work long hours, whereas the culture decrees, in silent and unwritten rules, that it is essential to finish the tasks at hand. The intimidation and innuendoes are unmistakeable and unyielding.

Many organisations comprise detached directors who demand increases in profit, market share, sales volume, and customer satisfaction, while insisting on reductions in staff, expenses, and capital acquisition. It was not uncommon for me to be told to cancel a project on which I had already spent $1.5 million. 'But that means we've wasted $1.5 million, and six months of hard work!' I would exclaim. The response was always the same, 'Yes Jonar, but it means that you don't have to spend the other million that you've earmarked for the project, so we save a million.' That was the level of myopic logic that we all had to endure from accomplished executives whose obscene annual salaries would have fed millions of starving children.

If your boss creates an environment wherein you feel obliged to work extraordinary hours without a clear offer to compensate you for your time, this would be sheer human abuse. We allow managers to steal people's time because we all treat *services* differently from products. Employees sell their services to employers, and this transaction is treated with contempt because services, time, and intangible intellectual property are the three areas that are commonly taken for granted. If you sold tangible products, such as computers, you would find it offensive if your client walked into your warehouse and took six extra computers for every eight ordered. You would call the police. Fancy thieving to such a degree! Yet it seems permissible that your employer (who is simply a client to whom you sell your services) can make such draconian demands.

It is well and good to be a conscientious employee, and sometimes it is in your interest to work back and learn as much as you can. Even so, it is rare that any employer would appreciate what you give away so freely. Besides, who wants to work with staff members who are unable to stand up for their rights? It *is* a question of attitude. If you want to claim your worth, you have to first build an attitude that allows you to realise that your time is valuable, and that you will charge for it.

There is nothing nasty, unfriendly, or unwholesome in being a good negotiator. No-one whose ethics are solid would be offended if you charged what you are worth. Only the manipulators and leeches of life create an intimidating environment wherein you do not dare speak up for your rights. If that is what you are subjected to, you need to engineer yourself out of there and find a new job where you can start on the right foot. That is not to say that your new employer is necessarily better, but at least you could state your terms from the outset, and if they are accepted, you would have stipulated your demands clearly.

When you can add value, price does not matter. There are consultants who can charge over $10 000 per hour, and they have more work than they can handle. Price is not the issue. It is the value that you can add.

You cannot get what you cannot negotiate

If your attitude is a self-defeating self-deprecating one that allows people to abuse you, I can confidently predict that you will not be able to earn a high income. No-one is going to give you anything for which you cannot bargain. You cannot get what you cannot negotiate.

THE COMMON APPROACH

After you have adopted a healthy attitude towards the services you sell, you might be tempted to ask for a pay rise in the traditional way. Although I am not a fan of the common approach, it can work if your expectations are not too high.

The first step is to find out what your boss is measured on, and set out to document what you do that contributes to the success of those areas. You need to be able to quantify your results by showing how many clients you are serving or how many orders you are generating. Your report must include figures that make sense to your boss, whether they be shown in 'time' or in 'money earned' or in 'money saved', or other factors such as how many documents you have processed.

Then you need to make an appointment with your boss to ask for guidance about the areas of importance. You might ask, 'How many clients would I have to serve to be eligible for a pay rise?'

Your exploratory meeting should be non-threatening, in that it remains a friendly chat about your performance and your financial aspirations. This should open up a discussion that would give you clues about your manager's views on the subject. If you detect that your manager is not interested, or is unable to help you, that is fine. Keep a happy disposition and walk away from the meeting knowing that you are the one who has to take charge of your career.

If the boss's response is a positive one, you need to set a measurable target that you can revisit in three months, at which time you can furnish your boss with a performance report.

If a modest increase excites you, the approach described above would work. Unfortunately, if your sights are set higher, you will be confronted by many obstacles, such as your boss feeling awkward about meeting your demands for fear of what the senior manager might say, or what your peers might think if they find out that you were given a hefty pay rise when they were overlooked. Some managers seem to think that it is better to offend one employee (you) who demands a pay rise, than to succumb, at the risk of upsetting everyone else.

HOW MUCH DO YOU WANT?

The standard approach of asking for a pay rise tends to work, but it begs the question; what type of a pay rise would you be satisfied with? What would you call a *decent* pay rise? In almost every field of endeavour, salaried workers say that they would be ecstatic if they were able to double their salary. Workers truly presume that happiness and prosperity can be found by doubling their salary. If that were true, why is it that those who are already in the higher income brackets are also striving to double their salary? Those who earn $30 000 wish they could earn $60 000. Those already on $60 000 presume that their life would be simplified if they could earn $120 000, and so it goes. Therefore, what makes you think that you can break away from life's pressures and not drop yourself into more debt the moment that your salary enables you to borrow more money with which to purchase material goods?

These days, most managers do not have the authority to determine the pay structure. They have to work within approved 'bands' and they can only issue increases if the budget allows it. Therefore, what tends to happen is that managers do not admit to being powerless. So they spin a lie about the hoops you have to jump through to secure an increase, all the while, knowing that they have sent you on a wild-goose chase. They would rather play mind-games with you than admit that they do not have the authority that you perceive them to have.

In smaller businesses, the traditional ways of asking for an increase rarely work. You might be able to negotiate a pay rise if you are allowed to innovate. Maybe you can make suggestions about new markets or new product lines. You might prepare a proposal to buy the business within a period of time, or even take out the option to franchise the concept or to open another branch in a new location.

STEP OUT OF THE MOULD

The common approach to asking for a pay rise forces you to play within limiting boundaries. It would be impractical to make you the exception to every rule in the book. The better approach would be to create a whole new job-role that does not exist. This gives you an opportunity to write a new job-description with its own measurement processes. You would have to present a cogent argument about why the role has become necessary, why the company would benefit from it, and how the job's success or failure would be measured. You might even show some projected figures, based on trusted industry trends, to show why the new role would increase in importance over time. Be sure to tie this new role to the core business because, unfortunately, most managers are blinded by the immediate demands. No matter how accurate you might be as a visionary, your idea could be overlooked if it does not address some of the pressing management issues that torment the CEO.

Then you need to describe the type of person that the job would require, outlining the qualifications and experiences that would be needed. You might write out a complete job-description to show your impartiality. In that way, you can also discuss what the salary ought to be. You can use market rates to demonstrate that the new role is of a certain calibre. (There is the risk that an outsider might be chosen. If that is the way you are treated for being innovative, either your manager does not deserve you, or you are lacking something that you need to address.) Finally, you can attach your credentials and an explanation about why you would be the ideal person to spearhead the new initiative. If you can quantify the objectives of the new role, you stand a better chance to fast-track your appointment, especially if you can show that you can groom someone to take your current role.

It is not unreasonable for your boss to appoint an employment agency to search for candidates, of which you would be one. You need to go along with that process, because your boss might be trying to show that your appointment at the new salary was won fairly and squarely after a comprehensive search. This would justify your extraordinary increase in salary, on the basis that you were the best candidate for the role.

ADOPT THE UNPOPULAR TASKS

A slight permutation to the suggestion above would be for you to find out what your boss absolutely and vehemently dislikes doing. It might be that your boss just hates preparing the monthly reports, or is not so strong in certain areas of the business. Whatever it might be, you can offer to adopt those tasks. For example, if you work for an owner of a small business, you might find out that your boss dislikes having to wake up so early to open the store. You could offer to wake up early each morning to allow your boss to sleep in. Another example might be to offer to fix a looming problem that no-one in the organisation has had the time to attend to. In return for your added or altered responsibilities, you would negotiate a pay rise to match. If the unpopular tasks are those that you enjoy doing, this suggestion would work well. If you lumber yourself with boring work merely to secure an increase, you will regret that move. Job-satisfaction must play an important role in your search for more money.

Although all employees are dispensable, some are more dispensable than others

Although all employees are dispensable, some are more dispensable than others. This means that some are more valued than others. This is not based on personality (although the least favoured tend to be the first to suffer when retrenchments have to be made) but based on what is considered vital or essential. For example, a forklift driver is essential to the running of a warehouse, whereas marketing professionals could be reduced in number if it all came to the crunch.

In many businesses, there are essential tasks, and peripheral tasks. Interestingly, in most industries, those who perform the essential tasks are in *safer* jobs, but they trade job-security for a low income. The pioneers of a new business venture or a new division are generally paid well, but their job is not secure because their services could be terminated at any time. If an initiative fails, it is harder to find an alternative job for them within the company because of the awkward nature of merging high-ranking employees with the broader staff pool — both in relation to status and the unpleasant aspect of asking highly-paid managers to downgrade their salary. Invariably, they would not want to contemplate that kind of backward step in salary, for fear of never being able to climb back to their previous level, or because their lifestyle and mortgage commitments do not allow them to take significant pay cuts. Generally speaking, employers are often suspicious of any high-ranking employee who agrees to a substantial pay cut. They fear that the move is temporary, and that they would have to deal with a resignation within a short period of time. Employers would rather cut the ties as soon as possible than suffer the inconvenience of having a demotivated employee in their midst and then inevitably having to re-appoint another candidate, causing more upheaval for all concerned.

Also note that those who are exceptionally good at what they do, tend to inadvertently lock themselves into a job simply because their boss is unable to find an equally competent replacement. For that reason, skilled employees need to be on the lookout for others who can be trained to take over.

NEVER THREATEN TO RESIGN

A colleague of mine (whom I will call Scott) was unhappy with his salary. Apart from wanting to climb the corporate ladder, he was upset about not being appreciated for the hard work he had been injecting into the company. Having secured large contracts worth millions, the only thanks he received was an inflated target the following year. To no avail, he asked for a salary increase. His manager felt that if she approved an increase for Scott, she would have to justify an increase for other salespeople. Additionally, the marketing folk would be likely to make similar demands because they were as much a part of the selling cycle as the sales team. The manager argued that certain roles had certain salary bands, and that no matter how good an employee might be, it would be difficult to alter the salary structures because it would trigger a messy chain of events.

Scott calculated that he was worth a lot of money to the company, and he felt that he was being treated unfairly. He set about to secure a well-paying job with a competitor. This type of strategy is relatively simple. More often than not, it is easy for a successful high-profile high-flyer, such as Scott, to secure a job with a competitor who would gain the services of a well-seasoned, well-trained, and successful employee who has good connections within the market. In addition, the competitor would delight in luring talent away from a rival.

The competitor in question did make an attractive offer to Scott. Mind you, he was already earning hundreds of thousands of dollars, so it is not that he was underpaid. Perhaps there was an element of greed. His *disposable* income was low. High-earning salespeople often trap themselves in a lifestyle that demands a constant stream of high income.

His job-offer was also attractive because there was an element of spite in his strategy. He was fantasising about the day when he could resign with glee. He wanted to see the look on everyone's face when he, the star performer, walked straight into the hands of the competitor.

As often happens with these things, information leaked, and everyone knew about the job-offer because some industries are too well interconnected. Scott went in to resign on a Thursday, hoping that his boss would ask him to clear his office on Friday, and that would be the end of that.

The resignation itself was a non-event, until his manager said, 'I knew that you were leaving, so I petitioned the CEO on your behalf and he wants to see you before I accept your resignation.' Scott told his boss that nothing would change his mind, to which the reply was, 'That's okay, but to keep the peace, you should at least extend the courtesy of seeing the CEO. You do not want to leave on bad terms.' Scott agreed, but the CEO was not available until Tuesday.

Over the weekend, the head-hunter telephoned Scott to enquire about the resignation. It is customary for head-hunters to keep tabs on candidates, just in case they weaken or change their mind. Scott explained what had happened, and that a meeting with the CEO was planned. Such news always terrifies head-hunters, so the head-hunter called the client to explain that the matter might go to auction (meaning counter bids would have to be made).

On Monday, the CEO's assistant sent an e-mail to Scott to confirm the meeting, which was set to take place at one of the best restaurants in town. Over lunch, the CEO painted a rosy picture for Scott's future with the company. 'Why throw out six years with us, all over a small misunderstanding. We can match any package they have made, because you're an important member of the team.' Scott was expecting that offer to be made, and he had promised himself that he would not weaken under pressure. The CEO was a clever negotiator whose strategy was to ask people what they felt would be the ideal situation, and then begin to paint an impromptu picture that matched every desire. By the end of the meeting, Scott was made an offer that was better than the competitor's.

Scott explained this to the head-hunter, whose response was, 'We spent ages working to secure you, and we don't want to lose you. I spoke with the client and they have decided to increase the offer.' Between the Thursday to the Tuesday afternoon, Scott's new attractive package had risen by another $100 000, and the new employer had offered a $100 000 sign-on incentive.

On Wednesday, Scott told his boss about the negotiations, to which his boss said, 'We have big plans for you. You are jeopardising your long-term career based on a short-term gain. The personnel manager wants to speak with you at 3:00 pm.' The personnel manager explained that Scott was being groomed to take over as the next CEO in two years' time. He said, 'Scott, all this is chicken feed. Look, if money is so important to you, we will give you half a million dollars at the end of the year. We would have to put it down as a bonus, not as a retention fee because headquarters would ask too many questions, but I think we can do it. But the CEO isn't happy about your disloyalty, so we would need your decision by 5:00 pm.'

Never let anyone talk you into staying after you have already threatened to resign

Well, it was a pleasant feeling to be wanted all of a sudden. Scott told the head-hunter about all of these counter-offers and made his decision to stay. He had no idea that it would be so easy. In a way, he found the whole exercise a little terrifying. He was tempted to go for one more round of negotiations, but his 5:00 pm deadline was fast approaching.

I told you this long story for a good reason. If you ever plan to threaten to resign, you need to study this story carefully because within it are clues about a modus operandi that seasoned executives know only too well. The series of events were meticulously planned by the CEO. Every move and every manoeuvre was premeditated. I suggest that you re-read this section and see if you can spot the tactics that contribute to the bigger plot.

Let me tell you what happened thereafter. Three months later, exactly to the day, Scott was fired. The way that execution took place was in itself a long and intriguing story. All along, from that fateful Thursday, the plan was to force Scott to stay, just so that he would burn his bridges with the head-hunter and the competitor, and so that he could be 'taught a lesson'. Never let anyone talk you into staying after you have already threatened to resign. It is a well-known trick to grovel at your feet, make you feel wanted, and when you least expect it . . . chop!

Bad news spreads much faster than good news

You walk out the loser who is distraught, demoralised, and unemployed (therefore less attractive to competitors who would wonder what you did to deserve to be fired), and you walk out under a cloud of darkness that follows you all over the industry. Just as easily as everyone discovers that you are job-hunting, everyone will also hear about your demise; and bad news spreads much faster than good news.

It is far better to look for a job while you are still employed. It puts you in a position of strength. Scott lost all of his bargaining chips. His story is not unique. It happens all the time.

When you set out to secure more, you had better be prepared to give more. The moment that you set your sights on a higher salary, you need to work out what you plan to give back when your employer asks, 'What are you offering in return?' Another good question you can ask yourself is *why* you need more?

THE MONEY OR THE BOX

The best way to secure a pay rise is not to have to ask for one. If all you can do is *ask* for a pay rise, you are limiting your opportunities and forcing yourself to operate within pre-established limits. To rise above the ordinary so that you can earn more money, you need to find ways to provide a worthwhile service for which people would want to pay handsomely.

The best way to secure a pay rise is not to have to ask for one

The best way to achieve a satisfactory level of income is to think and to plan three to five years ahead, whereby you can prepare yourself to answer some of the following questions:

1) What level of income are you hoping to generate?

If all you want to do is earn 'more', that would point to a lack of strategy or to an insatiable greed. If the level of income that you need for your quality-of-life requires you to work long hours, you will become trapped within a vicious cycle, whereby the very thing you are trying to improve suffers while you are trying to find a way to improve it.

2) What sacrifices are you willing to make?

As you begin to draft a mental picture of how much you want to earn, and after you have understood *why* you need to earn that kind of money, you need to understand your limits. For example, are you prepared to sacrifice your weekends, or your evenings, or are you willing to wake up at the crack of dawn? Naturally, all opportunities require some level of sacrifice. No success can be found without paying the price in some way, whether that be in the form of time, pressure, or risk.

> *No success can be found without paying the price in some way*

3) What are you not prepared to do?

Having identified what you are prepared to sacrifice, can you categorically state what you will *not* do? Some people refuse to work in industries that are cruel to animals, or in those that manufacture certain types of products (on moral or religious grounds).

You might dislike the political landscape or the added pressure associated with certain types of jobs. If you are lured into a new position by money, and you neglect to understand the peripheral pressures that you would be placing on yourself, misery would not be far away.

4) What type of work do you enjoy the most?

Some people decide to engage in unsatisfying, yet lucrative, work for a few years on the basis that they would rapidly attain financial freedom. They might decide to open a restaurant and endure long hours, hoping that they can eventually sell their business and use the income to pursue their dream. Unfortunately, this type of rationale traps some people whereby ten years later, they are more miserable than ever, still doing the same job. They become so entangled, that they cannot see a way out. They do not want to leave the business because they cannot sell it for what they think it is worth. Meanwhile, they live a life of drudgery, for which they have no solution.

5) What are your preferred hours of work?

Naturally, some jobs offer more flexibility than others in relation to the hours that must be worked and the time that the work must occur. If you do not consider some of these issues, your lifestyle could be affected. Not only must you choose between indoor and outdoor work, or dayshift and nightshift, you need to consider the pace that each profession demands. If you work in retail, you have to stick to a set timetable, whereas if you are an artist or gardener, you have some flexibility. Although senior executives appear to be free and easy, their diary is usually booked six months in advance.

6) What other leisure activities are important to you?

If an extracurricular activity (such as a team sport or a hobby) takes up your time on a regular basis, it is best to declare it to your boss prior to accepting your new job. Otherwise, your boss might presume that you are being difficult and inflexible when you are unable to work at certain times.

If your outgoings are always increasing, you could become a slave to your indulgences

7) Can you reduce your expenses?

Why do you need a pay rise? If your outgoings are always increasing, you could become a slave to your indulgences. Will a pay rise provide you with an improved quality of life? Merely working longer hours to obtain more money seems strange because if you continue that logic, it would mean that every time you need more money, you have to work harder and longer hours. Where would that lead, especially if combined with an open-ended expense mechanism?

The essence is really about reducing that which consumes your energy. Consider how you can spend less money, less time, less energy, less resources, and less agony, so that your skills can become potent fuel used to help you to achieve not only financial independence, but also 'career independence'. Career independence means that what you do not have, you can obtain. What you do not know, you can learn. What you do not own, you can access. What you do not want, you can discard. What you do not enjoy, you can bypass.

Career independence means that what you do not have, you can obtain. What you do not know, you can learn. What you do not own, you can access. What you do not want, you can discard. What you do not enjoy, you can bypass.

8) What would the market need?

As an employee, you sell services to an employer. What price can you command, and who really wants what you have to offer? Are you really offering something special, or are you just offering the same services and skills as everyone else?

High earners are those who can say, 'What I have to offer is something that anyone else can perform, but it would take them three years of training to catch up to me because I started training three years ago when no-one thought to prepare for this moment.'

The function of marketing is to engineer the future of business. As far as 'personal marketing' is concerned, it too requires that you look at ways to engineer your future success by pre-empting what the market and what society are likely to need.

9) Have you calculated the earning limits?

Some professions impose limits on your earning capacity. For example, a teacher can only work the hours that the school stipulates, unless part-time work is taken up after hours. Restaurateurs face similar challenges. Their potential to earn money is limited by the seating capacity, unless they improve their sales by offering a home delivery or takeaway service, or venture into corporate catering or pre-packaged product sales.

The function of marketing is to engineer the future of business

Sometimes, the limitations are geographic, in that a bakery is limited within its community because fresh bread has to be sold before it perishes.

The ultimate earner is the type of business that some singers enjoy, whereby they can earn money while they are asleep, selling music and merchandise around the world. They do not always have to be physically present to make money from their talent.

10) Is your profession portable?

In preparing for your future career, you need to consider the portability of your profession. This refers to how easy it would be for you to work in other countries or in other industries.

Hairdressers could work almost anywhere. Their tools are easy to carry. Musicians can also enjoy a life on the road.

In theory, lawyers and accountants could work anywhere around the world. Unfortunately, due to the different regulations in each country, new studies would have to be undertaken before they could be accredited or certified.

11) How crowded is it at the top?

Although there are no pre-defined limits to the number of carpenters or artists that a society can accommodate, there are some professions that are not plentiful in number. For example, how many presidents or prime ministers can the world accommodate? How many high-court judges can there be? As for commercial pilots, their quantity is limited by the number of airlines and their fleet. In such industries, the turnover tends to be reduced, meaning that high-court judges are less likely to leave their post because they have very few options. Unlike captains of industry who could expand their empire, some professionals have little room in which to move. Take airline mechanics. They tend to stay with the same employer for decades because their specialist skills are usually only useful to another airline. Unless they are prepared to work in another country, their prospects for changing their employer are limited by the small number of airlines that operate in each country.

WHAT WOULD MAKE YOU HAPPY?

Before you define your area of expertise, you have to be aware of whether or not your industry is unionised, and what that could do to your earning capacity. What about professions where rates and fees are regulated by governments, or where salaries are made public for all to see? For example, those who work in government positions are rarely able to negotiate a better salary because their employer would be fearful of the political damage generated by a perception that some public servants are earning 'too much' money.

While having lots of money might sound like a good idea, if it is pursued without a specific purpose, it can become a distraction and a drain on your energy.

Identify the lifestyle you want, and then work out what that would cost. If it means that you have to work unbearably long hours merely to earn enough money to attain your dream, something is amiss. By all means aim high, but plan ahead so that you are not driven into a corner.

Perhaps the issue of salaries is distracting you from the ultimate question; *what work would you ideally like to do, even if you had to work unpaid?* Rather than pursue work that will pay you 'more', you might find greater joy and job-satisfaction by chasing the type of work that you would be prepared to do 'free of charge'. Invariably, it would be a job that would enrich your life. It is also likely that it would be the job at which you would excel. High earners are often those who love what they do. If you can do that, you stand a better chance of earning more than you had imagined, because success invariably comes to those who are having a ball.

Success invariably comes to those who are having a ball

Often people speak about the 'salary package'. What about the 'employment package' that includes the atmosphere and attitude of the organisation, its policies and idiosyncrasies, and the job-satisfaction that you cannot readily see. The solution to this dilemma is to stipulate your own package, and present the future employer with a list of your requirements. These might include whether or not you are given an office, a parking spot, flexible hours, and other conditions that you value. If you can offer extraordinary talent, you will be in a position to demand an extraordinary package.

If you do not stipulate your requirements *before* you are hired, chances are that you will not be able to secure those benefits *after* you are hired. The oldest trick in the book is for an employer to say, 'Join us, and let's see how we go. All being well, we can review your package in three months' time.' I have never known that strategy to work, so I would never fall for that again. When

If you can offer extraordinary talent, you will be in a position to demand an extraordinary package

you can tantalise your prospective employer with exceptional skills, you will be able to say, 'Take it or leave it.' ▣

CHAPTER 14

I WANT *your* JOB

THE DANGERS OF PANDERING TO YOUR BOSS

*The sign of good leaders
is not what they do when the are good,
but what they do when they are mad*

If you aspire to take your manager's job, what would your strategy be? Would you *tell* your manager of your desires, or would you keep it a secret, for fear of being seen as a threat? Would your manager be a supporter or an enemy? These are valid and complex questions that you need to contemplate before you declare your intentions. If you shine too much, you might not be wanted on the team in case you make your manager's efforts look lacklustre. On the other hand, your manager might be delighted to groom you. Whatever the case, you need to know your position before you reveal your strategy.

As I was growing up in corporate life, I could not seem to get it right. I recall being interviewed by a marketing director who asked me where I saw myself in five years. I said that I was building a career in the technology industry, and I was hoping that in the near future I would reach the capacity of marketing director. I did not suggest that I wanted *his* job, but that my natural progression would lead me to that level, whether with his company or elsewhere. That made him angry. His face turned red as he accused me of being 'smug'. In a condescending tone he said, 'You seem to be sure of yourself.' I did not know what to say. I could see that my confidence disturbed him. Maybe he preferred to hire someone who lacked self-awareness.

Learning from this lesson, I went to another interview a few days later, and when asked that question, I was humble in my reply. I did not want to appear overly confident. That too, backfired, because I was accused of not having 'a clear direction'. I could not win.

Take time to understand your desires, to be clear about your direction, and to know your boss before you share your plans. Your boss might have no intention of vacating the chair, so any hint of your ambition might work against you.

BARKING UP THE WRONG TREE

What many people do not realise is that their boss is *not* the one who holds the key to their next promotion. If you want to take over from your boss, who do you think will be making that decision? While your boss might have some influence, the final say rests with the manager to whom your boss reports.

The ultimate skill in climbing the corporate ladder is in realising that if you plan to move up, you need to impress your manager's *manager*.

You now have two tasks to juggle. You need to keep your current boss satisfied that you are meeting the requirements, without being a threat. You also need to impress your manager's manager, without being disloyal or breaking the chain of command. Naturally, if you can move ahead with your manager's guidance and mentorship, all the better. Unfortunately, in this modern age, it is rare to find a mature, caring boss who hangs around long enough to be able to assist you in a practical way.

DRESS TO KILL, SPEAK TO WOO

To simplify the following example, let us call your boss 'John', and his boss 'Mary'. No matter how much you dislike John, you must never speak disparagingly about him to Mary (or to anyone else for that matter) because you will never know what relationship they have. In the corporate jungle, the first sad and sorry rule is that you must treat everyone as if they cannot be trusted. You just do not know what Mary is likely to tell John. Besides, if Mary sees you as someone who speaks badly about your current manager,

In the corporate jungle, the first sad and sorry rule is that you must treat everyone as if they cannot be trusted

she could easily assume that if you eventually reported directly to her, you might find it just as easy to discredit her to *her* superior. This would retard your chances of a promotion.

Another important aspect when maintaining a polished image in the eyes of your manager's manager is how you dress and present yourself. If you want to plant a seed in Mary's mind that you are 'executive material', she must always see you as such. What you wear and how you conduct yourself should lead her to think that you are someone whom she would like to have on her team.

Your best advocate is your image. Your actions must result in Mary believing that you possess star qualities. Nothing you

Nothing you say can override what another person believes

say can override what another person believes. For example, a person to whom you are not physically attracted cannot make you feel an attraction merely by asking you to reconsider your assessment. Similarly, you cannot *ask* Mary to think highly of you. She either will, or she will not. This means that your image will exude signals that Mary will interpret in her own way. You cannot ask her to translate your signals using *your* interpretation code. What *you* presume to be appealing might be off-putting to Mary. Naturally, it would be sensible to understand her preferences. What some people find alluring, others find repulsive. Beware what you do in the name of fashion and style.

Do not compromise your standards in an attempt to please others. The moment that you lose your own style, you become unattractive. I worked for an organisation whose entire management team enjoyed consuming alcohol at every opportunity. I was warned about my reluctance to drink, and told that the chairman would be offended if I did not share a beer with him. I would not acquiesce. There are some things I would not do in the name of corporate harmony.

It is vital to ensure that your image reflects your substance. What you project about yourself must be real. Those whose exterior is not a true reflection of their interior, end up living a lie. They will be able to fool some people, but they cannot fool those who matter most. Self-deceptive conduct is not only self-damaging, it is a resource-intensive Molotov cocktail.

You speak volumes by what you do not say. You expose your integrity by what you refuse to accept. You highlight your conviction by what you refuse to believe.

SECRET CODES, SILENT MESSAGES

In the same way that a brand can say a lot about a product, your actions and inactions send clear messages. Each and every social clique has its set of unwritten rules. You speak volumes by what you do not say. You expose your integrity by what you refuse to accept. You highlight your conviction by what you refuse to believe.

Astute people will determine your fibre by observing what you deem insignificant. They will construe your essence by what you overlook. They will interpret your actions by what you neglect. They will assess your grandeur by how low you stoop. They will examine your honour by what you hide.

Shrewd people will scrutinise your nature by giving you whatever you ask for. They will examine your morality by tantalising your pleasures. They will probe your ethics by sponsoring your indulgences. They will unveil your principles by extending your authority. They will know your limits by replenishing your power so that you will be able to reach your destination.

Leaders who are both shrewd and astute cannot be duped. They will see right through candidates. They do not mind clumsy people, but they worry about polished yobs. They do not mind the uneducated, but they loathe the ignorant. They can see value in a rough diamond, but not in fool's gold.

Shrewd people will scrutinise your nature by giving you whatever you ask for. They will examine your morality by tantalising your pleasures.

Take care to understand that you cannot reflect anything other than your reality. Those who fake their image give the game away through unintentional heedlessness. The tiniest detail exposes impostors. Vulgarity seizes glamour. Rudeness usurps style. Indiscretion smothers elegance. Insensitivity extinguishes romance. Selfishness destroys love.

BETTER THE DEVIL YOU DON'T KNOW

Some managers prefer to search for *external* candidates because they would have observed their internal aspirants long enough to be disappointed. This describes the 'familiarity syndrome' that plagues relationships. Often people lust over the unknown. For example, despite the fact that their current lover might be attractive in many ways, they gravitate towards another beautiful person in the hope of something new and unblemished. Distant strangers might not be perfect, but at least their faults are unknown. The old saying, 'better the devil you know', does not apply in these situations. People live in the hope that maybe the new lover (or candidate) might not possess the annoying habits exhibited by the person with whom they are familiar.

Mary could have seen or heard enough about you to form an opinion. If that impression is negative, you would have no chance of beating a candidate who comes from the outside — even if you have shown loyalty and if you possess extensive experience. Once the intangibles have been shattered, Mary might look outside and then explain it away with words like ' . . . the company is moving in a new direction, and it needs a candidate with new skills that you do not have'. Mary does not know about the new candidate's bad habits, but she is aware of yours. So despite your experience, you are at a disadvantage.

Distant strangers might not be perfect, but at least their faults are unknown

This means that in your quest to be considered as a potential replacement for your manager, you have to make a good first impression, and continue to uphold that image. This is where you have to learn how to adopt *two* languages. John, your manager, might want to speak with you about certain issues that concern *him*. Your conversations with him have to encompass what he finds of value. Invariably, John's pressures will stem from what he is measured on, such as 'revenue' or 'customer satisfaction'.

When Mary speaks with you, it is important that you learn *her* language. The best way to do this is to find out what occupies her mind. What pressures does her manager place on her? Maybe she is more concerned with 'market share' and 'gross profit'. You could glean some ideas by reading all her speeches, listening carefully to the points she raises at staff meetings and at media briefings, and by asking other staff members.

If you happen to see Mary at a staff function, and she asks you something like, 'Where do you think we can improve the business?' you had better respond in ways that make sense to her at her job level, not at your job level. Furthermore, never say anything that reflects badly on John. Besides, John's questionable decisions might have been carried out under Mary's orders, and you might not know the basis of her pressures.

SHATTERED ILLUSIONS

Once when I was the marketing director of a large organisation, several product and marketing managers reported to me. One young lady from the sales division had told me that she was keen to be given the chance to be considered for an upcoming role of 'product manager'. She impressed me with her enthusiasm, general knowledge, and keenness. As a result, I kept my eyes on her as a potential member of my team.

During our annual staff party, I saw the young lady in a new light. She entered with her boyfriend and looked stunning. As the night wore on, she became drunk, and her boyfriend was not much better. By the end of the night, he was a total write-off and she was a loud, sloppy embarrassment who had taken her shoes off and decided to sit on the floor. Her colleagues had to carry her to a taxi, all the while, she was a dead weight, protesting that she did not want to go home. This shattered my illusions about her and showed me her weaker side.

As a product manager, she would have to tour the world and attend dozens of events and parties. If this is how she would behave, how could I entrust her with such an important position? Several weeks later I appointed another candidate to the role. When she protested, I said to her, 'Would you ever go to a job interview while sloshed?'

I reminded her that her image is a 24-hour responsibility. She cannot behave in an unruly manner at a staff function and expect me not to notice. Her image was shattered that night.

Of course people are allowed to let their hair down. What I am saying is that once they reveal a part of themselves, they cannot ask others to erase their perception.

I have often warned people about drinking at business functions. They take certain liberties assuming that they are 'off duty'. Always remember that your image is important. It forms part of your brand. It can take years to build a brand, and yet only seconds to shatter it. For more on building your personal brand, see Chapter 3, 'Networking'.

IF YOU CAN'T CLIMB THIS LADDER, FIND ANOTHER LADDER

Talented managers are rarely revered within their own camp. Entertainers battle the same problem, whereby they have to go and prove themselves overseas before they can be taken seriously in their own country. As a result, strangers might appreciate your talent more so than your associates do. For that reason, sometimes it is a better strategy to seek to climb the corporate ladder by hopping on to a different ladder when you feel that you have outgrown your current role.

There is merit in grooming yourself to move to a new organisation where you can be taken more seriously, or where you can be seen in a new light. Just like parents find it hard to believe that their children have grown up, managers find it difficult to promote those whom they once knew as college graduates. I left school at the age of fourteen, so for many years, I was always working with people three times my age. It was hard to convince some of my managers that I had matured.

My youth lived on. My immaturity echoed for a while. Although no-one disputed my potential, it was difficult to move up the ladder. I found it much easier to promote myself by joining *other* organisations. I changed jobs every five years or so — an unpopular move in those days. Back then, those who did not stay at any one job for more than ten years were accused of having something wrong with them. These days, there is no stigma attached to those 'on the move'.

By changing jobs, I was able to start with a clean slate and turn a new leaf as far as my approach and outlook were concerned. Admittedly, there were many areas that I needed to work on. By changing organisations, I was able to start afresh, without any of the old baggage.

Changing jobs can be a good move if it adds value to your career. If you can enhance your chances to learn, grow, advance, and earn more, you need to move quick-smart. Waiting for your current employer to promote you might be a futile effort. Take charge of your career and seek to find your own avenues for promotion and growth.

DOUBLE OR NOTHING

When I was changing jobs, my strategy was to double my benefits. I had to either double my responsibilities, or my rank, or my standing, or my salary, or my job-satisfaction, or my learning opportunities. Otherwise, there is little point in changing jobs. If you cannot double one of those areas, you need to thoroughly investigate what the barriers are. Then you need to spend five hours each week undertaking a comprehensive and customised personal development program to boost your personal, communications, and negotiation skills. You have to be sure that you possess talent that you can use to add value to employers or to potential clients.

HOW MUCH DO YOU EARN?

A job interview is a two-way process. For that reason, I dislike being asked any question that the interviewer would not like me asking in return. The common irritating and irrelevant question is, 'How much are you earning at the moment?' I would dearly like to say, 'None of your business'. To keep the peace, I did divulge this information in the early part of my career.

In my latter years of job-hunting, I developed enough confidence to say, 'I do not wish to divulge that information because I believe that what I am earning now has no bearing on what salary I would accept from my next employer.' Immature interviewers pressed the point and made an issue out of my response. The serious players respected my decision and moved on to other areas of interest. (A friend of mine used to tell her nosy interviewers, 'My salary is confidential between myself and the company, but I am happy to discuss what I feel I am worth and what you feel this role is worth.')

You are strongly advised *not* to divulge your current (or most recent) salary package to a future employer. There are a number of good reasons for this. Here are five of them:

1) A person's salary is often used to measure seniority or capability. For example, if you are currently earning a low salary and you apply for a senior role, doubt would be cast over your level of seniority.

2) The interviewer might not understand the pay structures and ranking levels within your current work environment, and could presume that you are not paid well due to your current employer's dissatisfaction with your work.

3) If other candidates (who are earning more) compete with you for the job, it could be presumed that they have more experience.

4) The interviewer might wonder if you really want the job in question, or if are you simply lusting over the huge salary increase.

5) If you are applying for a job that pays *less* than what you currently earn, this would be met with suspicion because an

employer might wonder why you would be prepared to take a drop in salary.

SELLING SKILLS

Job jumping is an effective and honourable way to increase your salary. If you divulge your existing salary, you would find it difficult to negotiate more than a twenty percent increase. At that rate, it would be a long time before you could break into the higher stakes. It is for this reason that you need to protect your salary details early in your career. If each job that you jump to affords you less than a twenty percent increase, you would be losing valuable time. If you change jobs too frequently, you risk raising a different kind of suspicion, so you end up being a low-income earner for most of your life.

When you go to buy a product, you do not ask the manufacturer or the retailer to reveal the cost price. Brand names can command unbelievably high profit margins. The $250 running shoes might only cost $12 to make. How would you feel about parting with your money if you knew that kind of information? Similarly, your salary is your cost price. It should be no-one's business what you earn. When you go to sell your services, you should be aiming to sell your brand — being your reputation, your solid performance record, your knowledge, and the promise of the value that you can add to your new employer's enterprise.

In portraying the image that you want others to appreciate, you would be well served to have them *presume* that you are earning more than you really are. One way that some people do this is to lie about it, and they submit false figures in their job-applications. Although this could work, it is an unethical process to pursue.

It is far better to refuse to disclose private information and be thought a stubborn or secretive candidate, than to lie and be found out. Deceitful conduct would reveal a serious character flaw (as well as poor judgement), and it would be embarrassing for all concerned. I do not mind if candidates do not tell me what they are earning, but I do take exception to those who lie in their résumé.

SEE YOU AT THE TOP

Did you spend five hours last week to develop your skills? Are you keeping some energy in reserve at the end of each week to invest in your future? Are you doing brilliant things? If you are not, I can confidently predict for you a life of mediocrity. If you are, I can enthusiastically say, 'See you at the top!' **E**

CHAPTER 15

MOVE *over*

IT'S MY TURN AT THE WHEEL!

*Of course I like impromptu events,
so long as they are planned*

THE GRASS LOOKS GREENER on the other side, especially on the patch where the impressive ivory tower stands tall, housing senior executives who appear to be having a ball in their plush offices. We tend to associate the 'big guns' with luxurious lifestyles of fine dining and exquisite fashion, buoyed by whopping pay packets that make most employees salivate at the thought of climbing the corporate ladder for a stint on the throne. If wealth and power are the hallmarks of seniority, who would not want to strive for a share of the action?

Business people's level of importance is reflected in their job title, making senior executives more important than general staff, despite efforts by some managers to convince us that it is not true. The perceived power and authority of senior executives sparks a desire in many staff members to advance their own career in the hope that they might reach such celebrated heights.

If wealth and power are the hallmarks of seniority, who would not want to strive for a share of the action

Although consensus management and empowerment are often espoused, very few organisations give their staff members the necessary autonomy to make decisions that can shape their present or future environment. This results in frustrated employees who feel that the only way to effect change or to make worthwhile contributions is to 'get behind the wheel'. The desire to become the boss is born out of practical or egotistical needs, or of social expectations.

This chapter explores some of the issues that surround the notion of 'becoming the boss'. Chapter 17, 'Heads or tails?' outlines the fifteen personal qualities that will be important for bosses of the future.

SHOW ME THE WAY, THEN FOLLOW ME

Unfortunately, the impressions that are formed about what it means to be the boss are invariably inaccurate. Remember, if your fantasy starts from a distance, keep your distance. Although there is much satisfaction in being the boss, the rude shock of the experience can destabilise many managers.

Experienced debaters know that the best way to confuse an opponent is to make statements that cannot be disputed. For example, no-one would disagree with the statement, 'employees must have the right attitude' or 'human life is precious'. Similarly, no-one would disagree that 'successful bosses are those who can lead successfully'. Times have changed, and these days, the boss is not necessarily the one who sets the direction or apportions the resources. Tokenism is rife in corporate life, so take care to understand what you are letting yourself in for when you go after the top job.

Tokenism is rife in corporate life, so take care to understand what you are letting yourself in for when you go after the top job

In qualitative research, managers have admitted that what drove them to attain senior positions were intangible desires that were ill-defined or misplaced. In the same way that teenagers might plead with their parents to buy them a computer so that they can 'do their homework' (when in fact their real intention is to play computer games or surf the Net), many managers seek to be promoted for reasons that they never articulate, for fear of retribution. On the surface and at the job interview, they say that they would like the top job so that they can make a major contribution to the organisation. They speak about 'adding value' or 'leading the team', when in their heart they fantasise about their increased importance, bigger salary, and improved social status.

Like an embarrassing situation that no-one wants to deal with, managers avoid mentioning their real feelings about the remuneration package, pretending that the salary does not matter, when, deep down, they know it is an important part of their negotiations. They think that it would be 'bad form' to discuss the salary so early in the courting ritual. Nonetheless, those who seek the top job most certainly seek to maximise their income. Sometimes they seek to secure a salary package that verges on the obscene. For more about bosses who earn a huge salary, see Chapter 16, 'Bread in captivity'.

Other subconscious desires include the perception that reaching the top would look good on our résumé or make us more attractive or likeable. Some people want to be in a position to flaunt their title so that they can get what they want in terms of service, privileges, or special treatment. They might even have a deep-seated desire to make others feel afraid of them, although they would never admit to this, for fear of being called an egomaniac or a powermonger.

Although power can be intoxicating, the elation is short-lived

As you can imagine, these are feelings that can lead to disaster because they are not based on solid foundations. If you really want to become the boss, you must search your heart to identify what the driving force is. If it is a yearning for social acceptance or a longing for a dramatic life modelled on a movie character, you will be sorely disappointed to learn that your efforts will be in vain. Although power can be intoxicating, the elation is short-lived because the responsibilities of your position would soon weigh you down.

The best starting position would be your aspiration to create a better environment, whether that be for your staff or for your customers. It could be that you aspire to create a better

product or to deliver a better service. When these noble qualities ignite your quest to become the boss, you can feel confident
that you are starting your journey on solid foundations. The
best bosses are those who can see the big picture and then
improve their skills so they are well prepared to lead the team
to successful and honourable outcomes.

If your desires are fuelled by egotism, you will have a miserable time at the top. Only *you* will know your real intentions.
Naturally, like a child who is fixated on wanting a particular toy,
you might not want to listen to reason. Search your heart and
steer clear of desires that aren't based on a need to create better
environments or superior products and services.

Hopeless managers are those who say, 'Promote me now,
and I'll work on my weaknesses.' It is likely that they do not
have a clue about what their weaknesses are, and they would
not listen to advice. Successful managers are those who say,
'Before I undertake this important mission, I'll identify my weaknesses so that I can either eradicate them, or learn to work with
experts on whom I can rely to complement my strengths.'

HOW GREEN IS YOUR GRASS?

If you are unhappy about your current job, and you seek to
increase your job-satisfaction by climbing the corporate ladder,
take care not to harbour delusions of grandeur or misconcep-
tions about what responsibilities you would have to shoulder
when you become the boss.

A typical mistake is to presume that just because you are
good at what you currently do, you are worthy of a promotion.
Mature people will tell you that promotions must not be seen
as rewards. Naturally, because seniority tends to provide an
increased income, people see it as a *gift* when it is given to them.

Organisations should stop dangling promotions like carrots. Management positions require specialist skills. It would be a mis-take to award senior jobs to employees, loyal though they might be, if they do not have the appropriate skills.

Mature people will tell you that promotions must not be seen as rewards

Organisations distract and mesmerise their workers by pointing to the potential promotion in the distance. Workers presume that reaching the summit is the hallmark of corporate success. Erroneously, they visualise their crowning glory as the attainment of a management position that comes with all the trimmings. When the top job becomes vacant, anxiety sets in as each eligible candidate competes for it — only to be told that an external applicant is being interviewed 'because the company could do with some new blood'. This triggers dissension within the ranks, with loyalists withdrawing their support, totally offended that their hard work has been overlooked.

Do not look upon the top job as the jewel in the crown. If you cannot muster support for your current project, or if you cannot command the respect that you desire within your current circle, you will not enjoy the false courtesies that are sure to flourish when you are in power, because such attention will not fill the current gaps in your life.

Granted, people are easily impressed by titles and position. I recall times when my colleagues would ignore me, or not ask me to 'hang out' with them, because they did not consider me as being powerful or useful to them. I used to wonder what was wrong with me, and I started to observe what the 'popular' people had that I did not. I soon realised that they flaunted themselves and their power by dominating conversations. Their underlings and sycophants treated them like a 'queen bee' and hovered around them devotedly, in the hope that some of their power might rub off on them. I recall telling a joke around a conference dinner table one night. No-one laughed, because they did not feel that they had to humour me. There was an uncomfortable stretch of silence. Moments later, when the 'queen bee' told a joke, the group erupted in laughter.

The body-language that people display around the boss is fascinating to observe. The underlying source is a sense of desperation from both sides of the divide. Managers who enjoy such attention are likely to be immature, and employees who surrender to their manager's magnetism are likely to be insecure.

When you become the boss, pay attention to the social phenomenon known as the pecking order. The best time to start observing this is when you are still a member of the 'working class'. Watch how people will stand in a circle facing the boss, and how an immature boss will lap up the attention while ignoring other members of the group who cannot get a word in. It is best to bow out of that environment and find a more enriching circle of colleagues who can help you to build up more dignified memories of your days in corporate life. You need to build some memories that will uplift you when you look back on them in years to come. There is nothing worse than a past tarnished by snapshots of anxiety and emptiness.

There is nothing worse than a past tarnished by snapshots of anxiety and emptiness

EVERY BOSS NEEDS OBSERVATION SKILLS

Learn to hone your powers of observation. These can become a valuable learning tool. Over the years, people have complimented me on my ability to appear confident when speaking in public. 'Who taught you how to present so well?' they ask. I tell them that I learned by watching those who *did not* know how to present themselves well. When I sat in on boring lectures and dry presentations, I used to switch off and daydream or doodle. I once listened to a presenter who was so dreary and tedious that I entered a time warp: I took my watch off to adjust the time, thinking that it had stopped because it showed that only ten minutes had passed, yet I could have sworn I had been there an hour. I turned to the person sitting next to me and asked for the correct time, only to learn that my watch *was* accurate. I decided then that boring presenters were a waste of time, and that I would never subject an audience to that level of torture. I sat up and started to take copious notes on what the presenter was doing badly.

From that time on, I observed as many presenters as possible. I noted how they spoke, what they said, how they dressed, and what they did on stage. By observing speakers who performed badly, I was able to learn from their mistakes. The same applied to other areas of my career. I started to observe others intently. That kind of self-learning was immensely useful. No amount of reading could have helped me in the same way. I urge you to learn how to observe, how to question, how to watch, and how to interpret what you see. Most importantly, I encourage you to learn how to use such knowledge to fuel self-reflection and self-assessment, with a view to arriving at self-education. The best way to do this is while you are 'undercover' — when you are not yet 'the boss' and when you are not seen to be a person of importance. In this way, you can sort out the ethical operators from the selfish manipulators.

One of my clients owns a large international hotel. He wanted his staff to treat all their clients equally well. There was a problem with the service: famous guests would always be treated well, but unknown faces were often overlooked in subtle ways. To assess the situation, I walked into the hotel's fine dining room without a reservation and asked for a table. The restaurant in question was probably the city's most expensive establishment. A bowl of soup cost close to the average person's daily wage. The staff treated me courteously, but they did not deliver a level of service that was befitting the refinement of the hotel's credo. As the waitress was pouring a glass of water at my table, I asked if it was mineral water. She said no. I asked if it was filtered, and she said no. I pressed the point and found out that it was tap water. I explained that I did not drink tap water. She said, 'Oh, okay,' and removed the glass, but offered nothing more. No doubt I could have ordered a bottle of mineral water, but I deliberately did nothing and said nothing, hoping that she might offer me a bottle of mineral water as a gesture of goodwill.

During the hotel's staff training sessions, I was sitting behind the glass panel in the control room. I asked the analyst to ask that particular waitress to suggest a company policy that would have addressed that type of situation. First, she was asked which famous person she would most like to meet. After she mentioned the name of a Hollywood movie star, we put this question to her: 'Supposing that your superstar walks into your restaurant and indicates that he does not like tap water. What should the hotel policy be in that case?' Without any hesitation she suggested that a bottle of mineral water be brought out as a gesture of hospitality. The hotel's general manager then piped up and said, 'That's an excellent suggestion. I want you to adopt that policy, but I want you to make sure that it becomes standard practice for *anyone* and *everyone* who walks in, not just for movie stars.'

As you can see, she had the wherewithal to solve the problem. She knew right from wrong. She had failed to exercise her better judgement because I was an unfamiliar face.

Superior performers are those who perform at their best *all* the time. Those who know how to treat people well, treat everyone well all the time. Good managers are those who devise personal policies and stick by them at every opportunity. Unlike the waitress who knew what excellent service was but chose to ignore her better judgement, a good boss is one who understands how to deliver excellence, and does so as a matter of course. A good singer would find it difficult to sing out of tune. A good actor would be hard-pressed to act badly. A good boss would have to try hard to treat people disrespectfully. When you polish your skills and refine your talents, you will be able to deliver excellence consistently and effortlessly. Thereafter, you will be able to take over. ◼

A good singer would find it difficult to sing out of tune. A good actor would be hard-pressed to act badly.

CHAPTER 16

BREAD *in* CAPTIVITY

BUCKETS OF JAM FOR THE BIG CHEESE

*The only thing holding me back
from becoming filthy rich is money*

RECENTLY, THE CEO for one of the companies I worked for raked in over US$80 million for one year's work, and he took home another $60 million from stock options, and on top of that, he still had $270 million in unexercised stock options. This total of $410 million sounds high, but it pales next to the CEO whose package reached $910 million in the same period.

Far too many questions have been raised about exorbitant executive salaries. Can they be justified? Are executives adding sufficient value in return? What would happen if we did not reward executives with high remuneration packages? Is it fair that a few managers can, in one year, earn more than their entire workforce combined?

It is baffling to observe the theatrics that companies exhibit when they have to lay-off several hundred staff members, making people jobless and homeless (while blaming the economy; never their incompetence or ineffectiveness). Let us not pick on anyone who is earning $910 million, but let us take a closer look at someone who takes home $40 million in annual salary. That translates to over $750 000 per week, compared with a $7500 pay-packet that the President of the United States earns per week. That CEO on $40 million is taking home what 2000 low-wage workers collectively earn in a full year. And this is only calculating the single 'head of the tiger', not all the cubs who hang off the organisation chart.

Is it fair that a few managers can, in one year, earn more than their entire workforce combined?

When high-profile executives score lucrative senior appointments, journalists ask if an executive can be worth $40 million to an organisation. It *is* possible for experts to make a major contribution to an organisation. It would not be hard for a switched-on operator to help an organisation to increase its value by several billion dollars. Sadly, such scenarios are rare, and more often than not, executives who are paid obscene amounts are unable to justify their salary.

Excessive remuneration sends unhealthy signals throughout an organisation wherein workers become disgruntled about such inequity. Over the years, basic wages have increased at approximately five percent per annum for blue-collar workers, while some executive packages have increased at an annual rate of over fifty percent. At the very top, the figures are even higher. There was a time in the 1980s when a CEO could earn forty times the average blue-collar worker's salary, and that was considered flash. By 1990, that had risen to eighty-five times. In the year 2000, some CEOs were earning over 500 times what the average worker was taking home. While some CEOs are earning embarrassingly high amounts, their performance has been lacklustre, with their company's overall value dropping by as much as fifty percent over a five-year period.

Those who defend exorbitant salaries typically say that high-level CEOs are a *rare* breed, selected from a small gene pool. Perhaps the gene pool is not as small as we have been led to believe. Competent executives abound. There are managers who would be satisfied to exert their best effort for a few hundred-thousand-dollars instead of a few million. Take a look at mainstream authors, musicians, and artists. They give their all to their profession, yet contrary to popular belief, their earnings would put them among the lowest paid professionals. Doctors, nurses, plumbers, and public servants, who keep the social wheels turning, earn modest salaries. So what is it that CEOs do, to warrant

Who, in their right mind, would want to become the 'big boss' in today's work environment?

their astronomical packages? Besides, what would we miss out on if we did not remunerate these supposedly rare 'whiz-kids'? History has shown that the most significant inventions were given to us by geniuses whose salaries hardly paid for a loaf of bread. Would brilliant managers cease to exist if their salaries were not 500 times higher than a labourer's wage?

Perhaps it is not a question of finding talented executives who are prepared to take on the top job. Rather, it is one of finding executives who are prepared to *leave* their gene pool and allow themselves to be drawn into the spotlight. Could it be that high salaries are dangled to tempt executives who do not want the job in the first place? Those worth their weight in salt would have to be dragged out of the gene pool, kicking and screaming as they are moved up the food-chain. After all, who, in their right mind, would want to become the 'big boss' in today's work environment? Special skills will be required for survival and prosperity at that level. These skills are outlined in Chapter 10, 'Wanted: The boss of the future.' The personal attributes that will be needed are listed in Chapter 17, 'Heads or tails?'

The moment that they are subjected to the realities of life at the top, they regret having pursued such an unrewarding path

In organisations that focus on the short-term, CEOs are asked to forget everything that they believe in and kowtow to a board that surrenders to know-it-all analysts who can downgrade an organisation with the stroke of a pen. The innocent members of the public know that it is all a game, but they are forced to off-load their shares lest panic ensue. It is a sick sport that triggers a chain reaction. This explains why eloquent CEOs soon lose their wit and drive, and why many of them wish that they could resign. The moment that they are subjected to the realities of life at the top, they regret having pursued such an unrewarding path.

There was a time when sensible managers strived to reach the summit of their career. These days they duck for cover when the post becomes vacant. Those who are too ambitious for the position are ruled out automatically. Instead, the board goes in search of those who do not show interest, because such candidates are less likely to have formed grandiose plans to reform the organisation. Disinterest is thought to be a good quality for a candidate to exhibit. Manipulative boards want flexible, amiable, dispassionate CEOs because they are easier to mould — so long as they can be hooked.

The trick is to lure someone for whom several million dollars is an astronomical amount of money. It could be argued that enduring one year of hell is worthwhile, even if things do not work out, because the salary would go a long way to providing financial security. With this reasoning, candidates accept the post, but often underestimate the next step known as 'The Dealer's Grip'. This is a technique used by drug dealers who grip their traffickers by ensuring that they become addicted to the substance they sell.

Each board's mission is to ensure that the first two months on the job are blissful, so as to lull CEOs into a false sense of comfort and enjoyment. With newfound confidence and power-induced intoxication, CEOs are easily gripped when they are shamed out of their current affordable lifestyle and into the exclusive club that demands a plush house, a fancy car, and expensive accessories — thereby landing them in more debt than they had bargained for, all brought about by clouded judgement, mixed with an inflated ego and an invincible disposition.

MORE MONEY THAN YOU CAN HANDLE

It was young Steven Jobs of Apple Computer who, in 1983, made history by appointing John Sculley as the first CEO to break the million-dollar barrier. Sculley had to be lured from PepsiCo to head Apple. His package included a million-dollar salary, a million-dollar bonus, and a million-dollar severance, plus a car, home, generous interest-free loans, shares, and goodness knows what else. How did Sculley show his gratitude to his lord and master? He conspired to sack him, and succeeded. Perhaps all that attention went to his head. By 1990, Sculley and other CEOs were raking in over $10 million dollars each. Such record-breaking amounts now seem small by comparison to modern packages.

If you think that salary packages are high enough, then what about termination packages that are even more inexplicable? When CEOs eventually wrestle with their conscience and seek to bow out gracefully, they are offered even more dosh as a peace offering. Engraved on the gold watch is something like, 'Go in peace and keep your mouth shut, lest analysts catch wind of any of your vitriol.' What was known as 'the golden handshake' became known as 'the golden parachute'. These days, termination payouts are 'golden coffins' that encase shattered reputations.

These days, termination payouts are 'golden coffins' that encase shattered reputations

Many CEOs live in a world of tokenism. At times, they wonder why their position exists. Sadly, this good question cannot be contemplated because the world does not tolerate vacuums. It is not possible to vacate the throne because a corporation cannot exist without a corporal, no more than a monarchy can exist without a monarch.

MONEY FOR JAM

Ironically, there was a time when every soldier would have to die before Napoleon would suffer a bullet. There was a time when underlings were the scapegoats. It was not long ago when VPs shielded their CEOs, just like generals buffered their king. Regrettably, in the cruel networked world of ours, everything has been turned on its head. Today, CEOs are at the frontline and they must suffer whatever shrapnel is in the offing. When seen from this perspective, one can begin to understand that executive salaries are not rewards, but *compensation*. Several million dollars is not a lot of money when it is itemised into appropriate categories such as loss of privacy, humiliation, and a damaged career — not to mention a damaged reputation.

Why is the *brand* no longer a sufficient tool with which to boast about a company's reputation? Which organisation is true to its brand? Hardly any. These days, product quality and service delivery are so appalling, that even the biggest brands are lacklustre. Hence, in the absence of brand credibility, a 'human' has to be installed as the new (albeit temporary) figurehead.

These days, product quality and service delivery are so appalling, that even the biggest brands are lacklustre

As figureheads, CEOs are expected to have superhuman qualities. They must be squeaky clean, yet have battlefield experience. They must have the gift of the gab amid personal restraint. They must be strong leaders whom everyone likes. They must be courageous, without rocking the boat. Above all, they must be visionaries who can take direction.

So you see, the strategy is to pay heaps of money to herd CEOs inside a gridlock-style of package to ensure that leaving becomes more painful than staying. This makes for co-operative CEOs who will abandon all sensibilities and focus on the short-term gain. Sacking staff, dismantling the infra-structure, and damaging the brand are all considered fair play, so long as the share price can be manipu-lated upwards.

CEOs are expected to have superhuman qualities. They must be squeaky clean, yet have battlefield experience. They must have the gift of the gab amid personal restraint.

As a digital-age philosopher, my job is to ask the right questions. As an investigative writer, I am obliged to question the answers. Whichever way you look at it, organisations will never admit to operating unethically, because they say that they are operating within the law. Lawful behav-iour is not necessarily ethical. There is a solution. Dismantle the stock market and start to reward managers for the seeds they sow, not the crops they harvest.

Organisations ought to earn riches by delivering on their promises and by adding value to society. The stock market is the biggest cosmic joke of all time. If organisations cannot become wealthy through what they sell, then they had better get out of business. In the absence of share trading, one would begin to understand that having a great idea is not reason enough to start a business.

I fight a lonely battle because those in power (and those on the take) could not bring themselves to agree with me. Just for the record, I have always refused exorbitant salaries when shares were included in the package. I have told head-hunters that I would only sit on the throne if the board would stipulate its direction and leave me alone for five years. Invariably, they would pause for a moment and stare at me from the corner of their eyes to process what I had just said. When it clicked, they laughed, hoping that it was my dry wit, not my insanity, that led me to make such a bold demand.

I was doomed in corporate life the day I stopped lusting over my manager's job

If you are on a mission to reach the throne, be careful that you know when to abort your mission. For me, I was doomed in corporate life the day I stopped lusting over my manager's job. It was then that I decided to evacuate. I did not want to be *bred* in captivity, despite all the *bread* in captivity.

SOUR DOUGH

The topic of salaries always makes for sensational reporting. In time to come, organisations will be forced to disclose more information about how they reward their executives. Government departments will also be forced to operate amid greater transparency.

Shareholders are in two minds about this dilemma. On the one hand, they do not agree with the pay structures that inevitably erode the bottom-line and rob them of potentially higher dividends. On the other hand, they are beginning to learn that it is more important for the market to *perceive* that an organisation is credible and stable. In part, this is done by boasting about an organisation's CEO and its board of directors. Key players are rarely hired for their great ideas. In most cases, they are hired for 'who they are' not 'what they can do' — meaning that board appointments are often publicity stunts to signal to the market that an organisation knows how to rub shoulders with the rich, the famous, the influential, and the powerful.

Much of the world's business fraternity works on 'futures'. These days, this means having the ability to convince people that the future looks rosy. In the good old days, analysts were patient, and they were prepared to wait for new products to hatch from the labs. These days, no-one wants to wait longer than three months for projects to yield results. This is partly due to the compressed competitive cycle that sees rivals able to copy anything that anyone else does. This is spurred by international patent-exchange agreements that allow anyone 'in the club' to have access to the patents. For example, in the IT industry, most major manufacturers have cross-agreements that enable any player to use any of the newly-registered patents. It is for this reason that no sooner does one brand announce a new gizmo, than another brand is able to manufacture it.

Sadly, market supremacy is no longer measured by *innovation*, but by *efficiency*, whereby organisations are ranked by their economies-of-scale, and by their processes. Achieving 'world's best practice' once meant designing processes that delivered the best results to customers. These days, it means engaging in systems and procedures that are as mean and as lean as possible. Cost-cutting was always a priority, but now cost-efficiency is the order of the day.

Amid all that drama, someone has to face the public, and the more credible the face, the more 'time' that an organisation can buy. For this reason, a CEO has to be able to sell future hope. This intangible is powerful, if it is presented convincingly. Hope is cheaper to produce than a range of products. It requires no effort to design and manufacture. The only downside is that hope is also invisible, and it relies on the influencers to be able to see it and believe it. This brings us back to

A credible CEO can spin hope in any flavour and in any colour

the CEO. A 'credible' CEO can spin hope in any flavour and in any colour. So you can see that it would be cheaper to pay one 'spin-doctor' than it would be to build a new manufacturing facility. Hope does not need council approval to construct. The downside for society is that one spin-doctor (CEO) does not generate much wealth for the money cycle, whereas building a manufacturing plant generates jobs and taxes, and it injects vigour into the money supply.

The authorities, such as the tax departments, are beginning to question this new-economy shift in investment. Lobbyists are working to change the law so that executive salaries above one million dollars will no longer be deemed a legitimate company expense, and therefore will not be eligible for tax deductions.

Other legal aspects that are brewing include the argument for women to receive equal pay for equal work. At last count, it was estimated that women in the western world are earning approximately twenty-five percent less than what men earn, for doing the same jobs. This argument might be valid, but as with all statistics, it depends on the sample, and on the ways in which the numbers are divided. If, instead of gender, the division is made by age, race, colour, ethnicity, education, or one's suburb, the figures could be made to look just as interesting, depending on who is massaging them, and in whose interest it would be to pose each argument.

THE DAY OF RECKONING

There might come a time when governments will introduce new laws that place arduous responsibilities on the board of directors and the senior management team. Corporations will be forced to account for decisions that affect consumers, stakeholders, and minority shareholders. At the moment, corporations open and close subsidiaries without regard for who they impact. Directors are protected by insurance policies, and organisations are protected by limited public liability. Yet, they can still rake up billions of dollars in debt, and overnight they can declare their company insolvent or bankrupt. They exude some feeble pretence of humility by going into *voluntary* liquidation — they call it 'voluntary' but I have often wondered what the alternative is. The term conjures images of directors 'coming quietly and without a struggle'. What struggle can directors put up, apart from skipping town to live overseas in a safe haven?

The future law might simply read, 'Executives of failed organisations that are unable to repay their debts will be sent to gaol for a minimum of ten years.' When that kind of law is passed, it will trigger mass resignations because CEOs will know that they have no say in how their companies are run, and they will see that society will no longer tolerate the greedy giants milking innocent service providers and suppliers of their life savings, while they pretend to operate a business. In truth, they are just playing the money-market and stock-market to hype share prices to levels that will allow them to 'cash in' and put the money in their spouse's name while they cry asset-poor. When the conniving hounds sell their shares to unsuspecting fools, they tuck their fortunes abroad as they console the gullible with statements like, 'We are going through a market adjustment.' That is code for 'a market ripped off by hype merchants who knew what they were doing to the greedy who should have known better, but there is a sucker born every minute.'

Mind you, corporate greed is human greed. Let us not suggest that a corporation is a monster that is not human. We fight corporations as if they were a species unto themselves. Anyone who owns shares in a company is part of the corporate battlefield.

I believe that the day will come when directors and senior executives will be held accountable. I am not suggesting that the majority of directors act fraudulently. The premeditated crooks are few and far between, but the run-of-the-mill corporation can acquire goods and services, manipulate the share prices, and then tell the creditors to 'go jump'. Although this is called 'acting within the law', this type of behaviour might soon be outlawed. In a corporation's lifetime (and they are getting shorter on purpose) the majority shareholders can trade their shares daily. They do not see the corporation as a vehicle through which to make profits by delivering products and services. Rather, they use the shell of the organisation as an excuse to trade notional pieces of paper, knowing full well that the company is on its last legs.

Of all the species, we humans seem to be the least co-ordinated. Ants and bees do it better. We amass wealth without purpose. We grow without reason. We consume without need. In the end, what starts out as a quest to provide our families with daily bread, ends up as a mad dash for *more*. Do you want more? How much more? If you do not know what will satisfy you, you will never be satisfied with anything. As my sister once said, 'What will be enough, if enough is not enough?' There is something insanely brilliant about nature's revenge. It gives you all the freedom you *can't* handle just to remind you who's boss. **N**

There is something insanely brilliant about nature's revenge. It gives you all the freedom you can't handle just to remind you who's boss.

CHAPTER 17

HEADS *or* TAILS?

THE BIGGEST BET OF ALL

Equality isn't for everyone

AMBITIOUS PEOPLE TRY TO ASCERTAIN each other's aspiration by asking, 'Which would you rather be, the head of a chicken or the tail of a tiger?' In other words, would you prefer the autonomy of being the owner of a one-person small business (the head of a chicken), or an insignificant player in a huge organisation (the tail of a tiger)?

If you are a serious go-getter, you might be dissatisfied with both options. You might prefer to reach the pinnacle of your profession and become the 'head of the tiger' by going a few steps further up the ladder, to take the ultimate job.

If you hanker after the top job, you will need certain skills to navigate the journey's hazardous terrain. Chapter 15, 'Move Over', explores some of the *administrative* skills that you must develop if you are to become the boss. This chapter outlines the *personal* qualities you will need if you are to join the ranks of high-flyers who run their own business or who control giant corporations from dizzying heights.

Before I list the fifteen personal qualities that I have found to be present in over ninety percent of credible high-earning executives, try this exercise: ask your friends what they consider to be the important qualities that successful executives or business owners need to possess. Most people come up with politically-correct and socially-approved qualities such as integrity, vision, foresight, leadership, drive, energy, trust, respect, imagination, direction, confidence, and ambition.

Courage neither eliminates nor sedates fear

Next, ask your friends about what they understand these words to mean. It is all well and good to aspire to righteous and dignified qualities, but how do these qualities really become part of who we are? Personal characteristics are those behaviours that are ingrained into our life.

297

Let us examine one word that commonly crops up: *courage*. Courage is seen as being the opposite of *fear* (something with which we are all familiar). We know that fear can consume our whole body, making our heart pound faster and our mouth go dry. But what does courage do to our body? If we examine its essence, we can see that courage neither *eliminates* nor *sedates* fear. In fact, fear is a vital signal used by winners to understand their limits. Courage must co-exist with fear.

Courage is useful when we commit to do what must be done, and to fight for what must be won, even if it means losing friends, infuriating the establishment, and feeling scared out of our wits.

Courage enables us to face the facts, so that we can identify and then disregard the dangers. Courage is not about subliminal conditioning, but about facing the problems head-on, as they are, not as we would wish them to be. Courage prevents external dangers from extinguishing our resolve. We have to confront our fears with clarity, because only when we can see the problems as they truly are, will we be in a position to do what must be done.

Courage prevents external dangers from extinguishing our resolve

Furthermore, we have to understand the differences between *moral* courage and *physical* courage, and act even while terrified, opposed, threatened, intimidated, and/or humiliated. And even after we begin to absorb courage, we need to expand upon our understanding of it by learning about its 'moons', such as *bravery* and *audacity*.

Courage is just one example from the list of personal attributes that are usually deemed essential for successful executives. Additionally, high-flyers (sometimes called 'top-level' executives) possess qualities that most people would consider unpopular, irreverent, or unfashionable.

The fifteen personal characteristics that I have identified are discussed below. They are not for the meek or the fainthearted. Do not dabble in them casually. You must be intimately acquainted with each of them. Remember that your best strategies are those that your competitor least understands and least expects. For this reason, once these qualities become ingrained personal attributes, they must become *invisible* so that no-one will recognise the source of your strength.

| PERSONAL QUALITY # 1 • OBSTINACY |

If, in your résumé, you were to describe yourself as obstinate, you will likely be thought to mean pig-headed, stubborn, inflexible, or unreasonable. In fact, obstinacy can help you to overcome difficulties through boldness and daring. The wisdom of the ages tells us, 'When in doubt, don't do it!' I would venture to say that when in doubt, and you have no other feasible alternative, drive on, press on, move on, and confront the obstacles that are hindering or tormenting you. Leapfrog over those people who confuse and stifle you and your team. In a word: charge! Let no-one stand in your way.

Diplomacy is a waste of time. It saps your energy, gives your competitor legitimacy, and slows you down so that you can be attacked like a sitting duck. The only time that diplomacy is important is when the other party has the upper hand. If you know what you want, go after it. Grab what is yours, and then you can decide what you want to hand back.

The only time that diplomacy is important is when the other party has the upper hand

Inevitably, worthwhile treasures are hidden behind obstacles, and the only way to overcome relentless and indiscriminate difficulties is via relentless and uncompromising persistence. If you do not inject your project with obstinacy and persistence, you stand to be dictated to, by other people's whims and desires. For example, if you want to write a book and you give up

Inevitably, worthwhile treasures are hidden behind obstacles, and the only way to overcome relentless and indiscriminate difficulties is via relentless and uncompromising persistence

because publishers turn you down, what does that say about your determination? What a publisher might think of your project ought to have no bearing on your mission. Why would you allow a total stranger, who has no passion for your project, to tell you, via a simple rejection letter, that your ideas are not good enough? History is replete with examples of successful people who refused to let others stop them. They found a way. Allow no-one to rearrange your purpose for living.

| PERSONAL QUALITY # 2 • RELINQUISHMENT |

Learn to empty your mind, to erase your strategies, to discard the recipes, and to abandon your maxims. Then start again. If you arrive at the same conclusion, well and good. If you draft a new way, so be it. Whatever the case, be sure to test yourself by letting go of what you know, then go in search of the truth once more. This is just like hitting the reset button. You need to flush the system regularly, or risk burdening yourself with baggage that will weigh you down in the guise of customs and traditions.

The ability to relinquish old methods enables you to refresh your strategies. This helps to overcome the age-old problem known as 'the fear of change'. I have never understood that catch-cry, because I have always enjoyed change. When people resist change, they are not resisting variety. Instead, they are fighting against untested alternatives that might prove unstable and troublesome. In any case, if you ask someone to change, the onus is on you to prove why new strategies need to be considered. Whereas if you force people to rebuild their towers of logic, they will arrive at the most appropriate solutions without feeling that you have told them what to do. Smart people will come to the appropriate conclusions, without any debate about the notion or merits of change.

Allow no-one to rearrange your purpose for living

Learn to relinquish anything that can stop you from seeing clearly. Clarity in all things is vital for the top-level executive. Therefore, let go of any personal habits, beliefs, and vices that lock you into a routine, because they will dull your faculties of observation.

| PERSONAL QUALITY # 3 • IRRESPONSIBILITY |

The term 'irresponsibility' comes from the root word 'response'. When we ask people to be responsible, we are asking them to respond to stimuli that are generated by external forces. Being responsible means being able to hear and feel external signals. If they distract you, or cause you to react to uninvited and unplanned situations, you risk losing control.

Irresponsibility is a vital quality apparent in top-level executives. Here's how it works. In the world of opposites, we have to be totally and completely *focussed*, while being completely and totally *aware*. This requires an advanced level of *concentration*. To go one step further requires an advanced level of *self-control*. Using self-control, you can *fuse* the two skills of focus and awareness to arrive at one superior capability called 'prudence'. If you can operate with prudence, you will be able to make the decisions that you know are necessary to achieve your goals. This means that you can be attuned to know the difference between what is important and what is urgent. When you have determined your direction, and are conscious of the external factors, you are less likely to respond to situations that you know will slow you down.

Irresponsibility means having the ability to ignore distracting signals and those who do not add value to your mission. It requires you to have developed an ability to know who you can ignore and which energy-depleting tasks you can disregard. Irresponsibility does not condone recklessness or unruliness. In fact, it enables you to steer clear of those whose haphazard methods cause recklessness and unruliness through indifference to the main objective.

| PERSONAL QUALITY # 4 • PREPAREDNESS |

Winners are those who prepare for victory before they make their first move. As much as humanly possible, they leave nothing to chance. Nothing within their reach remains unchecked. They allow no-one within their command to tempt fate. Discipline and order might sound rigid and narrow, but they actually pave the way to a wider path through which we can safely pass.

Winners are those who prepare for victory before they make their first move

Preparing for failure is a pre-eminent way of maintaining success. Preparing for war is a sure way of securing peace. Preparing for an attack is a superior way of mounting a defence.

You might have read about army generals who advise that the *best* victory comes from the battle that does not have to be fought, because all battles are costly. They say that the *second-best* situation is to attack what cannot be defended, and defend what cannot be attacked. How do you suppose this can be achieved? Preparedness is the most powerful of deterrents, because your competitors will know that you mean business. Deterrence is infinitely superior to engagement.

Preparing for failure is a pre-eminent way of maintaining success. Preparing for war is a sure way of securing peace.

It is important to have a crystal-clear picture of what you want. Note that what you want, and what you can get, are two different things if you do not know *how* to achieve the results that you desire.

Achievement is not a matter of luck. Rather, it requires specific objectives, detailed calculations, exhaustive study, and scrupulous counter-measures that culminate in meticulous preparation. When all aspects of a project can be aligned with precision, you will be ready to synchronise your assault. To the bystander, your systematic execution might look frenzied and violent, when in fact, it is the epitome of orchestration.

| PERSONAL QUALITY # 5 • SECRECY |

For years I have maintained that the secret to success is secrecy. When secret plans are executed with *speed*, they generate the masterstroke that secures success. Can you work out what secrecy and speed produce when they combust? The answer is: *surprise!*

Only share your secrets with those who understand the importance of complete, ironclad confidentiality. Anyone who cannot be trusted must never be trusted. Eject immediately from your life anyone who seeks external rewards by betraying cabinet solidarity. No room exists for those whose ego prohibits them from feigning ignorance of your plans. Finally, do not tolerate carelessness, no matter how innocent in nature. If your efforts to weed out potential weaknesses are labelled ruthless, you can be comforted in the knowledge that ruthlessness is far better than carelessness.

No room exists for those whose ego prohibits them from feigning ignorance

Be aware that secrecy might become a currency with which people trade favours. If confidential information is known to exist, it will only be a matter of time before it is found. Supremacy for top-level executives comes not only when strategies remain secret, but when no-one knows of their existence. For this reason, it is not a good idea to stamp files as 'top secret' or 'highly confidential'. I have read memos from executives who allude to the formulation of a master plan, and they proceed to tell everyone that the details will be revealed on a 'need to know' basis. This could tantalise people by igniting their curiosity to the point where they will make it a personal challenge to find out whatever they can. They might then share that information with others to prove their capabilities or to fake their seniority.

Information is easily snatched from the hands of those who do not know its significance. The smallest sliver of information can destroy an entire project. A sophisticated plan is like a loaded spring: when released, the stored energy catapults the project forward at high speed. Remember that speed needs to fuse with secrecy, so that surprise can work in your favour to secure success. This means that anyone who can trip the spring by leaking what might appear to be insignificant information can destroy the whole project.

Do not put yourself in a position where your strategies can be foiled. Discipline in all things is the key with which you can lock away your secrets. Do not entrust your future to those who do not have complete self-discipline. Discretion and loyalty become the two fundamental qualities whose absence will jeopardise any plan. Pick your team members well, because their weaknesses will become your liability that will contribute to your demise.

Pick your team members well, because their weaknesses will become your liability that will contribute to your demise

Additionally, secrecy requires that you be unpredictable. Always keep something new in reserve. Do not let anyone know your full capabilities, because when your limits become known, your scenarios can be anticipated. Your competitors must remain in a state of apprehension. If they can read you like a book, you will soon be blocked. Do not be too quick to reveal your preferences or your passions. The more passionate you are about a subject, the more you will have to bite your tongue. Until you can turn your thoughts into meaningful and useful action, keep your mouth shut, lest you reveal too many of your 'hot buttons'.

| PERSONAL QUALITY # 6 • DECEPTION |

We are taught that it is wrong to deceive others. Yet, deception is the basis of all warfare. Admittedly, business activities are not usually conducted as seriously as all-out warfare. The principles of deception are vital in business because top-level executives must know how to appear weak in the areas in which they are strong, and strong in the areas in which they are weak. They must be able to duck and weave to avoid competitors' unwelcome and unwanted distractions. Although evasion is a resource-intensive strategy, it is nowhere near as draining as counter-attack.

Executives must know how to appear weak in the areas in which they are strong, and strong in the areas in which they are weak

Although your primary objective is to provide products or services to your customers via ethical business practices, you have to understand that your competitors are, by the nature of their existence, competing against you. If you ignore them, they will harm you. If you become obsessed by their presence, they will distract you. Therefore, you can use deception to keep them at bay while you get on with your work. They would delight in seeing you fail, so do not underestimate them.

Having said that, do not seek enjoyment from your competitors' demise. Your first priority is to deliver on the promises that you have made to your customers and to your business partners. Let that be your source of enjoyment. Do not take pride in destroying your competitors, but never assume that your competitors would not delight in eliminating you. For that reason, deception is the softest option that enables you to avoid your competitors while you solidify your relationships with those who matter most to you.

| PERSONAL QUALITY # 7 • DOUBT |

When I ask executives to list some of the important skills that they must refine, no-one has ever included 'doubt'. Yet, if you imagine the mind as a control-room with numerous monitors and consoles, 'doubt' would resemble that flashing red light in the centre of the ceiling that warns you to be on high-alert.

Top-level executives do not see doubt as an unwelcome intrusion, but rather as a saviour. They have learned to remove the triggers that trip false alarms. To them, that flashing red light is a precious tool. It puts them on high-alert to retaliate against saboteurs.

If you do not know what to do when the red light flashes, you are not sure of yourself or you are not attuned to your environment. Top-level executives would never tolerate that condition. They respond swiftly to intrusions. They place great value on the feeling of doubt. So much so, that they will stomp on anything or anyone who triggers the alarm.

Prudent executives must confront what must be confronted, resist what must be resisted, and reject what must be rejected. The difference between winners and losers is the ability to do *what* must be done, *when* it must be done. Timing becomes the single factor that determines victory. Timing is a perishable state. Its window of opportunity is never the same for any two situations. For that reason, the best time to strike is the instant that you know you must. When you can hone your sensitivities to use doubt as a tool for survival, not as a tool for torment, you will have adopted a lethal weapon — and like all such weapons, they can destroy anything or anyone who mistreats them. If doubt results in uncertainty, you might be harbouring a ticking time bomb that could lead to self-destruction. To avoid that disaster, learn to read your signals so that doubt becomes your trusted ally.

When you have a headache, do you take an aspirin and carry on, or do you rectify the problem? For me, a headache is a signal from my body, telling me to stop what I am doing because my constitution is not agreeing with the surrounding environment. Except in an emergency, I will not take an aspirin,

> *Prudent executives must confront what must be confronted, resist what must be resisted, and reject what must be rejected*

because I prefer to stay in touch with my faculties. Pain is an important signal. Learn to read your tangible (physical) and intangible (mental) signals. Although an aspirin tablet might stop my 'flashing red light', I know I am asking for trouble. (When a fire alarm sounds, would you be happy if someone just knocked the siren off the wall, without attending to the fire?)

Do not suppress doubt; use it to find and to attend to the cause of the problem.

| PERSONAL QUALITY # 8 • DISTRUST |

I once had a falling-out with a friend who could not comprehend what I meant when I said that she should trust no-one. 'Are you saying that I shouldn't trust *you*?' she asked. In view of the situation that she was in at the time, I felt that I had to say, 'The person you must least trust is the one who says, "Trust me", so I could hardly advise you not to trust anyone and then turn around and exclude myself.' She was not happy with that, and accused me of telling her that I could not be trusted.

I had overestimated her ability to understand her problems — the biggest of which was that she did not know how to trust *herself*.

Regular executives tend to distrust only those who have shown themselves to be untrustworthy. Top-level executives tend to trust only those who have shown themselves to be trustworthy.

Regular executives tend to distrust only those who have shown themselves to be untrustworthy. *Top-level* executives tend to trust only those who have shown themselves to be trustworthy.

No-one should access your trust in advance. It is not a question of credit. It is incumbent upon others to earn your trust, not on you to take the risk of giving it.

If you are forced to delegate tasks to people whom you do not trust, surround the project with sufficient fences so that you can contain the risk. Furthermore, do not proceed if you cannot handle the loss.

Do not look upon 'trust' and 'distrust' as expressions of 'like' and 'dislike'. Do not see distrust as an insult. Top-level executives know that trust goes beyond 'feelings' to include people's tolerances, weaknesses, skills, strengths, and capabilities. It is hard enough for people to know their *own* limits, let alone other people's limits. Supreme leaders leave nothing to chance, by endeavouring to know other people's limits. Distrust is your sensible shield that stops you from having to pay the price for someone else's frailties.

| **PERSONAL QUALITY # 9 • FAILURE** |

Which businessperson or creative genius do you respect the most? Now, suppose that you were that person's protégé — would you boast about the relationship? Would you be proud to tell your associates that you are being coached by one of the world's leading figures in your field of endeavour?

I draw this analogy to explain how 'success' is the protégé of 'failure' — meaning that success is coached by failure. There is no shame in that, simply because that is the natural and honourable process of achievement. I find it odd when people try desperately to hide their failures. Whenever someone is trying to pitch for my business, I want to hear about their failed projects so that I can garner information about their relationship with failure.

If winning is all that matters, then spare a thought for those who fail

Perhaps the taboo emerges because people burden the word 'failure' with unworthy descriptors, such as incompetence, mismanagement, blunder, disaster, misfortune, and bad luck. Although such descriptors can play a part in causing failure, it is important to note that failure can also occur in their absence.

I once designed a poster that read, 'If winning is all that matters, then spare a thought for those who fail.' I wanted people to treat failure with respect. It is not shameful to try one's best and to miss the mark. To me, failure is the process by which we can learn to succeed. In fact, it is the only process through which we can greet success honourably. A friend of mine once said to me, 'If you haven't learned the hard way, you haven't learned the right way.'

The only time that I criticise failure is when it is brought on by incompetence or stupidity. Bungled projects and inexcusable slip-ups are not something that I take to kindly. Ignorance, stubbornness, myopia, and sheer laziness are not qualities that I tolerate. These aside, I do praise those heroes who give it their best shot and inject their blood, sweat, and tears into a project, even if they fail. The lessons that they would have learned would be valuable additions to a company's intellectual property.

If you pull people off the team on the basis of their failures, you would be setting yourself up for another round of failure

In battle, as in business, if you pull people off the team on the basis of their failures, you would be setting yourself up for another round of failure — except that this time around, it would be called a 'disaster'. If you strip your team of those who have learned the hard lessons, you stand to repeat your setbacks.

Part of the reason that we do not know how to celebrate failure comes from the ways in which we discuss 'winning' and 'losing' in the context of sport.

For example, in tennis, I find it totally unreasonable that we can bring two world-class players together on the court, and broadcast their match to millions of people around the world who watch some magnificent tennis and a splendid display of human agility, stamina, and dexterity, only to declare one of them the *loser*. In some sports, we can watch a nerve-racking match snatched by only one point! What does that really say about how well we value talent and how we respect people's abilities? Instead of enjoying a day of tennis or cricket magic, we have to applaud a barbaric process of eliminating one player or one team — whereby the winner is the 'champion' and the runner-up is forgotten.

The Olympic Games makes a mockery of winning and losing. Every four years we assemble the cream of the world's athletes, only to humiliate <u>most</u> of them

The Olympic Games makes a further mockery of winning and losing. Every four years we assemble the cream of the world's athletes, only to humiliate *most* of them. They go home shattered and despondent because they 'lost'. They might have lost by only one 1000th of a second, but apparently, that is just not good enough! It is dandy to promote sportsmanship, but what about the losers? They are not given lucrative speaking engagements or sponsorship deals. There is no media exposure or publishing contracts for those who were one hair-width behind the first place-getter. Why do we do this to ourselves?

I am concerned about grand-final events that endorse the 'them and us' attitude and create unhealthy international rivalry. Why must sports teams be labelled by 'country'?

For some players, national pride weighs heavily upon their shoulders as they fret about how they will face the savages back home who could (as they sometimes have been known to) kill players who disgrace their nation. I saw a documentary about a bobsled team that contemplated suicide as an alternative to going home without the gold medal. In the luge events (derived from the French word for sled), competitors are timed to 1000th of a second. Can you comprehend how one second can be split into one thousand moments, of which only one millisecond will decide the winner? In sport, *money* and *pride* are alternating motivators. Unfortunately, they have both been known to ignite wars, and I am not sure which is the lesser evil!

Here is another example of the 'them and us' attitude in sport. When a sailing team wins the America's Cup race, people applaud the winning country, whether it be America, Australia, or New Zealand. What happens if the skipper and the crew of the winning team were headhunted to sail for Switzerland? Does that not make a mockery of the whole notion of national boundaries? We also see this in football and in Formula One motor racing, as players are lured by money to play for the country of their choice.

On the day of this year's football grand final, my eight-year-old niece asked me, 'Who are you going for?' She wanted to know which team I wanted to win. I said, 'I don't mind who wins, so long as it is a great game to watch.' She insisted that I had to cheer for one team, and in effect, wish that the other would lose. She sat there encouraging her side, while jeering the opposing players and wishing that they would fumble. This type of behaviour is macabre. We are teaching children to wish ill upon others for no reason at all. People hope that their team wins, and that the other team loses. If the

If the only way that we can feel good about ourselves is by wishing failure on others, we have much healing to attend to

only way that we can feel good about ourselves is by wishing failure on others, we have much healing to attend to.

Disregarding that warped sense of achievement, and if we concentrate on the importance and value of failure in our own life, we can start to understand that failure is an integral part of success. We must snap out of the delusion that failure is an embarrassment or a taboo. Success without failure is not possible for innovators. We must learn to embrace failure as earnestly as we desire success.

We must snap out of the delusion that failure is an embarrassment or a taboo. Success without failure is not possible for innovators. We must learn to embrace failure as earnestly as we desire success.

| PERSONAL QUALITY # 10 • TENSION |

Tension is not an external evil force. Rather, it is a tool that can be used to inject extra power into a cerebral challenge. Tension is to the mind, what muscle is to the body.

It would be incorrect to say that executives should be able to 'handle' tension. It is not a hot potato that must be dealt with. It is a vital ingredient that provides alertness. Therefore, it is not a question of *handling* tension, but of having the ability to *generate* it in sufficient doses to serve an important purpose.

Skilled managers can generate tension for their *own* use, and also ignite it in *others*. Carefully channelled, tension is an effective way to focus the mind. If it were ignited in people who do not have a common purpose and who are not able to take direction from the leader, it would be like an orchestra without a conductor. Mind you, beware the manipulators who ignite tension to maintain friction between people.

When you can learn to use tension as a positive tool, you might be tempted to increase the pressure from time to time. So long as you do this to a well-oiled team, you will become a force to be reckoned with. On the other hand, do not apply too much pressure within an environment where the players cannot cope with it. Choose your people well, and ensure that they have the mental, physical, and psychological fitness to cope with the adrenalin.

| **PERSONAL QUALITY # 11 • EXTREMITY** |

We presume that 'extremists' are fundamentalists who will stop at nothing and take no prisoners. That would be an inaccurate loading on the meaning of the word. Leaders know that life is far too precious to hover around mediocrity. I have never liked advice that urged me to do all things in *moderation*. Although it sounds like a sensible maxim, it tolerates inferiority and offers flexibility that soon becomes indecision.

Life is far too precious to hover around mediocrity

If you are going to do something, do it to the best level that you possibly can, and go all the way. Dancing around the edges will not produce the laser-sharp results to which top-level executives are accustomed because they are extremists. They put their heart and soul into every project they undertake. They reduce any unnecessary activities and do everything else with a sense of purpose. Whether it be writing a letter, launching a product, starting a business, or inviting friends to dinner, they leave no stone unturned in their efforts to make every moment a memorable and worthwhile encounter with life.

Admittedly, extremity in unwholesome pursuits will destroy one's foundations. For that reason, many people tend to steer clear of extremity for fear of overstepping their mark and demolishing their hard-earned position. A mature person uses 'discipline' to guard against self-destructive behaviour. If self-discipline is not protecting you from insalubrious temptations, you will destroy your empire in due course. The warning here is: you cannot join the ranks of the elite until you know how to

You cannot join the ranks of the elite until you know how to live the life of an extremist

live the life of an extremist; but you must never engage in powerful forces if you cannot protect yourself from yourself.

| PERSONAL QUALITY # 12 • AGGRESSIVENESS |

Ask your friends to demonstrate how an aggressive person might behave, and no doubt you will be treated to a display of unpleasant tantrums and abuse. It is a shame that some words conjure undesirable images. Aggressiveness has been unjustly detained in the sin bin.

Entrepreneurs know aggressiveness to mean 'resolute action at high speed'. Its opposite is called 'hesitation'. As any successful leader will tell you, hesitation spells destruction and defeat. When an aeroplane encounters turbulence, the pilot *increases* the plane's speed. This steadies the craft as it forces its way through unwelcome opposition.

Here is another example of what hesitation can do to an organisation. Imagine a long stretch of road with a hundred cars, all travelling in a single file and at high speed. If the car in front slams on the brakes to slow down to only half the speed and then immediately accelerates so that it reaches its original speed within five seconds, what do you suppose would happen to the cars at the back of the convoy? In fact, that slight hesitation by the car in front causes cars near the back to come to a complete standstill. A minor hesitation by the car at the head of the pack only wipes five or so seconds off the travel time for that car, whereas for every car behind, the delay increases to the point of a total standstill — presuming that no accidents occur as a result of each car having to slam on its brakes to cope with the sudden change in the flow of traffic.

An aggressive leader understands what a simple hiccup can do, and as a result, is averse to slowing down. The loss of *momentum* becomes a most costly burden to absorb. Although momentum is powerful and efficient, it is energy-intensive to generate. Aggressive people know what they want, and they go all out to get it. It is not a question of stubbornness or myopia. It has nothing to do with greed or inconsideration. It is all about careful assessment and unyielding determination being applied, when no other alternative could secure the desired outcome within the window of opportunity.

| PERSONAL QUALITY # 13 • JUDGEMENT |

'Don't judge people . . . ' 'Don't be judgemental . . . ' We have all heard these admonitions, which are meant to discourage us from being harsh or rash in our assessments of others. A judgemental person is thought to be unreasonable. In fact, ninety percent of the executives surveyed for this chapter told me that they rely on judgement to prevent them from drowning in data. They operate at such high speeds, and engage in so many projects simultaneously, that they could not survive if they did not make judgements about the inputs they receive.

An imperfect decision executed quickly maintains momentum. It is always preferred over a perfect decision that grinds everything to a halt.

Intuition plays a big part in supporting judgemental behaviour. The other major contributor is an ability to *discern* between useful and unreliable information.

A judgemental person focuses on improving the inputs, rather than challenging the information. Although not all decisions can be perfect, leaders know that they must be disciplined to make decisions with the available data. If they wait until perfect data becomes available, chances are that too many elements would have changed, rendering the decision obsolete or untimely. An imperfect decision executed quickly maintains momentum. It is always preferred over a perfect decision that grinds everything to a halt.

| **PERSONAL QUALITY # 14 • AUDACITY** |

Although 'bravery' sounds like a gallant quality, 'audacity' takes a bit of getting used to. It involves boldness and daring, and requires you to do things that you would normally feel uncomfortable doing. If it seems embarrassing, you might be getting closer to audacity. It is all about doing what has to be done.

The interesting aspect about this personal attribute is that when you are being audacious, almost no-one notices, because it does not relate to what you do to others, but to what you do to yourself — meaning that you force yourself to step outside your comfort zone.

Bravery requires you to find the courage to do what you know you ought to do. Audacity requires that you find the nerve to do what you normally tell yourself that you should not do.

Bravery requires you to find the courage to do what you know you ought to do. Audacity requires that you find the nerve to do what you normally tell yourself that you should not do.

| PERSONAL QUALITY # 15 • INTOLERANCE|

By all accounts, tolerance and patience are endearing qualities that contribute to peace and harmony. They are supposedly useful when combined with calmness to enhance communication. This is true if your environment is isolated from external forces and immune from energy-sappers. If you have to battle competitive forces, and if time is a luxury that you cannot afford, you have to learn the art of *intolerance* and *impatience*.

In the same way that 'failure' does not refer to incompetence, 'intolerance' does not refer to rudeness.

Timing operates within a law of its own. Timing is non-negotiable, because each window of opportunity has its own justifications. This means that if you want to seize opportunities as they arise, you need to be able to act in accordance with the law of timing. This might mean that certain decisions have to be made within specific and merciless time constraints. For this reason, you must make decisions with split-second precision, and that means you cannot allow others to slow you down. Intolerance towards those who stand in your way, or who threaten your chances of 'catching the wave', becomes the sensible approach that leads to success.

There is a point beyond which patience becomes useless

Do not confuse intolerance with impatience. When you can be certain that results can be achieved in the fullness of time, it would be prudent to exercise patience, because this will enable you to wait for the right moment. On the other hand, you would be reckless if you waited patiently for something that could never eventuate within the required time frame. Patience and impatience are decisions that relate to one's ability to discern between what is possible and what is impossible within certain parameters. There is a point beyond which patience becomes useless. For example, waiting patiently for a taxi to take you to the airport might be reasonable, but only to the point where you do not miss your flight.

Intolerance ought to be a premeditated state, not a knee-jerk reaction to displeasure. For example, if a friend borrowed $1000 from you and did not repay the loan, what would you do if your friend asked you for a *second* loan of $1000? What would you do if your friend asked for a *third* $1000 and made another hollow promise to repay it? An intolerant person would have already set the boundaries so that action could be taken to prevent abuse. It is preferable to stop situations occurring, than to try to rectify them *after* they have occurred. Intolerance is a calculation, not a reaction.

Intolerance is a calculation, not a reaction

Sometimes we use the term 'tolerance' in relation to equipment. We might refer to a rope having a tolerance of 300 kilograms. This means that the rope cannot hold a weight greater than 300 kilograms. The term is used to refer to predefined limits. A person who has predefined limits is one who knows what to do when certain situations arise. Intolerance is used as a protective barrier to trigger decision processes that have been carefully considered. This requires conviction to act when the limits have been reached. By the way, this is a personal characteristic rarely found in gamblers. They cannot quit while they are ahead, even though they enter a casino with the intention that they will cash in their chips if they have a big win. Unfortunately, their tolerance is so flexible that they do not stop until they have no choice.

HEAD OF A TIGER

Many people engineer a career based around the concept of being the 'tail of a tiger', working for an employer. Others choose to be the 'head of a chicken', operating a small business. Members of the elite minority look to become the 'head of a tiger', where they occupy the top job at a large corporation or start their own sizeable business. If you wish to become the 'head of a tiger', you need special personal attributes, including the unpopular and little-understood qualities of obstinacy, relinquishment, irresponsibility, preparedness, secrecy, deception, doubt, distrust, failure, tension, extremity, aggressiveness, judgement, audacity, and intolerance. These are personal skills that top-level executives tend to rely on for their business success.

Once you have mastered these attributes, you might like to explore ways in which you can live a zestful and enchanting life beyond your business concerns. To do so, you need to learn about the meaning of spirituality, valour, acuity, and perspicacity. Remember that knowing the *meaning* of words is not good enough. You need to know what each word *feels* like and *tastes* like.

Finally, never lose sight of the meaning of life and the value of living. Exceptional success is only achieved when you use your creativity to *enrich* your life. Along the way, be sure to walk alongside compassion, to play awhile with humour, to relax upon the bank of contentment, to sleep next to forgiveness, to rise to greet charm, and, in all things, to make learning your partner. When you do these things, you will be successful because you will understand that expertise is about knowing what to do when the rules run out. **S**

Expertise is about knowing what to do when the rules run out

PART FIVE

HANDLING *your* BOSS

*Those for whom philosophy is useless are those
who do not understand philosophy*

CHAPTER 18

OVER *my* DEAD BODY

IN THE LINE OF DUTY

*Angels rush from heaven to help those
who are engaged in a just fight*

I N THE WORKPLACE, the ill-conceived concept of 'consensus management' seeks to solicit everyone's *opinion* and then it tries to obtain everyone's consent. Managers are told that seeking opinion is *inclusive* and seeking consent is *democratic*. Managers who do not consult with others are accused of being dictators or autocrats.

We have conditioned our society to believe that if enough of us agree with certain information, then that information must be true; and if the majority disagrees with it, it must be false. We have reduced truth and justice to a democratic vote. Surely truth is not to be insulted by opinion — meaning that truth is not a question of popularity or expedience. Similarly, justice is not to be impaired by judgement — meaning that justice is not a question of proof and explanation.

When it comes to the notion of *agreement* and *disagreement,* people find it difficult to process information *neutrally;* meaning that they cannot help but judge, grade, rank, and categorise information.

This chapter outlines the burdens of acting on information that is presented to employees by the boss. Workers seem to think that if they disagree with the boss, it would be reason enough to mount a challenge. Workers presume that modern participatory approaches (fuelled by diplomacy and democracy gone mad) give them licence to challenge authority.

Some modern workers belong to the new order of liberated employees who have the temerity to defy their manager's decisions. Their behaviour ventures into the land of *disrespect* and borders on *recalcitrance.* Such liberated employees are more aptly called 'detached' employees who do not understand the bigger picture. They have no respect for authority — especially for managers whom they genuinely despise. Detached employees are a nuisance because they equate *authority* with *admiration* and mistake *position* with *popularity.*

If you are an employee who desires to do your best for your career, you need to start to do your best for your boss. The typical outcry is, 'How can I respect a boss who isn't deserving of such respect?' This can be overcome when you realise three things. First, when you do your best for your boss, you are in fact doing your best for your own sake. This does not mean that you should appease the boss just to receive favours or dodge scorn. It refers to the building of excellence through the daily delivery of excellence. Would champion swimmers protest against their unpleasant coach by reducing their speed while training? If you hold back your best, you are cheating yourself.

If you are an employee who desires to do your best for your career, you need to start to do your best for your boss

Second, I am not casting judgement about whether or not your boss deserves your loyalty. It is not a question of the *person* or the *personality*, but one of *position* and *office*. You might not respect your boss 'the person', but you must respect your boss 'the office bearer'. For example, when citizens salute their national flag, are they saluting the piece of cloth? Surely they are declaring their support to their constitution, to their form of government, to their leaders, and to their laws. When urged to respect the boss, employees are being urged to pay respect to the 'position' because it is their duty to pay *attention*, to give *respect*, and to provide *loyalty*.

Third, it is incumbent upon you to earn your right to demand respect and loyalty from your subordinates by behaving respectfully and loyally to your boss. Otherwise, on what basis would you be able to exercise your powers over your current or future subordinates?

IN THE LINE OF DUTY

As an employee, your first loyalty is to your boss, regardless of whether or not your boss is deserving of your attention and commitment. Even if you have to contend with an incompetent manager, you must deliver on your commitments. Avoid the temptation to treat bad bosses badly.

Are you honest with some people while dishonest with others? If so, what does that make you? Are you pleasant to some colleagues yet vulgar to others? What does that say about you?

Integrity is not something that can be applied selectively. Virtue is not a tool that can be called upon randomly. Honour is not a façade that can be erected arbitrarily. Loyalty is not a gift that can be given discriminatingly.

Integrity is not something that can be applied selectively. Virtue is not a tool that can be called upon randomly.

For beauty to exude, it must be all encompassing. For professionalism to survive, it must be un-deviating. If you allow another person's ethics to dictate your behaviour, you lack conviction. If you can be swayed by your manager's moods or values, you lack your own direction.

Excellence as an employee must be your aim, regardless of your manager's station in life. Would Michelangelo have painted a less stunning ceiling at the Sistine Chapel if he disliked his master? In fact, his master did torment him, but he did not allow that to affect his craft.

When you work, you must give your all, not so that your boss can be pleased, but so that you can grow. Michelangelo was not enthusiastic about leaving his projects to start on the Sistine Chapel. He had a team of painters assigned to work with him. He could have made his life easy by delegating the whole job to his workers. Instead, he dismissed them all because they were not achieving his level of workmanship, and he decided to paint the ceiling single-handedly in order to maintain the quality he demanded. He would neither compromise his craft nor allow others to lower his standards.

EYES ARE WATCHING

Incongruence shatters careers and reputations. By giving your best to your boss, you can fulfil your ethical and professional contracts. By exerting every bit of energy, you can work with a clear conscience. By adding value, you can claim your position. By working conscientiously, you will grow and enrich yourself. By immersing yourself in your craft and by doing a superb job, you are earning the right to demand the same diligence from your future subordinates.

If, along the road to high office, your colleagues see nothing more from you than a dubious demeanour, how can they take you seriously? What you serve upwards is what your staff will believe to be permissible. Beware that you do not lose your authority by your very actions. Your complete loyalty is not only scrutinised by your superiors, it is also observed by your subordinates and peers. When climbing the corporate ladder, do not allow your ambition to blind you. A fixation on the next promotion could easily lead to carelessness, which in turn guarantees your failure.

A fixation on the next promotion could easily lead to carelessness, which in turn guarantees your failure

EARNING RESPECT, BUYING LOYALTY

There is a lot of debate about whether respect can be 'demanded'. The traditional maxim suggests that people *earn* respect. It is not a question of the boss earning respect or buying loyalty. Employees who draw a salary of any kind are obliged to respect the organisation's hierarchy, its assets, its shareholders, and its customers. If employees cannot exercise their duty completely, how can they ethically command a salary?

Employees who have been lumbered with a bad boss seem to think that their manager's unacceptable behaviour gives them the right to withdraw their services. Can you see the irony in this state of affairs? It sets in motion a situation that inevitably leads to an environment depleted of energy and devoid of hope.

THE CHAIN OF COMMAND

There are many schools of thought about how managers ought to construct their team. I agree with a manager I once knew (whom we will call Bill) who disapproved of anyone going over his head. He made his position clear and supported his staff in their efforts to exercise the same discipline among their subordinates. He would welcome anyone into his office, and he would be happy to discuss any issue with any staff member. Regardless, everyone knew that Bill was a stickler for the chain of command. If other divisional managers called him to complain about a decision that one of his product managers had made, he would listen to each complaint and then assure the caller that he would put their case forward for consideration by his subordinate. He always made it clear that he would leave the final decision to the product manager in question. At no point did he intervene to change an employee's decision.

His product managers knew that he backed them. If he strongly disagreed, he would let them know. They had a solid relationship that enabled him to show his disapproval without them feeling that he was forcing them to change their mind. They respected and supported one another.

There came a time when Bill was interstate, and one of his advertising managers (whom we will call Jane) decided to go over his head to complain to the CEO about a promotions brief that Bill had stipulated. The creative director at the advertising agency was not in favour of Bill's ideas, so he encouraged Jane to convince the CEO that urgent modifications needed to be made in Bill's absence. Upon his return, Bill heard about the incident and asked the CEO to reverse the decision. Later that afternoon, Jane lost her job. The agency was also dismissed for encouraging the escalation.

There were several precedents that could not be allowed to progress. Drastic measures had to be taken. The greatest error of managers is when they say one thing, but do another. It is also an error to harbour dissention in the ranks. Things could have been different if Jane had gone to Bill and said, 'I know that you have your heart set on this campaign, but I believe that you are wrong. I need you to give me the authority to take charge of this project because I know that I'll be able to deliver a better outcome.' If she were half as clever as she thought she was, she would have stood her ground on professional terms, not on mutinous terms. All his subordinates knew that he would back them, come what may. Unfortunately, Jane deviated beyond her limits, and she committed professional suicide.

Do not commit such unforgivable sins within your workplace. Even if you get away with it, it remains unethical. If you wish to climb the ladder, you must do so ethically. As an employee, your duty is to your boss. You need to do everything you can to support the person to whom you report. Naturally, this is a difficult decision for those who have more than one boss. This is a problem that is plaguing the corporate world. It is brought about through the hideous practice of *matrix management*. If you have more than one boss to contend with, you need to seek unequivocal clarification, otherwise, urgently engineer yourself out of that environment. Matrix management is your ticket to hell. A whole chapter is dedicated to this subject in *How to Lose Friends and Infuriate People*.

DEALING WITH TYRANTS

What should employees do about incompetent managers who act like tyrants? If you are an employee, one universal rule is that you must never go over your manager's head. Although I disapprove of dictatorships, I understand that the work environment is not a sovereign political environment. Do not confuse how a country should be run, with how an organisation should be run. Although social dictatorships are ugly, organisational dictatorships are not evil. Managers have the responsibility to undertake certain projects, and to do so, they need to engage the services of workers in the form of staff, contractors, suppliers, or consultants.

Although social dictatorships are ugly, organisational dictatorships are not evil

The only time when it is permissible to go over your manager's head is when you know that your boss is acting illegally. If it becomes a question of law, you are obliged to inform your manager's manager, unless you believe that the corruption stems from the top — in which case you need to inform the appropriate authorities.

Some organisations that subscribe to the concept of 'the open door policy' confuse that to mean 'anything goes'. An open door policy works best when it encourages communication between employees of differing rank. It does not condone the loosening of the chain of command.

Abusive bosses need to be dealt with one-on-one. If your boss is rude or scathing, it is up to you to make an appointment and set out the rules under which you are prepared to work. If your efforts do not yield results, you need to find ways to engineer yourself out of the organisation. Under no circumstances are you to go over your manager's head to complain. The main reason for this advice is that you need to learn to stand up for yourself and to fight your own battles. If you cannot go to your manager and express your concerns about the way you are being treated, it means that you are not using the power within yourself to protect yourself.

As an employee, you are not a slave. You are providing services at a price. If you fear speaking up for yourself, you need to revisit your understanding about what value you are adding, and what services you are selling. No-one is doing you a favour by employing you. Employers need employees just as much as employees need the work. Even though everyone is dispensable, that is not a good reason to give the keys to your confidence and to your happiness to the boss from hell. The employment contract works both ways.

When you have to contend with a boss from hell, take care to strategise well. Learn when and how to fight the battles. For example, if your boss becomes abusive in front of your colleagues, you would rarely gain an advantage by hitting back with a snide remark. The moment you retaliate or react unfavourably, no matter how justified you might be, you throw down the gauntlet and signal to your manager that you are prepared to lock horns. I advise you to remain calm and to adopt the disposition of a respectful employee. Fights are won and lost on the thrust of timing, not justice. By reacting in public, you stand to lose in more ways than one. Therefore, take what is being dished out in public,

Fights are won and lost on the thrust of timing, not justice

remain calm, try to understand the insidious psychology behind your manager's stupidity, and consider your position. Then, in private, you can make your position clear. You can approach your boss at the appropriate moment and say something like, 'Out of respect for your seniority, I didn't react to the way you treated me yesterday. However, I want you to know that my agreeing to provide you with loyalty and respect doesn't give you licence to treat me abusively. So I want your assurance that this will not happen again. I'm not employed here to absorb that type of behaviour.'

Before you can win a battle, you need to understand its parameters. Your boss might not have meant to direct the fury at you, but used you as the buffer. This is a common strategy among immature fighters. Sometimes, what someone is directing at 'you' is really for someone else's ears. This is inexcusable, but it can happen. Therefore, there is no point in you taking exception to someone's immaturity or inadequacy. By fighting back, you could be triggering a fight that was never intended. Although there is no excusing rudeness and abuse, what would you stand to gain by trying to change the habit of a lifetime? It is not your duty to 'teach

A smart warrior conserves energy and picks the right moments to fight the important battles

your boss a lesson'. Surely you have better things to do with your energy. A smart warrior conserves energy and picks the right moments to fight the important battles. Besides, a public showdown of that sort relies on rank, and is often lost on the basis of rank. Your manager's superiors might find it difficult to back you, for fear of signalling that they condone your insolence. Duels of this nature are often reduced to bravado, ego, showmanship, and precedence — all fought in murky waters.

En garde

Remember that your worst enemies are those who do not make themselves known to you. Do not blind yourself with petty fights of principle if they are nothing more than energy-sapping distractions. Learn to tune your radar to spot the conniving and manipulating boss whose warm and friendly personality is a decoy. Distractions and decoys are the oldest tricks in the book. Do not let your guard down to someone who seems to be overly friendly. Whatever the situation might be, trust no-one. I know that this is a harsh and terrible thing to say. I wish life were simpler. Unfortunately, you just never know who is capable of what. It takes time, observation, and experience to know who you can trust. Fostering a delightful trusting relationship takes a great deal of nurturing.

Remember that your worst enemies are those who do not make themselves known to you

Many movies have used human betrayal as the central theme. Distractions are the cornerstone of offensive combat. The precepts of unarmed combat emphasise the use of distraction to penetrate the enemy's shield.

Your boss from hell might well be disguised as the unassuming friend who plots behind your back to locate your weaknesses and to prey on them. For example, it is not uncommon for senior scoundrels to snoop on employees' e-mails and telephone calls to amass a dossier of embarrassing or compromising information that could be used to apply pressure. Beware the flattering telephone call from a head-hunter who convinces you to meet for a chat. It has been known for head-hunters to be used to trap employees into showing their preponderance to contemplate external opportunities. A friend of mine once let a

334

head-hunter stroke his ego and extract his résumé. When he returned to the office, his manager asked him about his 'fling'. He was forced to admit that he had put his hat into the ring for another job. This compromised his position, and weakened his argument for a promotion. 'How can I promote someone who is not fully committed to this company?' exclaimed his manager. What my friend did not know at the time was that he was a victim of entrapment. It was all a dirty game masterminded by the manager to throw him off guard so as to put him on the back foot. For ideas on handling difficult managers, see Chapter 19, 'The boss from hell'.

PLAYING POLITICS

It is interesting to observe how the word 'politics' is used. During job interviews, candidates tend to say that they do not like playing politics. In this context, it is seen as a dirty word. Yet, as we learn more about life, we realise that it is a naïve thing to say because politics is an integral part of human interaction.

One of my managers believed that employees who did not engage in workplace politics were weak. He said, 'Anyone who does not play politics is either lying or stupid. If you want to develop your career, you need to use politics as a tool.' The confusion about this advice comes from the duality of the term 'politics'. For example, 'leader' is seen in two ways, depending on who one thinks of when the word is uttered. If it is used to describe a wholesome person who carves a new path for the world, it is seen as a noble quality. Yet, when it is associated with oppressive dictators, the word loses its appeal. Likewise, politics

Anyone who does not play politics is either lying or stupid

can be seen as either a dirty game that scoundrels play, or as part of a strategy to rightly protect and advance one's position.

Executives who do not understand corporate politics are like defence personnel who do not understand combat

Executives who do not understand corporate politics are like defence personnel who do not understand combat. *Politics is the peacetime tool used to protect one's power bases.*

While protecting *your* career, be sure to play by the rules. A renegade cannot find refuge behind the might of justice. If you are seen to undermine your manager's power and authority, watch out! **W**

CHAPTER 19

THE *boss* FROM HELL

FLYING WITH EAGLES WHILE SWIMMING WITH SHARKS

*If you don't understand your self-worth,
it's like having a box full of trinkets
and you throw out all the diamonds
in search of a penny*

IF YOU THINK THAT TAXIS are hard to find on a rainy day, try looking for one in the United States on the eve of Independence Day. After waiting two hours, and trying every kind of transport (even wedding car companies) to get back to my hotel, a taxi company took pity on me and sent a driver who was nearby training a new recruit.

The traffic was moving at a snail's pace. Eventually, as we neared an exit ramp, the veteran driver decided to dash into the right-hand lane to grab an opportunity to get out of the traffic jam. Everything the driver did was, in my assessment, reasonable and safe. Unfortunately, a state trooper who was parked by the side of the road did not approve of the manoeuvre. He pulled us over, stomped across to the driver's door, yanked it open, and started shouting obscenities. The driver followed his instructions and got out of the car, only to be further verbally abused by the trooper, who was obviously demented. I could not believe that anyone would strap a pistol to this maniac's waist.

When the driver returned to the car, he looked shaken and close to tears. I waited until he had settled before I asked him what he thought about the trooper's behaviour. To my amazement, he did not seem to think it was excessive. He said it was not unusual, and that people had come to expect that kind of treatment from law enforcement officials. He did not think he had done anything wrong in changing lanes, but he would pay the fine. 'That's how the system works,' he said.

The driver then asked me what I thought about the incident. I said that if the American public found such behaviour acceptable, the country would go to ruin. The trooper's violence and his abusive manner were one blink away from flashpoint. If the driver had so much as breathed at the wrong time, I would not have been surprised if the trooper had assaulted him physically. Yet, the driver did not want to lodge a complaint about the incident.

I encouraged him to take the matter to the authorities, and convinced him that we could not hope for a better future if people did not stand up and fight against that type of treatment. He was a forty-year-old family man who did not feel he had the power to change the system.

I gave him my contact details in case he wanted to use me as a witness. I did not tell him that I was an author on tour, lest he ask me the name of my book. He might have concluded that I was setting him up to lose friends and infuriate the police force! What I said to him must have weighed on his mind, because several days later, he contacted me and asked me to help him to make an official complaint.

The trooper had felt empowered to abuse the public because he had several weapons at his disposal: a gun in his holster; restraining devices strapped to his belt; and a badge that gave him the power to make other people's lives miserable while feeding his own ego. He was the trooper from hell.

The boss from hell uses similar weapons to intimidate employees and suppliers. Egotistical managers draw strength from their title and their position. They hand out fines in the form of reprimand notices, and engage in 'wrongful arrests' by threatening people with dismissal. Bosses from hell are usually small-minded people who would never get away with terrorising others if it were not for the power their title bestowed upon them. If they were ever stripped of their rank, their colleagues would eat them alive.

THE MIND BOGGLES

Whenever I meet abusive bosses, I try to fathom how they achieved their position of authority. Why does no-one put a stop to their oppressive behaviour? Why do staff members put up with it? How can people be so destructive? Do they know what effect they have on their organisation?

Over the years, I have come to better understand the issues surrounding abusive managers, and I have been able to categorise managers into several types. More importantly, I discovered some ways to handle them, or at least to minimise the impact of their actions on me. This chapter focuses on how the boss from hell operates, and what employees can do to shelter themselves from the fallout.

WHERE THERE'S ONE, THERE ARE TWO

I once managed to catch a rat at a community hall, and I boasted to the council rangers that I had solved their rat problem. One of them said, 'Where there's one rat, there's likely to be another.'

It is much the same in business. A manager who is prone to shouting at employees is likely to have a shouter as a boss. A mean-spirited boss probably treats subordinates in a way that senior executives have indicated is acceptable behaviour. This tends to answer the question about how the boss from hell can get away with sadistic conduct. When the chain of command is infested with the same disease, no-one in the chain finds it abhorrent to abuse staff members because the behaviour is considered normal and acceptable.

A talented boss can take average employees and turn them into superstars, whereas an abusive boss can turn superstars into a loose confederation of warring egomaniacs

When a company allows bad managers to flourish, its staff members lose respect for it. They start to mistreat the company's assets as a form of retaliation.

They might even believe that the boss from hell has some sort of a stranglehold on the senior manager. How else can employees justify the company's inaction?

Although staff members are *not* 'a company's greatest asset' (because employees do not *belong* to the company), they can make or break a company. Therefore any staff member who can *lose* a customer, must be treated with the same respect as any staff member who can *win* a customer. A talented boss can take average employees and turn them into superstars, whereas an abusive boss can turn superstars into a loose confederation of warring egomaniacs who will undoubtedly spearhead the organisation's demise.

DR JEKYLL AND MR HYDE

For years, organisations have tested job candidates in the hope of assessing their aptitude, intelligence, and personality. Remarkably, all the tests in the world will not alert them to a potential boss from hell. Such people are skilled at deceiving others with an acceptable 'front', while at the same time manipulating people and situations to their own advantage. Employees then feel helpless, convinced that no-one understands what is really going on.

There are cases where battered wives have resorted to murdering their abuser. Who of us can really understand the torment that must have led to such a desperate act? How many times had the women tried, but failed, to make other people understand what was happening?

In the work environment, few 'battered' employees would resort to *physical* violence when the hierarchy makes unsympathetic remarks like, 'Don't take it personally. Try to ignore your manager's tantrums and just do your job'. Instead, employees feel helpless and alone. In such cases, frustrations manifest into depression or into self-destructive behaviours.

THE FIRST CUT IS THE DEEPEST

The first interaction between people, sets the tone for all later personal dealings between them. In other words, if you start out on the wrong foot with your boss, it is not likely to improve.

It is advisable to practise what you would say and how you would react to an abusive boss. If you are ill-prepared, you could fail in your first encounter if it takes you by surprise. A friend of mine told me of how disappointed he was with himself when two young thugs accosted him in a dark street and demanded money. He said that he froze and, feeling defence-less, meekly handed over his wallet. He later realised that they were no match for him, and regretted doing nothing to defend himself. That kind of shock has a similar mesmerising effect on people in the workforce. When a new boss arrives on the scene and starts to intimidate the staff, few people react appropriately or are able to defend themselves effectively. If you do not stand up for yourself at your first encounter with bullies, you will lose ground that you might never be able to recover.

No response would be suitable for all situations. For example, if you decide that you will always 'give back as good as you get', you could risk perpetuating a culture of aggression within the organisation. Try instead to develop a repertoire of responses, designed to show that you will not allow others to intimidate you.

Here are twenty of the most prevalent categories of abusive managers, along with some tips on how to handle each type.

1) The absent-minded

This is the boss who asks you to do something, and then denies knowing anything about it. One solution could be to write a 'contact report' after every meeting, noting the details of the conversation with your boss and anything you were asked to do. This is common in the advertising industry between agencies and their clients. It is like keeping minutes of a meeting. In addition, submit weekly reports to your boss, outlining what you are doing and what your priorities are.

2) The anxious

It is amazing how one person's feelings can affect a whole organisation. The anxious boss is like a buzzing bee in a jar — heaps of energy is expended with little result. Anxiety burns up a lot of energy without giving any direction or adding any value. The distracting nature of anxiety ensures that everyone remains in a state of distress. It also keeps people preoccupied with peripheral technicalities to the point where they are unable to perform their core duties.

> *Anxiety burns up a lot of energy without giving any direction or adding any value*

I used to think that the best way to handle anxious bosses was to remain calm, so that I would not be drawn into their unproductive behaviour. Anxious bosses are worried about what could go wrong, and they do not feel comforted by what is taking place. Their anxiety tends to stem from the feeling that no-one cares enough, and no-one is doing enough. One solution could be to explain *what* you are doing, *how* you are doing it, and what *contingencies* you have in place, and to make it clear that you, too, care about achieving a successful result. If all you do is remain calm without giving assurances, your boss is likely to become more distressed, perceiving that you do not care about, or are unaware of, the potential hazards.

3) The avenger

This boss is not one to let an incident pass. The overwhelming distraction for this boss is the feeling that justice must be done. Those who cross an avenger will regret it. The avenger's idea of sweet revenge is not in attaining success, but in casting misery upon those whom the avenger dislikes or perceives as a threat.

> The avenger's idea of sweet revenge is not in attaining success, but in casting misery upon those whom the avenger dislikes

Such bosses cannot be trusted. Cover your tracks carefully and keep good records. The 'electric fence strategy' works well here. When avengers come anywhere near you, zap them every single time. Although it will infuriate them, and it could inflame the situation, they need to know that every attempt they make to get at you will trigger an unpleasant response. If you do not show that you will not stand for their underhanded attempts to harm you, they will see you as an easy and alluring target, and they will not stop until they tear you down.

4) The awkward

A normal reaction from the subordinates of an awkward manager is to hold their head between their hands, shut their eyes, and take a deep breath. They feel helpless and disappointed that they should have to endure another round of ineffective execution, all because their manager cannot seem to do anything right. They know that the manager means well, but projects keep on missing the mark because the manager keeps dropping the ball.

One suggestion is for the staff to request more responsibility to ensure that the critical work gets done by those within the group who can function under pressure. The most important thing is to assure the manager that you are neither trying to steal the limelight nor trying to take the credit. All departmental success must be given to the manager. Otherwise, you will not be able to strike a deal.

The awkward manager is not necessarily a mean manager; rather, someone who wants to shine, and therefore pushes to the front to try to score every goal. Let the accolades go to your manager, and just concentrate on doing your part of the job well.

5) The bully

Most bullies do not realise what they are doing. Not all of them set out to harm people. They are merely doing what they have found to work. Bullies might be lacking in communications skills and might find it difficult to engage in any rigorous debate. Over the years, they have realised that their short fuse and impatience are effective in warding off those employees who might ask pertinent questions or mount reasonable challenges. Bullies cannot cope with any deviation from their plan. For that reason, they behave in such a way that no-one dares to question them. When employees exhibit discomfort, the bullies do not understand that their harsh treatment is causing pain. Instead, bullies presume that the employees are weak and therefore are unable to cope with the harsh realities of business.

The best way to confront bullies is with a stern will

346

I have found that the best way to confront bullies is with a stern will. Respond to them assertively, but do not stoop to using bad language, and do not defame them. Even bullies have feelings! Do not insult them or give them cause to think that you are attacking them personally. Instead, show them that you can talk their language. No matter how much they try to insult you, ignore the personal aspects of the conversation and fight back with a clear focus on the job at hand. They will soon realise that you want to understand their issues.

One powerful question to disarm bullies is, 'What is it you are trying to achieve?' Let them tell you what they want, and what they are trying to do. Then you can talk to them about what you plan to do to help them to achieve their goal. A 'good' bully (meaning someone who is not out to harm you, but simply to win) will find it refreshing to be able to communicate with someone about what they really what.

Be aware of the tactics that bullies might use to try and terminate a conversation. They will try to 'break' you so that you will become submissive. They might say, 'What I'm *trying* to do is get this machine fixed, but it is obvious that an idiot like you can't get anything done.' That type of statement is designed to ignite your anger. In responding to this type of attack, do not focus on the insult but on what you can do to get the machine fixed. A good response would be, 'By when do you want this machine fixed?'

If you are forced to work with bullies who *do* mean to harm and intimidate you, remain calm and unresponsive. When, later, you are being reprimanded for not having done what you were ordered to do, you can say calmly, 'When you can treat *me* like I treat *you*, I will happily get on with the job.' In this way, you are not attacking the bully personally, but merely explaining what works for you. If they want something done, you have given them the clue as to how they can get you to do it.

6) The bureaucrat

Although some people like the sound of their own voice, bureaucrats like the sight of their own reports. They feel safe and protected when they can follow procedures and back everything up with

Although some people like the sound of their own voice, bureaucrats like the sight of their own reports

sufficient studies and ample proof. Much like tightrope walkers who cannot muster the courage to perform without a safety net, bureaucrats see the administrative aspects of their work as their safety net. They do not necessarily enjoy amassing piles of paper and attending lots of meetings. Their pleasure comes from knowing that they are protecting their bases. This might have something to do with the bureaucrat having been caught out in the past when deviating from the rules.

The other type of bureaucrat to watch out for, is the one who plots and schemes to slow everything down to the point of inactivity. Such a person is trying to stop you from achieving success. That type of obfuscation can only be overcome if you can work out what the bureaucrat is threatening you with, and to whom you would be answerable if you were taken to task. For example, if you are held back by threats that your actions could land you in 'legal' difficulties, short-circuit that threat by speaking with the company's legal adviser to come to an agreement about your course of action.

The clever bureaucrat will always find a reason to tell you that your 100-page report is missing something. No matter how much information you submit, you will be told that you failed to include some vital data. In working with such people, I learned never to submit a full report in one go. I would submit, say, a five-page outline first, so that the bureaucrat could take pleasure in telling me which areas of the report needed to be expanded. I would then submit a ten-page outline to show my 'work in progress', so that my boss could see that the report was taking shape slowly and with due diligence. Only when my boss had approved the outline would I submit the entire report, knowing full well that, by then, almost everything had been discussed.

7) The deadly silent

It is up to you if you choose to be a silent brooder, but not if you are the boss. A boss has a duty to communicate. Hiding in one's shell and indicating displeasure or indifference can be frustrating for those who get the cold-shoulder treatment without knowing what the real reason is. Conscientious employees will be driven to distraction trying to fathom what made their boss unhappy. Deadly silent bosses might well be in a state of resignation; they might no longer care, so they cope with their dissatisfaction by disengaging from the business.

Rather than unsettle this type of boss with probing questions about what is wrong and why, take a step back and ask questions before you engage in a new project. Perhaps you could ask, 'What would you like to see as the outcome of this project?' If you can listen to what your boss requires, you will be in a better position to deliver a satisfactory result. Be sensitive to the communication process. If shyness is a compounding factor, try to communicate with your boss in writing, showing as many visuals, mock-ups, drawings, or pictures as possible, and attach a list of questions that your boss could respond to in writing. This could assist those who are unable to verbally express their feelings and ideas.

8) The demented

The only good thing that could come from working with a demented boss is the opportunity to appreciate one's own sanity. What is most baffling about such bosses is that they tend to get promoted. I once asked a CEO why he continued to employ such managers, and he said, 'Because they get results.' That might be so, but at what cost?

The only good thing that could come from working with a demented boss is the opportunity to appreciate one's own sanity

You cannot reason with demented managers, because their value system is hard-wired. They do not care about anything other than the task at hand. If you find yourself entangled with such a manager, you will have no choice but to look for a way to get out of the department or out of the organisation as quickly as possible. If you remain, there is a real danger that you could pick up some bad habits. I have seen many young people become immoral in their business dealings as a result of mixing with bad company.

9) The egomaniac

Egomaniacs crave attention. They seek acceptance, and they need to feel wanted and appreciated. Their behaviour might cause people to steer clear of them, which might ignite in them a sense of panic that results in their trying *harder* to step into the limelight. Egomaniacs seem to ooze confidence, where in fact they lack confidence. They project a sense of superiority because they feel the burdens of inferiority. They want to be understood despite not understanding themselves. In most cases, they are harmless. Unfortunately, egomaniacs who wield power attract sycophants who feed their insatiable appetite for attention. The result is an endless loop of 'give and take' that shuts out other colleagues, making them feel unwanted and unimportant.

Although it is not advisable to pander to an egomaniac's hunger for attention, it would be prudent to avoid making snide remarks of any kind. If you intimidate the egomaniac, or say anything that could be misconstrued as an attack, you could encourage future attacks upon yourself. Remember that the primary objective of such a person is to shine and to be appreciated. Therefore, only *constructive* criticism would be appreciated, so long as you do not pass

> *Egomaniacs seem to ooze confidence, where in fact they lack confidence. They project a sense of superiority because they feel the burdens of inferiority.*

any kind of judgement in public. If you can help by adding value or by teaching the egomaniac some new skills, you would be seen as a valuable asset. Although your efforts would be appreciated, do not hint at the need for any public recognition. You will not be given credit for your efforts, apart from being seen as a useful employee who provides practical support. If you can boost your manager's image without leaking the fact that you are the private mentor, you will be protected only if you do not pose a threat to exposing what you know about your manager's weaknesses.

10) The fallen angel

The corporate battlefield is an unsafe place, even for the 'good guys' who are sometimes unjustly wounded. Inexplicable decisions can result in hardworking, dedicated managers becoming targets for attack. For no apparent reason, a blossoming career can be cut short. Talented managers who find themselves embroiled in political battles in the workplace might be shot down, either because they are seen as a threat to incompetent colleagues who do not want anyone to outshine them, or because they are unwilling to engage in the dirty tricks that would be required to meet those colleagues head-on.

Fallen angels are those who were once decent. Unfortunately, they become bitter and twisted when they lose their ability to climb back up the ladder. Fearful of slipping any further, they anchor themselves and hang on for dear life. Having lost their self-confidence, they attack anyone who threatens them. Such managers are confusing to deal with. Their good nature still emits inviting signals that lull employees into a false sense of security. Unfortunately, when least expected, those same employees can find themselves being ravaged.

When working with fallen angels, you need to be sensitive to their feelings about the past. Do not do anything to cause them to lose any further ground within the hierarchy. Learn to understand what *they* hold dear. If you do not perform to the desired standards, you could find yourself in the firing line.

11) The fault-finder

Life can be seen as a series of battles that require complex decision-making, including some compromises. Along the way, we have to forego some opportunities as we take what we consider to be the best options at hand. At every junction we are faced with multiple choices that branch out like a tree. Backtracking is almost impossible. Having carefully made the best decisions at each junction, we arrive at a solution that we present to the boss for approval. The professional fault-finder only needs a few seconds to fire a series of questions that could leave us speechless, because it would be difficult to explain and justify every twist and turn that was taken to arrive at the present position. It does not take much brainpower to find the limitations within any rec-ommendation. Therefore, fault-finders desire to prove three things: that they are interested in the project at hand; that they are penetrating observers; and that they are superior thinkers.

Fault-finders desire to prove three things: that they are interested in the project at hand; that they are penetrating observers; and that they are superior thinkers

The fundamental issue with fault-finders is that they are aware that they cannot add value in any other way. They lack the necessary skills and an overall knowledge of the subject mat-ter, so they pretend that they are adding value by looking to see what 'could have been' or 'what is missing' in the hope of giving others the impression that they are useful to the group. With this in mind, you can see that it would be in your interest to educate fault-finders. Avoid using language or terminology that is unfamiliar to them. Otherwise, it will rub salt into the wound. They are more inclined to send you away to rethink your strategy as a way of postponing a tough decision regarding a situation about which they know little.

Over the years, I have found a strategy that works. I start by asking fault-finders what their desired outcome is. In this way, we can agree on the results that we are looking for. I then ask for clari-fication about the budgets and my level of authority. As much as possible, I push for autonomy, while promising to meet all my obli-gations. This tends to work, because fault-finders ultimately want a successful result so that they do not look bad. What they fear most is missing the mark and being called up to their superior to explain themselves. They do not fear failure so much as dread being exposed as frauds. The priority in negotiating with fault-finders is to convince them that you are capable of delivering a satisfactory outcome. Once you have done that, you will need to negotiate your autonomy. Emphasise that you cannot deliver if you are prevented from operating at your own speed or from making important decisions that can affect the end result.

Be specific when asking for help. Fault-finders would be intimidated if you were to thrust a huge report at them and ask an open-ended question such as, 'What do you think of this?'

12) The frustrated

It can be quite a drag working with a frustrated individual who complicates every issue and makes everything seem futile. You might have heard it said that anyone who is afraid of failure cannot attain success. Frustrated people see every hurdle and every challenge as a precursor to failure. They do not understand that failure is part of the journey to success. They delude themselves into thinking that unless everything is going superbly well, failure is imminent. Their defeatist attitude and lack of confidence often lead them to change course prematurely and to try different approaches.

Anyone who is afraid of failure cannot attain success

One possible way of overcoming the negative impact of a frustrated boss is to approach challenges in a relaxed way, injecting humour if possible, so as not to alarm your boss unnecessarily. This is like the tactic that works on infants who fall over and hurt themselves. If the adult immediately distracts the infant by laughing-off the incident, it usually passes without the child becoming upset or frightened.

13) The immature

There are some companies that blossom far too quickly for their founders to mature appropriately. If the business grows faster than expected, managers might have to take charge of bigger budgets and larger departments than they have coped with previously. This could mean that inexperienced operators are being forced to direct a large number of people, many of whom have far more experience. Other types of immature managers could be the children of rich parents who are appointed to senior positions to which they are not ideally suited. Yet another, is the first-time investor who injects capital into a business and ends up having an influence on the company's direction.

If anyone can solve the dilemma of immaturity, the world would change forever. We cannot do much to help immature people who do not seek to help themselves. One approach could be to urge immature managers to partner with mentors who can act as a sounding board. People respond well to third parties who can act at arm's length. They can explore ideas with a mentor who is not part of the business, and who would not be a threat to their ego or to their position of power.

If anyone can solve the dilemma of immaturity, the world would change forever

If your boss is immature, the best thing you can do is to remain consistent in your approach. Immature people might not like what you have to say, but they usually learn to appreciate your methods. It is through your consistency that they learn to understand what you stand for and what you believe in. Over time, they will begin to understand why you do things in a certain way. Once they can start to see that your ways yield

355

results, they will be able to pre-empt your methods and adopt your ways. This requires patience without judgement.

None of us can say that we have never suffered from our own immaturity. The only differences between people are the length of time that they need to overcome their immaturity, and their ability to learn from their mistakes and to apply what they have learned to other areas of their life.

14) The indecisive

Indecisive people are often heard to say, 'I don't know what I want, but I can tell you what I *don't* like.' These people are hard to please; they do not give specific briefs, yet they expect others to make suggestions that they invariably reject. Despite having grand plans and wild ideas, they settle for the simple and the bland.

More frustrating are managers who make decisions far too quickly, and then change their mind within hours, depending on who they spoke to last. I once had a manager who agreed with everything I said, yet when any of my colleagues walked into his office, they were able to change his mind. My colleagues and I were often in dispute, adamant that each of us had the manager's approval. In fact, we *all* had his approval because he was trying to appease each one of us, hoping that we would sort it out among ourselves. When we took a deputation to him, he felt trapped, so he would suggest that we take the matter up at the next meeting. Obviously, that was no way to run an organisation.

Eventually, I stopped believing his decisions. Even when he fervently encouraged me to press on with a project, I would wait a while, knowing that, before long, he would change his mind. I do not remember him ever sticking to his word. I cannot remember a single decision that he did not overturn. Eventually, all those who reported to him stopped going to him, and they relied on their own influence or personal power to force their hand.

The only thing you can do with indecisive managers is to help them to understand the parameters, which I call 'fences'. The fences might be pegged by virtue of a limited budget or a limited time frame. Your boss needs to understand the equations at hand: 'If we do this, that will happen.' By putting things in measurable terms, you stand a greater chance of painting the right picture. For example, I used to say to my manager that if we did not drop the price of our product by five percent, it would not be featured in retailers' Christmas catalogues, which meant that we would not receive an order for $3 million worth of the product, which meant that by January, we would be stuck with obsolete stock because a new model was being released. By explaining to him that no-one would buy our old models, and that we would then have to write-off our stock, I was able to get him to see what his indecision would do to the bottom-line that he was judged on. When he could understand the impact on *his* performance, he was able to see why we had to take action. Almost everything had to be articulated in terms that impacted his bonus or affected his credibility with *his* boss.

15) The insensitive

It can be a delicate affair to strike a balance between being sensitive to people's needs and being honest about our own thoughts and feelings. If we speak up, we could offend people. If we say nothing, their behaviour could infuriate us. It is this type of juggling act that workers have to contend with when they consider the question of sensitivity.

Rigorous debate and the sharing of views and ideas ought to be encouraged. It is regrettable that more people cannot express their thoughts and ideas without being accused of upsetting others. It is amazing how people seem to allow themselves to become offended. I have often been accused of upsetting someone. My typical response is: if ever I *meant* to upset them, they would know about it. I maintain that no-one has the right to be offended by what I say unless I *intend* to offend them. It hardly seems right that people can accuse me of offending them when it was not my intention to do so. It is like being accused of a crime that one did not commit. I liken insults to assaults. In the same way that one cannot be blamed for *perceived* assault, I maintain that no-one should be blamed for *perceived* insults (although certain courts in some countries do not subscribe to this philosophy).

The term 'insensitive' does not refer to managers who speak their mind. Rather, it refers to managers who are unaware that what they are criticising is not something the other person can do anything about. The blunt end of insensitivity is not a person who is offended, but someone who is helpless. Insensitive managers are those who complain about inadequacies or situations that cannot be helped by the employees in question. People cannot do anything about the way they look, or their heritage, or their family situation. Therefore, it is inappropriate for managers to criticise them about such matters. I knew of a worker whose abusive husband used to pick her up after work. If she took any more than one minute to leave the factory floor, he would become irritated and obnoxious. She would then have to contend with an uncomfortable drive home. Her boss would often ask her to perform a few last-minute tasks, and this made her uneasy and unhappy. She would be seen crying as she tried to work out how she could please two masters, both of whom gave her a hard time, and neither of whom she felt she could stand up to.

I remember asking the manager why he always chose her to carry out the last-minute factory checks, and he said, 'She drives me mad. Every time I ask her to do something simple, she becomes agitated and upset. She's not a team player.' That manager made it a personal mission to 'break' her so that she would stop being so difficult to deal with. When I explained the situation to him, he was unsympathetic. Nonetheless, he agreed to let her go the moment the factory bell sounded. He eventually noticed a marked improvement in how she responded to him.

You cannot expect to convert insensitive managers, because they rarely have the ability to empathise with others whose pain is different from theirs. The best that you can do is to explain the bigger picture and express your concerns with a view to finding a way around the problem. It might also help if you can explain the potential benefits of finding a solution. Insensitive managers are not necessarily nasty by nature, so they would usually be willing to find a compromise, even though they might not be able to relate to other people's problems.

16) The lonely

Given that our work environment has become a major part of our life, it is not surprising that many of us form friendships in the workplace. The fragmentation of communities means that many employees no longer have their extended family close at hand. They might be strangers to their suburb. Away from family and friends, they have to forge new relationships within their new neighbourhoods. It is understandable that, for them, colleagues become the most likely contenders for friends, companions, or lovers.

In the normal process of human interaction, people test the waters with each other, trying to see if a mutual attraction exists.

The usual courting rituals take place — some more gracefully than others. In the end, both parties give each other certain signals about their intentions, which might include an invitation to pursue the relationship or a signal that no interest exists.

The awkward aspect to such a communication process emerges when one party feels obliged to entertain the other. Some lonely managers take advantage of their position, and invite a subordinate on a social outing, confident that their invitation is unlikely to be refused. There is no crime in a lonely person trying to make friends. In such instances, employees need to be especially careful not to encourage the attentions of a lonely boss. If employees respond enthusiastically, hoping that personal attention from the boss would translate into special treatment, such as better career prospects, difficulties will emerge if the boss misinterprets the reason for the enthusiasm. (Incidentally, in some cases, managers are legally obliged to declare any relationship that could be deemed to be a conflict of interest. Organisations are facing troubled times with expensive litigation in relation to alleged sexual harassment in the workplace.)

Miserable people are critical without seeking a solution, and they are unhappy without trying to locate the source

If your boss invites you on an intimate excursion, and you accept while harbouring unwholesome intentions, you would become just as responsible if the relationship turns sour. Keep your distance, and offer other alternatives, such as a group luncheon that might introduce the boss to a wider group. Some employees criticise their boss for not going out to lunch with them, when it might be that the boss would like to fraternise with subordinates, but does not know how to go about it, or feels unwelcome.

17) The miserable

Some people never seem to find anything interesting or fascinating. If the weather is warm and sunny, they complain about the heat. If it is cold and wet, they complain about the rain. Nothing seems to please them. Their attitude contaminates the workplace, casting a dark cloud of discontent over every project.

Miserable people are critical without seeking a solution, and they are unhappy without trying to locate the source. When such managers are let loose on workers, organisations suffer. Be wary of miserable managers who rope you into their projects so that they can have you alongside to share the blame or to take the fall. There is nothing you can do to appease miserable people, except to show them that happiness is possible.

If you cannot restrain yourself from being affected by such a negative influence, your fate will be sealed with endless depression. If you have some energy to spare, use it to *resist* miserable people, not to *fight* with them, for once you come into contact with their negative force, you will be drained. Their negativity is stronger and more consistent than your cool-headedness. Miserable people do not know when to let up. If you attack them, you will merely feed their depression and confirm their position.

> If you have some energy to spare, use it to resist miserable people, not to fight with them, for once you come into contact with their negative force, you will be drained

18) The oppressor

An oppressor is kept buoyant by finding people to oppress, such as those who make their own weaknesses known. Weaknesses are known when temptations are exposed. Temptations are exposed when desires are revealed. Desires are revealed when pleasures are satisfied via such means as fame, money, and status. The craving for

Weaknesses are known when temptations are exposed. Temptations are exposed when desires are revealed. Desires are revealed when pleasures are satisfied.

personal attention, affection, acknowledgement, and social acceptance could point to weaknesses that the oppressor can play on.

If your boss is trying to probe into your comfort zone, your least confrontational solution would be to use cunning as a form of distraction. I once worked with a colleague who indicated that he hated international travel. He said that he disliked the crowds, and he had a fear of flying. Our CEO took great pleasure in forcing him to go to remote locations overseas to conclude major deals. I recall travelling with him to several countries during a three-week tour. When we returned, it dawned upon me that we had both really enjoyed the trip. I called him at home one night and asked if he had in fact enjoyed himself. He said that yes, he had loved the trip. 'But I thought you hated travelling?' I said, wondering if perhaps he just felt better having a colleague travelling with him.

'Jonar, I forgot to ask you this favour. Please don't say anything at the office about us having an enjoyable trip, because [our CEO] would take me off this division.' My colleague knew that our oppressive boss would be unhappy to learn that we were enjoying what we were doing. So my colleague pretended that he disliked travelling, knowing full well that he would be made to travel as a form of punishment. He had the situation under control. Unfortunately, I was not as smart as he was, and I had made several mistakes in my relationship with the CEO. So much so, that I paid the price. The twelve months I spent working with that oppressive boss rank as the worst in my corporate career.

19) The shouter

Many people do not realise it when they shout. They are so focussed on commanding the listener's attention, they are unaware that their voice has risen to a pitch that is uncomfortable for those around them. When I am with a shouter, whether it be an excited child or an adult passionately trying to convince me of something, I just ask, 'Why are you shouting?' It usually does the trick.

Some bosses (like some insufferable parents) use shouting as a way of silencing their critics. They do not care to engage in any form of negotiation. They become stubborn and agitated, hoping that they can walk out of the room without having to explain or defend themselves. At other times, they might use shouting to disarm or admonish employees who have failed to reach their targets. Some shouters are not only trying to insult or to inject fear into the other party, but they are also insisting on a better outcome in the future. Their fury is caused by frustration, disappointment, and helplessness.

The initial reaction from employees is to interpret the act as one of abuse. Although one could be forgiven for taking exception, there is some merit is trying to bypass the tantrum and to understand the crux of the matter. If, in fact, employees are not taking their job seriously, they would do well to examine their performance with a view to improving their professionalism, rather than just take offence.

If your performance is beyond reproach, and your boss shouts at you for other inexplicable reasons, you can grin and bear it, or ask for a private meeting to discuss the matter calmly. In trying to explain what you dislike about the communication process, do not appear to be highly offended or hurt. Merely ask that you be given the opportunity to hear what the issues are in a calm and rational manner. It will not help matters if you get on your high horse and criticise your boss at this stage. Do not pass judgement on your boss, because if the shouting is a result of low self-esteem, your meeting might be seen as criticism, to which your boss might react violently to shun your criticism — the very thing that your boss might be trying to avoid.

20) The thief

A young neighbour of mine got into trouble with the local supermarket where he worked because he was accused of stealing money from the cash register that he operated during his two-month tenure. He was finally dismissed, and his parents offered to make up the shortfall to avoid complications.

Months later, word got out that more casual workers were in trouble for pilfering. Three of the parents decided to complain to the head office. Upon investigation, it was revealed that the shift supervisor had quite a racket under way: she would pocket the money herself and then accuse the junior workers of stealing it.

Internal corporate theft takes place at all levels. The CEO who uses a company credit card to pay for a lover to go along on a business trip, or the financial controller who puts friends and colleagues on the company payroll, even though they do not work for the company, are both guilty of theft. Then there are law enforcement officials who help themselves to some of the loot that passes through their hands during an investigation, and the warehouse staff who conveniently leave products out by the door for the afternoon courier to pinch 'accidentally on purpose' and sell them on the black market. The underworld of stolen goods is a multibillion-dollar industry.

You might think that such an underworld relies on secrecy and exclusivity. It does not; at every level, it requires accomplices who can lean on each other for support while at the same time threaten each other with exposure. The more people who can be implicated, the less likely that anyone will dare to blow the whistle, because too much would be at stake and too many people would apply pressure on anyone who weakens. The best way to get rid of such 'traitors' is to frame them. The overwhelming evidence would be sufficient to discharge and discredit those who threaten to topple the cartel.

I forbid staff members from going over their manager's head, except where illegal matters are concerned. Notwithstanding, if you suspect that even the senior managers cannot be trusted, it would be best to seek advice from a lawyer or the police.

Resist any temptation to share in ill-gotten gains

The first step is always to resist any temptation to share in ill-gotten gains. What might seem harmless 'because everyone else is doing it' could later haunt you. Think of any supposed 'reward' in the context of the bigger picture. What might seem attractive and lucrative now would be insignificant if your reputation or your résumé were shot to bits as a result of your involvement.

THE DEVIL IN DISGUISE

It no longer surprises me when hardened criminals are described as being shy and unassuming. Even those who might have masterminded the slaughter of millions in concentration camps, or who might have been notorious serial killers, often appear to those around them as timid people who never made a fuss or who never stood out in a crowd. There is no such thing as a standard way of behaviour for criminals. For example, one serial killer who was facing several charges of rape and murder was let off by the jury because he was handsome, well-groomed, well-spoken, and 'not the type to be a murderer'. Years later, after he had committed several more atrocities, he was sentenced to life in prison. Even then, he received many letters from women wanting to marry him because they still believed him to be innocent.

In life's parade, few of us can look at strangers and guess what their darkest secrets are. Nor, on first meeting executives, can we be sure of what kind of managers they are. I recall warning a colleague to watch out for a manager whom I knew to be manipulative. She refused to heed my warning because that manager was clever enough to hide his evil traits. After six months, he showed his true colours, and she called me to apologise for doubting me.

When you are going for a job interview, take the opportunity to stipulate your demands, and make it clear what type of boss you are looking to work with. Ideally, your boss should be able to add value while also accepting the value that others can add. Do not be afraid to ask for verbal references from people who have worked for that manager in the past. Also, ask to speak to the person whom you might be replacing. Two-way reference checks are not a bad idea when so much is riding on the temperament of one person.

Keep in mind that while you are trying to avoid the *boss* from hell, it is vital that you regularly examine your own profile, lest you become the *employee* from hell. If locating evil traits in others is hard, imagine how much harder it would be for you to spot your *own* weaknesses. Re-examine the characteristics described in this chapter to see if any of them apply to you, then decide how you might rid yourself of them. Usually, the worst devil is the devil within. **E**

CHAPTER 20

GO AHEAD, MAKE *my* DAY!

FIRED UP AND NOWHERE TO GO

Irresponsibility is such a wonderful luxury
that I am looking forward to being
able to afford it soon

EVERAL YEARS AGO I instigated a new index called The Firing Line, whereby ex-employees were asked *how* they were fired, retrenched, or made redundant.

In the old days the standard line was, 'You're fired!' These days, to avoid any legal backlash, we hear more delicate phrasing, such as 'This job no longer suits you.' Firing lines are now usually scripted by the personnel department and approved by the legal eagles.

The latest firing lines are being delivered via arm's-length methods, such as e-mail, voicemail, or by letter while the employee is on leave. During corporate collapses or corporate takeovers, the first that employees know of their fate is often through the media.

THE FIRE DRILL

Are you prepared to be fired? In other words, if you were fired tomorrow, do you have everything in order? Would you be in a position to walk out the door within the hour with all your personal effects? Would you be ready to start looking for another job? Employees who are prepared for this eventuality are likely to have their important personal e-mails archived on a disk at home. Their office computer would contain minimal personal information because it is cleared regularly. And there is nothing in their filing cabinets that might prove embarrassing if found by someone else. These are examples of *administrative* readiness.

Given the volatile nature of the current business environment, it is surprising that an estimated ninety-nine percent of workers are not adequately prepared for the loss of their job. Most people know that they do not have a job for life, and that it is up to them to protect their own interests, yet less than one percent of staff keep their résumés up-to-date in the event of their job being unexpectedly terminated. Having an up-to-date résumé is the first important step.

What would you do if you left your job tomorrow? Would you have to pound the pavement to let potential employers know that you are looking for work? Or would you sit at home at your PC and enrol in the Web-based job-search services? Some executives who are happily employed still keep an iron in the fire by keeping their details on file with employment agencies.

The key to finding a job is having a thorough understanding of the job market. Who are the key decision-makers? Do they know that you exist?

It is a good idea to peruse the weekend newspapers and select a few jobs that interest you, even if you are not actually looking for work. In this way, you can learn about the skills that are being sought, and you will benefit from the experience of going through the interview process. It will also give you an understanding of current wage structures, work environments, and 'who's who' in the industry. Naturally, it would be ethical to let the interviewer know that you are happy in your current position, but that you want to learn more about what is on offer to see if any opportunities exist for you to contemplate a serious move. In this way, you can shop around without misleading potential employers. They will understand that you are merely testing the waters.

It is vitally important that you are known to those who matter

It is vitally important that you are known to those who matter. Why not contact head-hunters and ask for a brief meeting so that you can let them know about your skills and career aspirations? If you then keep in touch with them by telephone every six months or so, they will come to understand your strengths. Provided that they like your skills and social

370

graces, they will think of you when the right opportunity arises. If you do not develop a relationship with the key decision-makers, how are they going to know that you even exist? If the first time you contact them is when you have just lost your job, the timing, and the fact that you are a complete stranger to them, are likely to work against you.

THE FIRING SQUAD

These days, some employers assemble a firing squad that includes: the 'executioners' who bear the bad news; security guards to restrain unco-operative employees; computer administrators to disable their access codes and security swipe cards; pay-office clerks to decipher their final payslips; and a counsellor to introduce them to the outplacement agency that will help with moral support as well as some practical advice as to how to go about getting a new job.

If you feel that you are being fired unjustly, do not sign any documents. Seek legal advice from your union or industry association, or from your lawyer. There is no harm in putting up a fight if you believe you are being victimised or treated unfairly. If there are good reasons for your dismissal, it is best to accept them and move on. Any hearing or settlement would take a long time to resolve, and it would only hold you back from moving on to a new chapter in your career.

Being fired is high on the list of most people's worst nightmares. Some employees might find it so embarrassing to be fired, that they go home and pretend that nothing has happened. For weeks, they go through the motions of getting up early and dressing for work, just so that their family members do not suspect anything. They never thought it could happen to them, so they were completely unprepared for it. They live in denial until, sooner or later, their family finds out and they have to face the music.

People who take pride in their work and career might be loath to admit that they have been fired, because of the stigma they associate with it. They question what happened, why it happened, and how it could have happened to them. Initially, fired employees might presume that it was a personality clash; they might then think that it had something to do with a decline in their skills. Some might believe that they failed to impress the boss, or that their performance was inadequate in what might have been a high-pressure environment. As they search for an explanation, they might react with shock or anger. They might desperately look for a solution, hoping that a compromise could be reached, but they feel that no matter what they say, their boss would not listen to them. They might become consumed by a sense of frustration when they realise that their fate is not subject to negotiation. They are caught between feeling 'this can't be happening to me, I must be dreaming' and 'I'm disposable, and all my foundations have been destroyed.' During this first stage, the main question they ask is, 'Why?' Unfortunately, for many people, this question is never answered satisfactorily because of their self-denial or because of the lies that employers spin.

When one's mind and time are occupied, one is lulled into a sense of achievement

The second stage of coping with the shock might be manifested in a fight-back strategy, fuelled by a sense of outrage: 'How dare they do that to me! I'll show them!' After several telephone calls to lawyers, unions, and government authorities, some employees hatch a plan to retaliate and 'fight fire with fire' on the grounds of unfair dismissal, unfair termination of contract, or discrimination, or some other means to restore their dignity. This phase is an exciting one because it consumes the mind and takes up time. When one's mind and time are occupied, one is lulled into a sense of achievement, even though nothing is being achieved on the front that matters most — finding a new job.

Employees who embark on a legal battle might enter a long period of hyperactivity during which documents and statements are exchanged between all the parties. If everything goes according to plan, offers are negotiated and settlements are signed, hopefully out of court. For senior employees who were also directors of the company, this stage includes the formalities of officially resigning as directors. There have been cases of directors who had forgotten to officially resign, and they were later roped into litigation when their ex-employer landed in hot water over corporate negligence.

The third stage is when people start to review their employment history in search of clues about what could have led to their perceived failure. They start to question their moves, their relationships at work, and their demeanour. They search their memory, trying to find clues as to what went wrong and why they did not twig to the potential danger of being fired.

Self-examination is a useful process of weeding out the habits and faults that could stifle your progress

The fourth stage is when they develop a healthy attitude about the past, and put their job in perspective. The majority of ex-employees feel a sense of relief at having been forced to leave their work environment. This might be because they are relieved to be out of the rat race, or because they have new-found hope about the future. The overwhelming response is, 'Being fired is the *best* thing that could have happened to me!' Some executives later admit that they desperately wanted to change their job, but they were too afraid to do anything about it. They either lacked the confidence to go through the process, or they did not know how to start the ball rolling, always fearing that their mortgage and family responsibilities were far too important to risk. Some try to commit 'professional suicide' by sabotaging their own success in the hope that they will be asked to leave after being offered a lucrative golden handshake.

Be careful not to incubate your faults by covering up your mistakes

It would be presumptuous to say that the boss is always the fiend. There might be times when the person who is fired needs to examine what happened and why. It could well be that there are important personal and professional issues that they need to rectify. Again, this is best done *before* there is any hint of a problem. Make it a habit each week to reflect on the events of the previous week to see if you could have improved on anything you did. Think about how you reacted to certain situations and decide if you might have over-reacted in some circumstances. Self-examination is a useful process of weeding out the habits and faults that could stifle your progress.

The first response to being fired is usually one of defence and denial. Be careful not to incubate your faults by covering up your mistakes. Have the courage to admit your faults to yourself, and have the maturity to undertake some steps to rid yourself of your shortcomings. It is not important that you agree with your boss about why you were fired, but it is vital that you understand yourself sufficiently well to pinpoint any problems. They might be linked to your personality, your professionalism, or your ethics. Carefully examine what you find appropriate or inappropriate, compared with what is deemed acceptable or unacceptable in your chosen industry.

FIRE IN THE BELLY

There is an old Chinese expression that encourages warriors to 'have a cool head and a fire in the belly', meaning that one should maintain a calm disposition in a crisis, and have the determination and stamina to undertake arduous tasks.

Remaining calm does not mean switching off one's senses. It does not mean that you should take a break or have a holiday to get over a bad experience at work. Cocooning yourself at a time of uncertainty could cause you to harbour a defeatist attitude. For example, those who have lost their job might say that they will look for another job soon, but first they need a break in order to come to terms with what has happened. This sounds like a perfectly reasonable thing to do. Except that, unless they already have a job or a project lined up, this ought to be the *last* thing on their mind. Understandably, people might yearn for a recovery period so that they can heal, but if it is not managed carefully, 'recovery' could turn into 'escape'.

> *Getting ready to look for another job is something you should do when you are still happily employed*

As tempting as it is, taking a break is not an appropriate response in this situation. Ignoring the problem will not make it go away. Of course, you might need time to gather your thoughts and to prepare yourself. That time ought to be invested *prior* to the unfortunate event. Getting ready to look for another job is something you should do when you are still happily employed. It is like the philosophy behind a well-stocked pantry. When you purchase salt, sugar, flour, and other basic ingredients, you do not always know exactly when and how you are going to use them, yet you buy them because you know that you are likely to need them at some point. Being prepared is the key to harmony and freedom.

Are you prepared to absorb the major shock of losing your job? Are you *financially* prepared to be out of work for several months? The worst thing is to be forced to take on low-paying, time-consuming, energy-sapping, menial tasks that distract you from your main mission, all because you do not have enough money to meet your basic living expenses. Once you fall into this trap, you will find it exhausting to clamber your way out.

Most people are keen to purchase non-essential items yet they do not think to acquire the most important luxury of all — independence

Most people are keen to purchase a computer, a camera, a car, and other non-essential items (usually on credit), yet they do not think to acquire the most important luxury of all — independence. Those who do not have six months' financial security will not be able to operate with a cool head if the axe falls, leaving them unable to pay the rent, and incapable of looking after their welfare. For most employees, no matter how much they earn, they still have to contend with a low 'disposable income' because their spending priorities typically include unnecessary luxuries. By all means, purchase that new car and the gold watch, but only after you have a reserve of cash that can act as your buffer. Once you have achieved this, you will feel a remarkable sense of freedom. The fire in the belly is less likely to be extinguished if you know that you are no longer perpetually one pay-packet away from the poverty line.

The fire in the belly should not be fuelled by anger or discontentment, but by strategy and clarity. For high-school students, the toughest question is, 'What do you want to do when you leave school?' Very few teenagers have any idea about the path they want to take in life. This sense of disorientation plagues many adults as well. Most wage-earners could not answer the same question in relation to their career. They cannot articulate a strategy about targeting and securing their next job. Plodders tend to live one day at a time, not because they have adopted the popular maxim for healthy living, but because they do not have a clue about what they would like to do with their life. For that reason, when push comes to shove, and they are forced out of their safe haven, they are like children lost in the wilderness. Having one's job terminated is not unlike losing a loved one, or breaking up with a lover — the intense feelings include despair, distress, a sense of dislocation, and confusion. A friend said, 'When I was fired, all the same feelings I had when I was divorced came flooding back.'

THE FIRE EXIT

Some employees fear that 'contemplating their future' smacks of disloyalty to their current employer. When it comes to our career, we need to understand that it is an ever-changing part of our life, especially in these times of corporate collapses, takeovers, mergers, downsizing, and fierce competition. If we deprive ourselves of future planning and if we do not constantly nurture our thoughts and ideas, we can easily suffocate our career. If we do not fuel our fantasies, hopes, and dreams, we will extinguish the fire in our belly. As for a cool head, this is not possible amid despair.

THE BUSHFIRE

Mass retrenchments are on the increase. When they happen, hundreds of skilled workers become available, all willing to compromise on their salary package in return for a secure job. The oversupply of applicants creates a new level of competition. For this reason, it is inadvisable to sit on one's laurels after a corporate calamity. In addition to immediately hunting for employment, successful strategies include staging attacks on multiple fronts. For example, in addition to looking in the newspapers and contacting employment agencies and well-placed friends, it would be prudent to contact companies directly, including industries in different markets and different locations. Avoid falling into the 'pyjama trap' of staying up late each night, watching mind-numbing television, or sleeping-in each morning as your sense of ambition seeps away. If you have lost your usual routine, it is vital to get out of the house to attend seminars or to undertake short courses, or to read books to improve your skills.

A recently-retrenched employee, Joel, told me: 'I made the mistake of leaving my future in the hands of the employment agencies. I met many of them, but they just used me as a "viable alternative candidate", sending me to all sorts of interviews for which I wasn't suited. They wanted to show their clients that they were offering a variety of qualified candidates. But they just sent me around town, at my expense. They were playing with my emotions. I resented them for that, and I soon realised that they didn't care about my career.'

Joel was a senior member of the medical profession who was certain that his qualifications and experience were sufficient for him to secure a new and exciting job. Summing up his current situation, he said, 'I now realise that I should have had many more irons in the fire. To me, job-hunting is now all about having four or five opportunities spinning simultaneously so that I can leverage my time and increase my chances. I'm looking at all sorts of opportunities, some of which bear no resemblance to my previous role. I love dogs, so I'm thinking about a dog grooming business. I enjoy consulting, and I'm looking at starting my own consultancy. I already have a business plan for that, and I've registered my business name and printed my stationery. I've contacted several companies and let them know that I'm available to undertake project work.'

Joel had wasted six months before learning this lesson. Meanwhile, his finances were becoming depleted. The longer it takes to secure satisfying work, the more pressure one will be under to find a source of income. Invariably, when forced to find work for the sake of survival, people start to lower their standards to secure any job so as to avoid financial ruin.

THE FIRE EXTINGUISHER

The most powerful personal position is the one that affords complete control. Having control over one's career can certainly help to shape one's destiny. Unfortunately, control is not within everyone's reach. For that reason, it would be wise to bolster one's activities that can help to achieve the second-most powerful position — choice. In the absence of control, choice is the next best thing.

Having control over one's career can certainly help to shape one's destiny

One way to extinguish fear and anxiety about employment instability is to own a business. Self-employed people have a lot of things to worry about, but being fired is not one of them, unless the business fails. (By the way, the failure rate for small businesses is high within the first five years. This is mostly due to a lack of planning and the absence of clear goals and professionalism.)

In the absence of control, choice is the next best thing

The path of self-employment is not as smooth and autonomous as many people might think. Owning your own business enables you to exercise your creativity. You can work at your own pace and to the beat of your own drum. The downside is that becoming your own boss does not mean that you no longer have people who can harass you. The demands on you can still come from employees, customers, business partners, banks, suppliers, government departments, and competitors, all of whom can make your life difficult.

Notwithstanding the obstacles, business owners are quick to defend their move, saying that stepping out of corporate life to run their own show was the best move of their career. Even though their earning capacity is initially nowhere near as high as what it was, the new rewards can be invigorating and uplifting. They speak about having a new lease on life through new challenges and exciting opportunities.

So, what is stopping you from starting your own business? If you are like most people, *fear* might be the main hurdle, rationalised as a lack of funds. Fear is a legitimate and normal inhibitor. There is nothing that you can do to remove it. Instead, if you fancy the idea of starting your own enterprise, start investigating every aspect of your project. When you can methodically study the environment of your chosen industry, you will find that your confidence will overcome your fears.

A friend of mine told me that he wanted to escape the clutches of his boss to start his own business, but he could not muster enough courage to resign and delve into a whole new area. Taking that first step can be terrifying; not unlike the feeling

one gets when standing on a high diving platform just before taking the plunge. Hesitation puts a halt to all reasonable processes,
and inactivity becomes the most com-
fortable option.

My friend said that he would like
to open a restaurant, so I encouraged
him to learn as much as he could about
real-estate prices, venues and locations,
fixtures and fittings, equipment costs
and leasing arrangements, licensing rules
and council regulations. I also urged him
to visit the best and worst restaurants he

*Hesitation puts a halt
to all reasonable
processes,
and inactivity
becomes the most
comfortable option*

could find, and to work part-time as a waiter in several establish-
ments. I accompanied him to industry lectures, and suggested that
he attend a few cooking classes.

Once he had a mission in mind, he was able to talk to
friends about their experiences with restaurants. He started to
collect data that could help him to paint the bigger picture about
his future project. Within a short period of time, I could sense
his enthusiasm. Fear no longer played a part in his judgement,
because the mystery of the unknown had evaporated. One
afternoon, he said to me, 'I can't wait to get started! I know
exactly what I want to do.' That type of attitude is not one that
he could have arrived at merely by confronting his fears head-
on. If he did that, he would have failed, because fear is a
formidable opponent. Instead, he educated himself and found
answers to his doubts.

If you fancy yourself as a business owner, you too must
engage in thorough research. Your confidence about jumping
into your own enterprise will grow when you understand every
aspect of your decision.

The first stage requires comprehensive research. The second

stage requires a crystal-clear dream. The third requires that your dream be supported by administrative and business skills. The final element relies on personal qualities that most people do not harness because of the lack of social mechanisms available to teach each other about their substance and importance. Some of these personal qualities are listed in Chapter 17, 'Heads or tails?'

IN CASE OF FIRE, YOU NEED A LIFT

You might not appreciate this when you are fired, but there are many good jobs out there. You *can* find something that will stimulate you. If you have prepared yourself for that big day, you will not become disoriented when you lose your job. Having said that, it is important that you develop a relationship with friends who can understand what you are going through, and who can give your spirits a lift.

Apart from needing a good morale booster, you will need some practical assistance with your career development. Start to talk to a few of your trusted friends about what each of you would do if you were fired, and discuss the subject seriously so that you are able to brainstorm some viable options. This type of mental training is similar to the visualisation that musicians and actors undertake before a major performance. With their eyes closed, they run through every movement, giving themselves uninterrupted rehearsal time. You, too, need to rehearse your exit, in case you are fired.

It is all too easy to slip into indulgent self-pity and to take on undesirable habits in the name of stress relief

Do not underestimate the stress that you will be under when you lose your job. There is no doubt that you will feel the pinch. It is an unpleasant experience, no matter how geared up you might be. Therefore, your emotional health is one of the key areas that you need to protect at a time of rejection. You need to plan for your therapies in this area. It is all too easy to slip into indulgent self-pity and to take on undesirable habits in the name of stress relief. When colleagues lose their job, the first mistake they make is to go down to the local bar and drink themselves silly as they wallow in their sorrow and gossip about 'the dirty rotten scoundrels' who fired them.

During times of confusion, you need to lift your spirits, not sedate your senses. Therefore, plan now what you will do, and what activities you will undertake during the healing process.

During times of confusion, you need to lift your spirits, not sedate your senses

Decide on the videos you will watch and the places you will visit for solitude and reflection. Alert yourself to the dangers that you might subject yourself to as a result of your bad habits. Prepare a list of things you would like to do, so that you do not sit around all day watching television in your pyjamas.

At times like these, some people spin out of control. Without a predetermined rescue package, they fall by the wayside because of their strong tendency to drift towards failure.

Careers are *built* as a result of careful planning, not as a result of reactions to problems. Successful people plan so that they can *avoid* problems. They also have a fallback position so that the turbulence does not throw them off course. Ultimately, career development is about career choice. When confronted by a disaster for which you have no strategy, your choices become limited. You are forced to *respond* and *react*, rather than *command* and *control*.

FIRE STAIRS

The winners are those who are completely familiar with the corporate ladder, as well as being fully aware of the fire stairs. Knowing when to evacuate is a skill that requires acute awareness of one's environment.

Winners are those who are completely familiar with the corporate ladder, as well as being fully aware of the fire stairs

There is a game called Beat the Bomb. The host calls out an escalating prize pool of money, saying, 'One hundred, two hundred, five hundred,' and so on. The player has to halt the host before the 'bomb' creeps in unexpectedly and nullifies the prize pool. There are two main types of players. The first is the ultra-conservative who will call a halt almost immediately, thinking that it is better to walk away with a few hundred dollars than to push one's luck. The second type of player goes all the way, hoping to become rich. This type of player tempts fate and is prepared to walk away empty-handed in the hope that such a risk might yield a big windfall.

This is the type of behaviour that workers seem to adopt. Some jump ship at the first sight of another opportunity. They might regret their move, but they feel satisfied to have quenched their curiosity. Their impatience works against them, and they end up burning too many bridges. Conversely, some employees never know when to call a halt to their current employment. They build an enviable track record and amass much-desired credibility at the risk of burning out. Unfortunately, it is not greed, but fear, that stops them from cashing in their chips and trying their luck in the big wide world. They become so comfortable in their position, that the tables turn and they start to feel uncomfortable. Their job-satisfaction dissolves into dissatisfaction. After many years in the same company, their contentment slowly transforms into discontentment. Their job security becomes prized because of their personal insecurity. Strange things begin to happen, because those who do not know when to bow out of their comfort zone soon end up prisoners in what I call 'the hostage zone'. Then the big diseases take over, when they no longer have to worry about burning out, but about *rusting* out. They become like hopeless and helpless sitting ducks — and they

Those who do not know when to bow out of their comfort zone soon end up prisoners in what I call 'the hostage zone'

know it. It must be a terrible feeling to be lame in a tumultuous industry. The hostage zone is a place from which people do not even *try* to escape. They do not realise that they are stuck there, because they delude themselves by thinking that they are happy where they are, and that they can leave when they choose. Sadly, when they try to escape, they are catapulted back into familiar territory because their tolerance for failure is low.

Emotionally-drained workers cling to memories of when they were the superstars in their industry. Alas, there are no prizes for good memories. In a competitive world, currency provides vitality, meaning that one must remain current by trading-in one's current job for a new one, before the expiry date is reached.

How are you playing the game? Do you have your finger on the pulse so that you will know when to run down the fire stairs and leave your current job while you are still in your heyday? Remember that the best time to look for another job is when you do not need one. Naturally, if you are happy where you are, and are satisfied with your work, you might choose not to leave it.

But can you be certain that you will not be *asked* to leave? These days, mergers and acquisitions flood the workplace with an air of uncertainty. Even those who work in government departments have to endure endless policy changes and funding withdrawals, making their positions uncertain.

The best time to look for another job is when you do not need one

If you are satisfied with your current job, and if you feel safe in it, you can count your blessings. All that would be required of you is to answer this simple question: if you decided to leave your job, or if something untoward happened that forced you to leave, are you prepared to vacate your position? Would you know what to do, who to contact, and how to go about it? If you have not had any job-seeking experience for a long time, you will inevitably be 'stale' and are likely to become your own worst representative.

The best job to be in is the one that you absolutely love. The second-best job is the one that you absolutely hate. The worst job is the one for which you have *no* feelings. This is a dangerous situation that will lull you into inactivity; before you know it, the grass will grow around your feet and you will look back and wonder where the years have gone. Indifference is the chief contributor to discontentment. If you cannot say that you either love or hate your job, where will the impetus come from for you to do something about it? Poke the fire and see what comes out. Whether it be warm flames of contentment or choking black smoke of displeasure, either one is preferable to not having any fire to stoke at all.

OH NO YOU DON'T!

Have you seen TV comedies where two of the characters are arguing on the telephone? The showdown culminates in threats about who is going to hang up first. 'You can't talk to me like that, I'll hang up on you,' threatens one person, while the other says, 'Oh no you don't. I'm going to hang up on *you*!' And so the script goes until one person does in fact hang up.

Similar routines are sometimes played out when bosses are about to dismiss employees. Before employ-ees can be fired, they jump in with, 'I resign!', hoping to avoid the stigma of being fired. Of course, the worst sce-nario would be the one that my friend found himself in when he jumped the

> *The best job to be in is the one that you absolutely love. The second-best job is the one that you absolutely hate. The worst job is the one for which you have no feelings.*

gun. His boss had asked that they meet for lunch at the end of the week. The boss wanted to promote my friend. Unfortu-nately, due to a guilty conscience, my friend thought that he was being summonsed to 'the last supper', so before the boss could explain the purpose of the meeting, my friend pulled out his letter of resignation.

It is often said that one must never walk around with a loaded gun, because someone might get hurt. Apparently, being *too* prepared for losing one's job might backfire. Notwithstand-ing that, the ultimate state of preparedness, and supreme test of self-confidence, is to have a resignation letter in your bag. If you can prepare yourself sufficiently to the point of feeling comfort-able enough to carry a resignation letter around, you will truly be ready to face the consequences of your actions.

For the last seven years of my twenty-year career in corporate life, I had a resignation letter on my computer and in my brief-case. I was not trigger-happy, but I was not about to let anyone intimidate me. I'd had enough of that in the past. Sure, there were times when I was tempted to tell the boss where to go, but luck-ily I was able to distinguish between revenge and reason. I felt better by knowing that I could resign when and if I wanted to.

This heightened state of readiness kept me aware of the realities of corporate life, and it gave me some satisfaction to know that I could resign if I could no longer stand it. It was like a safety blanket, a life jacket, or a parachute. It made me feel safe. Mind you, some of my friends thought that carrying my resignation letter around was more akin to carrying a suicide pill. For me, it was a symbol of my acceptance that nothing is certain, and of my determination that, in the dog-eat-dog world of the corporate battlefield, I was not about to be bullied by anyone.

By becoming financially and administratively prepared, I eliminated the fear of being fired. This sense of independence felt like a great weight had been lifted off my shoulders. I was able to be 'me' and to respond to situations in ways that were true to my conscience. I was no longer held hostage by anyone. My real personality was allowed to shine, and I was able to be true to myself. My friends would comment on how relaxed I looked and how calm I was. I was able to perform my duties professionally and creatively, without having to worry about the thick and murky waters we call 'office politics'.

I was the kindest and most generous of employees, and the fiercest and most forceful of opponents. If someone stepped out of line, I had the courage to stand up for myself and for what I believed in. I was no longer going home feeling like I had betrayed myself. I took the opportunity to make each day count. If my colleagues, no matter how senior they were, pushed too far, I would stand up to them. They soon scurried back into their bunker — no doubt determined to plot their revenge, but what could they do? Have me fired? That did not matter, because all I could think was: 'Go ahead, make my day!' ▣

CHAPTER 21

HEROES *from* HEAVEN

MANAGERS WHO ENRICH YOUR LIFE

The best gift you can give someone is a dream

PRODUCTS SUCH AS DIAMONDS are sold on the basis of their *scarcity*. Their pricing structure is delicately balanced between supply and demand. If anyone were to find large diamond deposits that dramatically tipped that balance, they could push the price of diamonds down to that of glass.

Within our social structure, many things are precious because they are rare. If scarcity is the key to our economic system, should we make anything available in plentiful supply? For example, would we want everyone to be in good health? Even if we were able to eradicate the common cold, think of the millions of people who would become jobless, and the hundreds of factories that would have to close down. The health industry wants to make us better, but it cannot afford to rid the world of all its ailments because an oversupply of healthy people would send it broke.

What about management? Would industries thrive on an abundance of skilled managers? Or is it important to maintain a level of scarcity on that front as well? Surely it does not make sense to wish upon ourselves bad bosses and oppressive leaders.

There are two issues to consider. The first is that good managers are *not* scarce. There are plenty of them. The problem is that they quickly become 'bad managers' amid corrupt environments that drag everyone down to the lowest common denominator. One good boss can rarely survive a diseased environment because evil always wins over good, and therefore it is easy to thwart wholesome efforts with corporate cancer. The second issue relates to the difficulty of recognising intangibles. A broken chair is a tangible object that is easily identified, whereas a good boss is hard to spot because the intangible qualities are not readily evident.

As a result of this dilemma, good bosses are often revered in *hindsight*, not at the time of their reign. Often people fantasise about how exciting it would have been if they were able to work with Albert Einstein, George Patton, Napoleon Bonaparte, Oliver Cromwell, Sun Tzu, Frederick the Great, Julius Caesar, or Henry Ford. The same could be said about poets and artists. It seems that the dearly departed command more respect than the current crop.

If you can identify 'the boss from heaven', it would mean that you are able to identify modern-day heroes who will be saluted by future generations. Do not pass up an opportunity to become a student of skilled managers. Your challenge would be to identify who they are, and then to look, listen, and learn.

HEAVENLY QUALITIES

When asked what they would consider to be the hallmarks of an ideal boss, employees ask for someone who is friendly, caring, fair, intelligent, supportive, happy, approachable, helpful, and knowledgeable. Although these qualities are desirable, they ought to be normal attributes for *all* managers.

The boss from heaven should possess *exceptional* characteristics that are above and beyond the call of duty. The following are some of the special qualities that define the ideal boss who can turbo-charge your career.

Coaches are those who urge you to take paths whose outcomes are of benefit to you, whereas taskmasters are those who urge you to undertake assignments purely for their own benefit

1) The ideal boss is able to coach

How would you know what a coach looks like? What is the role of a coach, and what would be your role as a student? Coaches are those who urge you to take paths whose outcomes are of benefit to *you*, whereas taskmasters are those who urge you to undertake assignments purely for *their* own benefit.

A good coach will allow you to make mistakes, because the function of the coach is not to tell you what to do, but to alert you to the potential consequences, and to guide you through decision-making processes.

The most important challenge for a coach is to teach you the sense of timing. Much like a conductor who keeps the orchestra playing to time, a coach will assist you to develop your career by helping you to learn when to deviate from the path, and when to apply certain disciplines.

In modern corporate environments, managers are not obliged to act as coaches. Their role is to run departments with the help of skilled employees. If you are fortunate enough to have a boss who is willing to coach you, and if you want to seize the golden opportunity, it is incumbent upon you to learn how to listen and how to ask the right questions. Above all, you must reciprocate with discipline. Talk to young people about discipline, and they will presume that you are asking them to lead a boring, uninteresting life. They see discipline as the thief of fun. The application of discipline is not aimed at suppressing desire, but at eliminating self-destructive habits to the point where the triggers are eradicated.

The application of discipline is not aimed at suppressing desire, but at eliminating self-destructive habits

A good coach will never expect anything in return, but will insist on discipline from every student, because coaching is a resource-intensive affair. For that reason, take care that you do not drain your coach to the point where you will lose the opportunity to stride into a successful future.

2) The ideal boss is confident

When managers act with confidence, it is not unusual for bystanders and critics to accuse them of lacking humility. For some reason, people feel uneasy around confident operators.

Confidence does not translate into perfection, but into excellence. Yet excellence does not guarantee success.

Confidence does not translate into perfection, but into excellence. Yet excellence does not guarantee success. The function of excellence is to align elements in the best possible manner, given the conditions at hand. This means that a confident person is not someone who knows that success is imminent, but who is certain that everything possible has been done to ward off failure.

If you can learn to observe the ways in which confident operators work, you will see that their attention-to-detail does not come from a desire to live in an orderly world. Instead, it comes from an understanding that they live amid chaos.

Apathy leads to complacency, whereas confidence leads to self-satisfaction. Observers who do not understand this, tend to accuse confident people of being smug.

To appreciate the art of confidence you need to learn the art of planning. Remember that confidence is the end-result of careful planning. It is a veneer, behind which is intricate detail. If you can learn to discern between detail and clutter, you will be able to operate confidently. Failure in the face of confidence is called experience. In the face of confusion, it is called carelessness.

3) The ideal boss is consistent

Some people are considered predictable. Take them to a restaurant, and you can guess which meal they will order. Predictability is not the same as consistency. Predictability refers to the outcome, whereas consistency refers to the processes used to arrive at an outcome.

Consistency is not related to stubbornness or rigidity. Rather, it refers to solidity and firmness that come from conviction. When one's values are solid and one's ethics are firm, one is able to navigate through life's dense jungles without losing direction.

If your manager is consistent, consider yourself lucky. It takes a fair amount of energy to resist the temptations to deviate from the straight and narrow.

Consistency allows us to land on our feet, no matter what happens. At the administrative level, consistency saves time. At the personal level, it saves heartache. At the business level, it saves guesswork. At the professional level, it saves energy.

If your manager is consistent, consider yourself lucky. It takes a fair amount of energy to resist the temptations to deviate from the straight and narrow. Entering a life of mediocrity looks appealing amid relentless opposition. Within a thankless environment, the quick-fix approach is expedient and alluring.

Note that 'consistency of method' does not necessarily translate into 'consistency of outcome'. This means that what you see is not necessarily what you will always get. For example, people who are consistently kind and caring are not pushovers. They know how to stand up for themselves, and they will react unkindly to anyone who abuses them. It is due to their rock-solid ethics and values that they will retaliate against anyone who violates their trust or who threatens the foundations from which their gentleness emerges.

When you start to appreciate the benefits of consistency, you will begin to see how enjoyable it can be to work with those who say what they mean and mean what they say, and with those who are prepared to fight to protect their values.

4) The ideal boss is decisive

If you have observed remarkable musicians, you might have wondered how many years of practice would be required to reach a high level of competence. No matter how easy they make it appear, we appreciate their talent because their dedication culminates in a form that can be seen and heard *immediately*. When skill and talent combine to produce tangible results that can be assessed in their totality (such as music we can hear), we are able to appreciate their depth.

What about intangible skills such as the ability to make good decisions? The process of decision-making also requires years of practice. Unfortunately, there can be no accolades for the decision-maker because not every decision results in a tangible masterstroke. Besides, few people can appreciate what it means to be a maker of good decisions.

Music teachers have an advantage in that they can tantalise students by giving a demonstration and then saying, 'If you continue with your lessons, you too could play like this.' They are able to demonstrate the desired end result. Unfortunately, decision makers cannot demonstrate their skill. To

If your manager seems to be a good decision maker and a maker of good decisions, you would be advised to learn as much as you can about the reasons behind each action

make matters worse, they have to battle opponents who cannot understand the strategy. The game of chess is a visual interpretation of mental dexterity. For the uninitiated, it appears as a game of warfare. For those who appreciate the complexity of the human brain, chess gives them an insight into the ways in which the trillions of brain cells interact under pressure to produce short-term moves for long-term outcomes.

Try to observe your manager's every move, and then try to unravel the decision-making process. You would need both observation and memory skills to notice a pattern that culminates in successful outcomes. If your manager seems to be a good decision maker *and* a maker of good decisions, you would be advised to learn as much as you can about the reasons behind each action. If you can learn from a skilled strategist, you will be well on your way to joining the ranks of winners who can plan for long-term victories by undertaking prudent short-term steps.

As a keen student, your challenge would be to ask the pertinent questions so that your boss could impart some of the clues about the complex processes involved in decision-making. When you can learn to be decisive, you will delight in the mental thunderstorms that spark to produce lit pathways to success so that eventually you can traverse any terrain without fear.

5) The ideal boss is discreet

The art of discretion is multifaceted. The common understanding of its application pertains to keeping secrets. Immature managers tend to select a small number of subordinates to whom they disclose secrets as a way of buying loyalty. In no time, cliques are formed whereby some staff members have an advantage over others.

Good managers do not divulge confidential information to anyone, regardless of friendships. They know how to treat all subordinates impartially. To them, discretion is maintained on the basis of honour, as well as good judgement.

Prudent managers are discreet because they do not want to jeopardise the success of a project. They understand that it would be unwise to burden people with information that they might not be able to handle.

Compassionate managers understand that discretion is also concerned with not forcing people to divulge personal information. They are careful to resist the temptation to pry into other people's affairs.

Managers from heaven will use discretion as a tool of grace. This means that they will disregard past failures or irrelevant personal frailties when negotiating with subordinates. You might have come across such managers who never ask awkward questions. Do not mistake their grace for ignorance. They might pretend to know nothing, simply because they might have the perceptivity to know that they would be causing you some grief if they were to pursue a certain line of enquiry. By the way, my definition of grace is 'not burdening others with your expectations'.

If your manager gives you the freedom to make mistakes and does not hold your prior misdemeanours against you, consider yourself fortunate. All too often in this selfish world, people delight in pinning evidence on others. It is common to find people who delight in others' weaknesses. They reveal the fact that they know more about you than they should, and then they suppress their knowledge, so long as you show them that you are grateful. If ever you waiver from the path that suits them, they will threaten to divulge your secrets to others.

The ultimate skill in exercising discretion is knowing when not to ask questions that might embarrass others or put them under an intrusive spotlight

If you have noticed that your manager does not play these underhanded games, be sure to reciprocate. The ultimate skill in exercising discretion is knowing when *not* to ask questions that might embarrass others or put them under an intrusive spotlight. People harbour several nerve-racking fears, including the fear of being forced to divulge their private affairs. If your boss has spared you, and helped you to 'save face', you can count your blessings because all too often, curiosity and mischief are tools used by managers who try to tame their subordinates via psychological bullying or via intimidation.

6) The ideal boss is eccentric

Conventional wisdom has it that successful people are those who can 'ride the wave'. Business schools teach would-be high-flyers that the secret to 'making it big' is being able to jump on the bandwagon of the day. Undoubtedly, there is money to be made by rushing to seize new opportunities.

What bounty hunters do not realise is that a 'wave' is symbolic of a lot of people rushing to cash in on a new idea. The clever people are those who are *ahead* of the wave, not on top of it. They are the pioneers who forge through the dense bush, unaided and unappreciated. Sometimes pioneers are ridiculed for daring to venture alone to pursue what seem to be bizarre ideas. Their courage or foresight is sometimes seen as eccentricity.

Eccentric people are those who do things that others consider to be odd. Sometimes their unusual behaviour amuses observers who cannot help but smile at their peculiarity.

To classify eccentrics as just those who *act* differently, would miss other types of 'oddballs' who also *think* differently and who are non-conformists in their strategic approach. They are reasonable, except that they reason differently. They are rational, except that they rationalise differently. They are methodical, except that they use different methodologies. Those who are not prepared to take the conventional routes to solving problems, invariably clash with people who accuse them of being erratic or unpredictable.

Eccentrics are reasonable, except that they reason differently. They are rational, except that they rationalise differently.

The essence of an eccentric is not to think differently, but to allow different inputs to be assessed on their merits. Assumptions are not permitted until all the inputs have been reviewed. This does not mean that an eccentric seeks to be different, but rather operates from the belief that each situation should be judged on the evidence at hand. When working with others who prefer to jump to conclusions, eccentrics are not appreciated. For example, they might insist on being meticulous when others are prepared to be careless. That alone is seen as an irritating trait. Eccentrics never jump to conclusions — they browse to conclusions after surveying the environment and assessing all the possible options. If they cannot find solutions easily, they are prepared to go looking for them.

If your manager is an eccentric thinker, you stand a greater chance of being ahead of the wave. You would have to pave your own path as you search for new opportunities in uncharted territories. Those who are ahead of the pack are those who find the treasures — thereafter, they are swamped with instant believers.

7) The ideal boss is an experimenter

The most annoying thing for experimenters is to work with impatient colleagues who do not understand the essence of experimentation. If your boss likes to experiment, you might be tempted to ask, 'What are you hoping to find?' This is not a useful question because your boss might not know the answer. Innovators and experimenters understand that the most important generators of ideas are wildcards and 'accidents of invention'. For example, while practical people tend to question the value of investing in space probes that are sent to Mars, experimenters delight in the 'process' because they are creating environments that could trigger accidents of invention — that means, they create sufficient tension from which springs new problems and new discoveries that might not otherwise have been created.

Some of the most significant inventions of our time have come about by accident

Accidents of invention are the unknowns that surface after unlikely events occur. It is no wonder that some of the most significant inventions of our time have come about by accident as a result of sheer experimentation.

You can learn a lot by observing how experimenters work. They are like the children who derive greater pleasure in *fixing* a go-kart than in *riding* it. The thrill of experimentation is not in achieving an end result, but in observing the remarkable processes unfold, triggering new ideas that might not otherwise have emerged. People who can capture sparks of ideas are called geniuses. Geniuses do not sit still and come up with ideas. They are agitators who observe the most unlikely of situations in the hope of finding the glue that binds their wild thoughts to form a germ of an idea that later takes flight with hard work and skill. Musicians, writers, and artists find their inspiration in the most unlikely places. They are never actually doing what people think they are doing. They might go to a shopping centre merely to observe the million-and-one aspects of life inside. They might undertake unusual trips or they might venture into unfamiliar territories. They do not know what they are looking for, but they know that if they poke the fire, sparks will fly.

If your boss is an experimenter, learn to open your eyes so that you can see with peripheral vision. Central objects rarely capture their attention. Although they appear aloof and disinterested, experimenters are actually observing things that other people are not looking at. At parties, they do not look at the eye-catching person, but at those who are looking at that person.

8) The ideal boss is generous

Our society functions best when the learned are generous with their information. This means that the 'educated' ought to become 'educators'. Graduates need to realise that their education must not be seen as a 'commercial advantage' or as intellectual property, but as a 'social responsibility'. They have a duty to *share* their knowledge.

Our society functions best when the learned are generous with their information

If you can benefit from your manager's experiences, you stand to save a lot of time, energy, and effort. Heroes from heaven are generous because they do not subscribe to the antiquated attitudes of 'knowledge is power'. They know that the greatest power comes from an informed and enlightened group. If information is only rationed to the chosen few, it suppresses creativity, thwarts opportunities for victory, and minimises the potential for synergy.

When people are generous with tangible gifts, their actions are easily detected. When you are given a box of chocolates, you are able to see generosity in action. Unfortunately, when people are generous with intangible gifts, such as their time or their spirit, you might not recognise it, because intangible gifts often pass unnoticed. Your biggest challenge would be to know when you are being showered with intangible gifts.

9) The ideal boss is a mentor

There are differences between coaching and mentoring. A coach is someone who can guide you through practical aspects of your job or your craft, whereas a mentor is concerned with your over-all personal strategies. Mentors in the workplace are rarer than coaches, despite the trendy so-called 'mentoring programs' being implemented by organisations whose high staff-turnover is an indication of the lack of communication between the ranks.

A good mentor is akin to a *tormentor* — someone who shakes you out of your comfort zone and asks you per-plexing questions that cause you to sigh at the overwhelming challenges that are being put before you.

> *A good mentor is akin to a tormentor*

If your manager torments you, maybe you are being assisted to empty your knowledge base so that you can reset your system and refresh your attitudes. The hallmark of a good mentor is the ability to answer your questions with even better questions. The role of the mentor is to prepare you to think for yourself, not to give you the answers. Therefore, next time you feel that your manager has not been forthcoming with immediate answers, con-sider the possibility that you are being challenged for your own good, and are being given clues to help you to find a better way.

10) The ideal boss is passionate

Passionate people are sometimes told to relax and to stop being intense. This would drive them mad because they are serious about their work. After querying the status of a project, I was told to 'relax'. This led me to exclaim, 'Don't tell me to relax. Relaxing makes me nervous!'

Passionate people do not understand what it means to 'take it easy'. They take life seriously and they immerse themselves in their craft. They enjoy what they do, and they are highly focussed on the process *and* on the outcome.

Don't tell me to relax. Relaxing makes me nervous!

It seems to be socially acceptable to be passionate about sport. Passionate players are cheered on by passionate spectators. They excuse their intensity on the basis that they are enthusiasts who love their sport.

Similarly, there are people for whom *work* is stimulating and just as rewarding. The last thing that they want to hear is people urging them to be indifferent. Passionate workers derive as much pleasure from their work as any serious sportsperson might derive pleasure from playing sport.

If you are fortunate enough to work with a passionate boss, see if you can learn about the stimuli that make it all worthwhile. Your work is something that consumes a lot of your energy, so it is in your interest to understand how you can be energised by it. It would make sense to sharpen your appreciation of your profession. If you cannot do that, you might be in an industry or in an environment that does not suit your temperament.

11) The ideal boss is playful

For some children, their playfulness comes to an abrupt halt in their mid-teens when they convince themselves that it is no longer 'cool' to smile. They walk about with a stern look on their face, hoping to project an image of seriousness. They presume that a demure look gives them an air of intelligence. What they do not realise is that they appear more aggressive than pensive. Some adults seem to have not grown out of that unapproachable disposition. Their sternness becomes their shield.

Sometimes, a stern approach to business seems to be an expedient way to ward off unpleasant attacks or insensitive probes. For example, there are many celebrities who are unable to cope with the attention that they receive from their overbearing fans, so they appear aloof.

There could be many reasons why managers project an unfriendly image. Whatever the reason, the signals are unimpressive. If your manager is playful, approachable, and friendly, be sure to not abuse that relationship by overstepping your mark. Maintain the protocols and due respect, and do not presume that a happy manner gives you licence to become sloppy or to get personal.

The greatest mistake would be to assume that happy and playful managers are frivolous. They are serious about maintaining a happy working environment. It is for this reason that they will pounce on those who jeopardise the cheerful environment.

If your manager knows how to have fun at work, go with the flow, but never assume that anything other than excellence would be tolerated.

12) The ideal boss is resolute

There are two types of resolute managers. The first is the type that leads the way and sets the tone for everything. This type of manager wants employees to obey all the rules. In so doing, the manager is seen as the strong leader who sets the direction and leads from the front, saying, 'Please don't deviate from this plan. If there are any problems, come to me.'

The second type of manager is the supporter who hires experts, gives them all the tools, and then sits back and waits to be called to assist. When called, the manager springs into action with guns blazing, ready to defend the troops against anyone who gets in their way. This type of manager says, 'You do what you think is best, and I'll be here to support you.'

Resolute managers can be trusted to adhere to their decisions and to follow-up on their promises. Once they have made up their mind, they do not take kindly to anyone who jeopardises their authority. They are the type who would dig their heels in at all costs because they would be more concerned about the precedent of having one of their decisions overturned. Stalwarts such as these are a joy to work with because their word is their bond.

HEROES EVERYWHERE

Imagine if you could hone your skills to spot heroes in all areas of your life. Living today are numerous gifted people who are like Custer, Edison, Ghandi, Gibran, Mozart, and Rembrandt. Fame is not the only measure of brilliance. Your next-door neighbour might be a person who could enrich your life. Learn to look deeper than people's veneers and you might find that you are rubbing shoulders with fascinating people from whom you might learn new skills.

Fame is not the only measure of brilliance

What is better than having a great idea? Being able to recognise good ideas! What is better than being a hero? Being able to recognise heroes!

Learn to embrace the generosity of those who can help you to raise your standards. If ever you ask what you can do to repay such people, the answer is likely to be, 'I ask nothing from you except that you promise that you'll one day go out and show the same kindness to someone else who could benefit from you.' After you have been blessed by heroes from heaven, it would become your responsibility to go out and bless others. In the same way that heroes are every-where, so too are deserving people. It

What is better than being a hero? Being able to recognise heroes!

would not be up to you to decide who is worthy of your gifts. A giver gives to all who wish to receive. ∎

sample CHAPTER

*The following is a sample chapter
from the book
'How to Lose Friends and Infuriate People'*

CHAPTER 1

WHAT CAN *you* SEE FROM THE BALCONY OF LIFE?

TIME IS RUNNING OUT

Imagine, way up in the sky, a balcony that resembles a view-ing platform where you and others stand looking down on Earth. You are but a spirit. From the balcony you can see the marvellous and wondrous things on Earth — spectacular surf, exotic fruit, delicious vegetables, tantalising ice-cream, mouth-watering pasta, remarkable flowers, awesome gardens, stunning animals, breathtaking mountains, splendid rivers, people in love, exquisite fashion, fast cars, exhilarating snow skiing, and romantic sunsets.

The one in charge, Spirit-Superior, approaches you with a clipboard in hand and says that the next tour to Earth is about to depart. The problem is, only 10 percent of those on the bal-cony can be granted permission to go to Earth for a period not exceeding eighty years. Would you put your hand up? Would you ask to be considered? Are you enthusi-astic enough? Do you really want to wear a human body and experience the beauty of life on that planet below?

Who is stealing your chance to walk barefoot in the sand?

According to Spirit-Superior, all candidates promise to make the most of their time on Earth. They are eager to start their journey. They cannot wait to take their first swim, to enjoy a juicy orange, to bite into a scrumptious cake, to walk in the park, and to make love with a beautiful com-panion in symphony with the cool breeze. You push to the front of the queue and plead, 'Please pick *me*. I promise to make the most of life on Earth.'

Well, here you are *on* Earth. Not long to go before you have to return to the balcony. Not long when you compare eighty-odd years to eternity. What are you doing about it? Did you bite into a delicious apple today? Did you take a swim? Did your heart skip a beat as the stars came out to bid the sunset a fond farewell? Or did you waste the day and insult Spirit-Superior by allowing anger, that elusive intangible, to take hold of your body and spoil your moment? You are not guaranteed the full eighty years. Only 'now' is your guarantee. Tomorrow is not in the contract. You have no way of knowing when your tour will be terminated.

Every night, as you put your head to sleep, Spirit-Superior visits you and asks, 'Would you like to go back from whence you came — back to the balcony of life where you will never again have the opportunity to come back to Earth? Or would you like one more day to give it another go?' What would you say? Most people say, 'Oh please, give me one more day. Tomorrow I will live. Today I messed up, but tomorrow I will go to the beach and grab an ice-cream, and feed the birds, and make my friends laugh.'

Doubtless, some do choose to terminate their stay. They cannot see what all the fuss is about. They want life no more. So, Spirit-Superior grants their wish and takes them back to the balcony. Tragically, others tamper with the process and take their own lives when they can no longer believe that tomorrow will bring relief. Some of my dear friends have decided to leave me behind by terminating their contracts.

Yesterday is gone, tomorrow is not yours, and today is already packed with drama

One young man of nineteen asked his mother for some money. As loving mothers do, she obliged and asked no questions. He bought a rifle, went back home, and did the deed. He used to love life, but a door shut in his face. He was convinced that the door would never re-open. Faced with that prospect, he bowed out.

Where are you at in life? Are you battling with time thieves? Are you being robbed of *your* moment? Who is stealing your chance to walk barefoot in the sand?

FLIGHT 101 NEVER RETURNS

In the airline business, everyone knows that once an aircraft departs, any empty seats on that flight cannot be filled again. The opportunity to recoup that lost fare has gone. This is why many airline companies overbook their flights. They do not mind inconveniencing their travellers, so long as they can be sure to pack the aircraft.

For undersubscribed flights, and since the advent of the networked world, airlines are trying to sell the last remaining seats via Internet auctions, hoping to fill every seat, even if at cost. It is better to cover costs than to fly with an empty seat, because empty seats cost money.

Your life can be likened to this challenge. Every day that you allow to slip through your hands is irretrievable. You cannot decide to return to yesterday or 'turn back time' to mend the broken dreams. You cannot return to last Monday. So, yesterday is gone, tomorrow is not yours, and today is already packed with drama. Is this what you planned when you were standing on the balcony of life? If not, stand up and do something about it.

Do you divide your day into work, rest, and play? Is work something you do out of obligation? Is rest something you do because you are exhausted? Is play something you do to forget about work? This is not a pleasant cycle.

You know what needs to be done. You do not need 'motivational' speakers to pep you up. This is *your* life. No-one is authorised to upset you. This is *your* turn. No matter how generous you might be, you cannot pass it on to someone else. If you choose to skip a turn, you will not be doing anyone a favour. The one thing you will be doing is ringing the alarm bells in the control room, and Spirit-Superior will have to take a closer look at your files. (For more about motivation, see Chapter 3, 'The secret destroyer' in How to Lose Friends and Infuriate People.)

EVERY MINUTE OF EVERY DAY

Have you considered that the Olympic Games would not have progressed if it were not for technologists' ability to slice time into tiny bits we call a second, a tenth of a second, a hundredth of a second, and so on?

Electricity and the entire power grid, including street lighting and traffic controls, rely on disciplined and regimented pulses that must beat to time. The loss of one beat could stop a city. Traffic would grind to a halt, and the city could very well become grid-locked, meaning that no-one could move because no-one can move.

Computers operate to time. Not only for calendar and date-stamping purposes, but for internal microchip operation. One tiny beat out of rhythm and the computer fails.

Time, at its smallest, is precious. Even the big chunks we call day and night are great punctuation marks that herald a new week, a new month, a new season.

How well do we manage time? As a society, we manage it well. Things tend to work more often than not — despite that 'year 2000 computer issue' that many will remember with fury and laughter as the 'Y2Kaboom!'

How well do *you* manage time? Do you divide your day into work, rest, and play? Is *work* something you do out of obligation? Is rest something you do because you are exhausted? Is *play* something you do to forget about work? This is not a pleasant cycle.

Life is life. To allow manipulating hounds to steal your life at the office through bureaucratic and politically poisoned meetings is theft of the highest order. Life is now, not after work. Life is shopping, not when you get home. Life is every minute of every day. So, how well are you managing your life? How well are you managing your time?

Time management is not about a list of things in order of priority that must be completed by a deadline. (How apt that we call it a deadline.) Time management is about life management. The issue is not what you do, but where your soul is at.

Do you put your pleasures on hold when you clean the house? Do you accept misery and boredom as unavoidable traits of your work domain? Do you accept domestic unrest as your lot in life?

UPS AND DOWNS

Life management is not about a delirious state of affairs. You own your life, so only *you* can live your life. Take charge of it. This does not mean that you must seek to be happy at all times. This is impossible. Not because it is too difficult in this day and age, but because *happiness* can only mean something to you after you have experienced *sadness*. From a young age we are taught that if one achieves happiness, one has achieved something worthwhile.

Time represents seconds. The seconds measure the division between the sun and the moon and these, in turn, ultimately measure the distance between life and death.

However, although sadness, pain, and sorrow are not mentioned, or under-valued, or avoided, they are *vital* for the attainment of more happiness.

After one of my presentations, a young man approached me to thank me. He had the brightest disposition. He told me that although his colleagues were looking to build their careers in medicine, business, and the like, he just wanted to be 'happy', so it did not matter to him what profession he chose. He looked happy, but I knew that he did not know what he was saying. 'How happy do you want to be?' I asked. 'Very happy,' he replied. We sat for a while as I explained to him that if he wished to attain ten lots of happiness, he would have to endure ten lots of sadness. He finally grasped the concept and became scared. He specifically does not want to be *unhappy*. So he froze. I felt sorry for him, but such is life. Eventually he began to understand and assured me that he would brace himself. He valued happiness because he had experienced much sadness. However, he was unaware that more happiness could only be appreciated in the wake of more sadness. Even then, the process is not automatic, and much building is required. The trick is to use the sadness to build for yourself tools that can help you to get back on your feet again. You need to be ready to attain additional wisdom, to build shields that protect you, to enhance your attitude to cope with the situation. This is important because sadness knocks you down, and it is much easier to stay down than to lift yourself against the inertia.

We are taught to be eternally tolerant, yet intolerance is just as important when you can use it to protect your life against time thieves

Life management is not about being happy through ignoring society, or shedding one's responsibilities, or resigning from corporate life to take up subsistence farming, or filing for divorce. These things in themselves do not make you happy. They might be important steps that you choose to take, but on their own, they do not lead to happiness. Life management is about being *well adjusted*. This means taking the good and the bad, and being able to stand against the wind of disappointment. It is the realisation that solutions do not come from escaping. Running away from unhappiness does not build happiness. A well-adjusted person responds well to what life dishes out, and builds new shields. In responding well to what life dishes out to you, be sure to arrest those who steal time — the essence of life.

Time is not really the important element. It is what time represents that matters. Time represents seconds. The seconds measure the division between the sun and the moon and these, in turn, ultimately measure the distance between life and death.

LIVE BY HALVES

Although life is not so easy to measure, time *can* be measured. Assess your time and how you expend it. Do you really need to watch so much television? Is it important that you spend so many hours surfing the Internet? How about halving all of the things that do not add value to your life?

If you watch twenty hours of television per week, why not cut it back to ten? If the loss of your precious ring causes you to become angry for two days, try to get over it in one day. If the loss of your pet causes you to cry for six weeks, try to overcome your grief within three weeks.

By halving the things that you know are unproductive or soul-destroying, you are starting to manage your time. Continue to live by halves until you can take better control of the impact of your environment upon you. This does not mean that you ought not to spend your time any way you like. In fact, that is the point of the exercise. By ridding yourself of time-consuming life-wasters, you will have the time to do the things you really *want* to do, not the things that *force* themselves upon you, or command your attention without your permission, or that you do out of habit.

Some habits cannot be halved. They can only be ampu-
tated. The diseases of gambling, alcoholism, drug abuse, and the
like, need to be obliterated without negotiation. Only the life-
owner can choose to do that. If people's enjoyment of such
things is greater than the value they place on their life, they are
not ready to do anything about their addictions. In those cases,
it is better that they do not try because the emotions and turmoil adversely affect the life of those around them as well.

In truth, time-wasters are life-wasters. Anyone who wastes
your time is wasting your life. Do not stand for it. Typical time-
wasters include: the way in which a meeting is managed;
people's inability to stick to their word; not meeting deadlines; and being tolerant of people.

TOLERANCE VERSUS INTOLERANCE

If you consider tolerance a virtue, beware you do not fall victim to
virtues. Patience, tolerance, and empathy are all noble, important
qualities in life. However, you need to learn how to set your
boundaries. Supposing that you agree to meet a friend but that person does not turn up at the agreed time. How long are you
prepared to wait? Ten minutes? One hour? Seven hours? Most
people would not consider waiting seven hours. Well, why is ten
minutes acceptable? Why not five? If you think that five minutes is
a little harsh, then pray tell, would you leave at precisely ten minutes, or would you give your friend just a couple of minutes more?

The point to time management in such cases is to reduce
the guesswork. You and your friend ought to have made an
agreement that says if one of you is late by more than ten minutes the meeting will be cancelled. This has nothing to do with
being nasty. It is all about setting expectations and understanding the boundaries.

Meetings at work should start on time. Do you start on time, or do you wait for the stragglers? I live a fair distance from the main city, so when people invite me to an early morning meeting in the city, I need to be up at 5:00 am to get ready and leave home before 6:00 am so that I can get there at 7:00 am. I need to do this even if the meeting is scheduled to start at 9:00 am because if I were to leave home at 8:00 am, I would not get through the unbearable traffic until 10:00 am. This is a tricky juggling act. So I arrive early, wait two hours until 9:00 am, and have to put up with life-wasters who say, 'Oh, let's wait a few minutes for those who might be caught in traffic.' Then they say, 'Oh look, it's 9:30 am, why don't we have an early morning coffee break while we're waiting?' By 10:00 am, when the meeting starts, I would have been up for five hours!

At first, I give some people the benefit of the doubt, but I later become nonchalant, or do not arrive on time, or choose not to go. When will people learn that adults are just like children? If a child gets the chocolate after ranting and raving, that child is being conditioned. If chairpeople wait for late-comers, I would rather a few extra hours in bed, and they can wait for *me*.

Needless to say that most meetings are life-wasting rituals, devoid of content, lacking direction, and ultimately useless. The same is so for any meeting where the guest speaker reads a speech at me. If I have to get up early, iron my clothes, shave, shower, endure the heavy traffic, pay for petrol and parking, only to have some slow, uninteresting presenter read at me, I would prefer the speech be sent to me via fax or e-mail so that I can read it in the bath when I awake at a godly hour.

We are taught to be eternally tolerant, yet *intolerance* is just as important when you can use it to protect your life against time thieves.

WHEN TIME IS MONEY

Organisations measure the productivity of each employee. When they hire hundreds of people, they are effectively buying time. More people working on a project ought to result in greater output within the financial year. Productivity per head is one of the vital measures of success. If you are a chief executive officer (CEO), ask your financial analyst to estimate your corporation's profitability if your workforce were to double its output. What would become of your share price if you were twice as productive?

Sure, many organisations understand the need for more productivity. That is why they maintain the pressure and make everyone miserable while, at the same time, trying to improve productivity. Employees are having to work intolerable hours amid job insecurity and unfulfilling environments.

I long for the day when a senior manager congratulates the staff for a job well done without spoiling the whole ceremony with a plea for everyone to 'work harder'. And I cringe when I hear calls for employees to also 'work smarter'. How depressing. How ungrateful. Forget about working harder. Never mind about working smarter. If, as CEO, you want to improve productivity, start doing things by halves. Navigate your way through your spaghetti-like systems and policies and chop the time-wasters. Remove anything or anyone who steals time through bureaucracy, through stupidity, and through strangling red tape cast upon the masses by the almighty headquarters. Even if you cannot eliminate them, just halve them! What difference would that make? You do the numbers and work it out. If what you see does not make your blood boil, then you are sailing smoothly, and you have a well-adjusted organisation.

If you could double the productivity of your organisation,

would such a project not be worthy of your attention? If so, get on with it. By the way, once you, as CEO, have removed the time-wasters, you need to search your soul and come clean with your conscience and check to see if you are the chief time-thief. Have you created an environment in which your actions create a domino effect?

It is laughable to see how many CEOs increase the revenue targets as a small buffer, so that their people strive harder for the bigger number, knowing that if they miss a little, the original target will be met, and the CEO will look like a hero in front of the board. I have seen numbers eventually doubled after they have gone through a buffering process from headquarters, to regional headquarters, to country, to division, to department, to individual. What a joke. At the end of the line the individual has to strive for a number that is twice as big as the original without the same level of growth in operating expense and headcount. This unrealistic target-setting is demoralising.

I have seen the aftermath of this wicked accounting process. The individual would have battled in spite of having unco-operative colleagues who were also stretched to unreasonable limits. The individual would have tried hard, increased the revenue by 70 percent on the previous year's figure, but still be declared a failure because the ridiculous target was missed by a few dollars. How ungrateful! Organisations make employees work a miserable year with no time for life, no time for a decent lunch, and at the end of all that hard work: a slap in the face. Then the chiefs of the land, who exceeded their revenue targets in real terms, end up scoring healthy bonuses. Every way you look at it, this is theft — and it starts at the top. Oh, the burdens at the top! ❗

INDEX

MEMBER SINCE 1990

Jonar Nader has been a member of the
Australian Society of Authors since 1990.

He encourages professional authors and budding new authors to join
the ASA in Australia or the NZSA in New Zealand.

AUSTRALIA

ASA@ASAUTHORS.ORG
WWW.ASAUTHORS.ORG

NEW ZEALAND

NZSA@CLEAR.NET.NZ
WWW.ARACHNA.CO.NZ/NZSA

USA

STAFF@AUTHORSGUILD.ORG
WWW.AUTHORSGUILD.ORG

HONG DONG WAH

If you enjoyed this book,
check out the companion products published by ABC Audio
and available at all leading bookstores or at www.LoseFriends.com

PLUTONIUM

Plutonium publishes the following books by Jonar C. Nader

How to Lose Friends and Infuriate People, Third Edition
How to Lose Friends and Infuriate Your Boss
How to Lose Friends and Infuriate Thinkers

Other books in the Series are currently in production.

If you would like to join our confidential mailing list,
we would be delighted to keep in touch with you
about our developments and inform you of Jonar's latest projects.
Please register at the Contact section at
www.LoseFriends.com or write to Mail@LoseFriends.com